THIS MOTORING

THIS MOTORING

Being the Romantic Story of the
Automobile Association

by

STENSON COOKE

Published by
The Automobile Association
Fanum House, New Coventry Street, London, W.1

Printed in Great Britain

TO HER

CONTENTS

PROLOGUE

(AUGUST, 1905)

HE stood at the Piccadilly end of Shaftesbury Avenue, wondering what to do next. Six o'clock in August didn't really mark the *end* of an imperfect day—imperfect because business had been bad. Hardly sold a thing. Selling and dealing was indeed an overrated amusement. This freedom that folks belauded was all very well— when it paid. When ! There was the rub.

These workers swarming into horse-buses bound for home and high tea had much to be grateful for. The coming of Saturday for them would spell " pay." However modest, there it would be, chinking pleasantly in its little envelope ; whereas—— What was a one-man business, after all ? A hand-to-mouth struggle for sprats, which so infrequently caught a mackerel. It didn't lead anywhere.

Here was the Highbury bus. In forty minutes he could be home, to meet the never failing welcome, to answer the inevitable query, " What sort of a day ? " and get the comforting reply, " Never mind, dear, it's bound to be better one day if we keep a good heart and work on ! "

Permanency. Was there really any to be had ! That tide in the affairs of men, did it ever flow for people of thirty ?

Another Highbury bus ! Why not go home ?

His mind ran over the day's work. Streets and stairs, stairs and streets ; receptions for the most part curt ; undercurrents of resentment voicing, " Nothing in your

line to-day, so why bother me ? " or, " Why weren'
you here last week, when we *did* want you ? "

Why couldn't one divine by telepathy a customer'
needs at the right time, and so economize those unendin
stairs and streets ?

Another Highbury bus ! Away, then ! But—just
moment. Had anything been left undone that ough
to have been done ?

Yes, there was that decent chap in the lawyer's offic
near Temple Bar. Six weeks ago they had had a dea
—yes, a real deal, netting ten perfectly good sovereigns
A perfect day ! But the clean-up showed a debit of
pound or so due to the Decent Chap, and it hadn't bee
paid, for reasons obvious. It still couldn't be paid, fo
reasons just as depressingly obvious.

Ten past six. In forty minutes he could be home
but why not pop along to the chap's office, and explai
that the spirit was still willing though the bank wa
weak. The debt still stood, and should certainly b
cleared.

Right ! Across the Circus for a pennyworth to Templ
Bar. A tide in the affairs of men ? Perhaps—perhap
not. Good ! The Decent Chap wasn't gone. He sa
in his chief's chair as befitted a particular " personal '
assistant when the Boss had left him to finish off.

" Good evening, old man ! "

" Evening ! "

" I've called about that little balance. I haven'
forgotten it ; but sorry—I can't give it to you, yet."

" That's all right ; sit down for a minute. Funny yo
should call in just now. There's a job going, would i
be of interest to you ? "

He caught his breath. " Would it be of interest
Oh ! go on, please."

" It's like this. A bunch of men have formed
motor-something or other to fight somebody or other
Here's the prospectus. My Chief is in it. He is givin
it house-room, and I'm the Honorary Secretary ; bu

f course we can't go on running it indefinitely. Our business is Law. They want to put the whole thing on a permanent basis. There must be a paid man—a whole-time job. They're looking for one. Why shouldn't you have a shot ? You never know what it might lead to."

A whole-time job ! Permanency !

" Surely I will, and I can't thank you enough. What do they want ? I know nothing about the business. I've only been in a motor car twice. But never mind that. Consider me a starter for the motor-something-or-other stakes here and now."

" Good ! Away you go and write in to us. Let me have the letter in the morning. This is Wednesday—the Committee meet on Friday. Be here at half-past three, on the chance that they will look at you ! Good-night ! "

" Good-night ! and whether it comes off or not, I'll never forget."

A bee-line home—to her.

Was this the tide in the affairs of men, to be taken at the flood ? Take it, anyway.

And now for the letter. It must be brief, to conceal ignorance. It must be deferential, to get an interview. Then—the Committee, who and what were they ? Care, not to show eagerness. Wit, to answer questions promptly. Caution, not to get rattled by cross-fire.

" Oh, Friday, hurry up ! "

Friday came.

" The Committee will see you ; this way, please." The lawyer friend, Decent Chap, was sitting at the foot of a long table, acting as secretary ; Monocled Majesty was ensconced at the head, grey, big and impressive. Some with darker hair sat around, keen and businesslike, eyes kindly ; some inscrutable, equally impressive.

He felt rather lonely. He was up against the biggest selling job of all—not *things* to boost, but *himself*.

" Care ! Don't look cheap," had been Her last word that morning, as she set his tie and brushed his hat, and kissed him good luck.

" Sit down, please ! " said Monocled Majesty.

" Thank you, sir."

" We have your letter, applying for the position of secretary. We are looking for a capable organizer."

" I can organize."

" How do you know you can ? That is to say, what have you done in that line ? "

" It's difficult to explain, sir, but I know I can. In my Regiment, a Volunteer Regiment, I—— "

" Oh ! We know all about *that* kind of organizing " (he was a Colonel of Militia), " but—well, leave that for a minute. What else can you do ? "

" I can sell stuff. I can interview people. I've had a sound business training. I can keep books and write a good letter. I can handle men. I can—— "

" Are you married ? "

" Yes, rather ! I mean, I am. I put it in my letter."

" Quite right ; but we like to see a man's eyes when he answers that question. What do you know about motoring ? "

" I—I—— " Were there no friendly eyes round that table—had none of them ever been up against it ? (Care ! Don't look cheap.)

" I know nothing, sir, yet. But does that really matter ? "

Monocled Majesty looked round. " Would any member like to ask a question ? No ? Very well ! That will do, thank you. Good afternoon."

" Good afternoon, sir, and thank you, gentlemen." How would he get through the door ?

Well, that was that, and now back to the streets and stairs.

Decent Chap's colleague, bless his big heart, fielded the hopeless applicant in the corridor.

" How did you get on ? "

" Oh ! Clean bowled, stumped, L.B.W. and swallowed my bat. They asked what I knew about motoring, and I know nothing. Yet why should that matter, if I could run their show ? And I can, I know I can. Oh, let me get out ! "

" Steady on," said Big Heart. " It isn't entirely hopeless. Come into my room until the meeting's over, and we can get information straight from the stable."

The meeting finished. Decent Chap shook the last hand in his capacity of Honorary Secretary, and resumed his lawful occasions.

" It's like this ! That fellow two from the right of the Chairman has a pal who wants the job. He can ride a motor-tricycle, and that seemed to impress the Committee. Yet somehow you must have made them think a bit. They are all top-sawyers in their own particular lines. It has been decided to form a sub-committee to select a Secretary. With power to appoint, mark you. There are only two of you in the running. The other chap's pal is one of the sub-committee of three, but the remaining two will see fair play. So cheer up."

" What's the next move ? "

" How about another letter ? "

" But *can* I ? "

" Of course you can. And I'll try to get you an interview with that chap who sat on the extreme left. We do business with him and he's one of the brightest. Now, off you go to get out a draft and submit it to us. We'll form a sub-committee on our own to consider and improve upon *the* letter, where it may be deemed necessary and advisable ; and one of our girls shall type it for you. We're seconding you in this contest."

" Jolly good of you. Cheero ! " And as he went down the stairs once more he felt less lonely.

When the two " seconds " had added their experienced and calculating efficiency to the effort, the letter was indeed a letter. It glossed airily over the disability of lack of motoring knowledge. It set out boldly what a motoring-something-or-other should do in order to become a force, and ended on this high note :

" You need, above everything, a man of tact and discretion, competent, when called upon, to interview persons of whatever social standing, without embarrassment, and in a manner befitting the dignity of a great organization. This, gentlemen, is what you appear to want. I can do it."

Rather cheeky that ! But let it go. Faint heart never won fair anything.

Monday came.

" It's like this," said Decent Chap. " The sub-committee meets on Wednesday, and I've got you ten minutes with Him at his office this morning. Your letter has gone in. They haven't asked you to be present on Wednesday, but—go ! I shall be there, and I'll let 'em know that you are."

Meanwhile, ten minutes with Him. Inscrutable eyes shading a kind heart ; and, withal, strictly business.

" Sir, it's awfully good of you to see me. I feel I can do this job. I can make it something. What does it matter, really, whether a man can ride a motor-tricycle or not ? Surely the work is more than that." And so on.

Hardly a word from Him. But anyway—something attempted, something possibly done. One never knew.

Wednesday. Great Marlborough Street, Motor show-rooms. Clean-limbed young men, with shiny hair and shiny shoes, and socks to match the coach-work, added tone to the exhibits.

The sub-committee was meeting in an office no bigger than a bathroom. Black Hair presiding, supported by Inscrutable Eyes and the Other One's friend. Honorary Secretary in attendance.

He was introduced to the Other One.

" Good afternoon ! "

" Good afternoon ! "

" After this job ? "

" Yes."

" Me, too. I can't very well wish you luck, but no bad blood, eh ? "

" No ! " They shook hands.

The sub-committee was sitting. A shiny-haired acolyte said, " Come this way, please ! "

Black Hair, quite genial, opened the ball. " It's like this." (That phrase was getting familiar.) " We've had your second letter, and we are deciding this matter here and now. Would you like to add anything ? "

Now for it !

" Thank you, yes. There's only one thing which troubles me. The pay isn't enough. A man can't live on it, and he can't turn out the best work when worried for money. Of course, there's my little business, but that must die slowly. This is a whole-time and a whole-heart job, and——"

" But it won't stand any more money until it grows," said Black Hair. " We have all been dipping into our pockets, and it's time the show should stand on its own feet. That's why we want to find the right man. It's a chance in a lifetime for the right man. We want——"

" Yes, I know. You want members and money. The fierce light of publicity. Get people talking, and do things to keep them talking. Energy, enthusiasm, and imagination. I have all three."

The Other One's supporter chimed in. " But about riding a motor-tricycle. What about it ? You haven't got one, have you ? Can't ride one ? "

" No ! I haven't got one and can't ride one, but is that everything ? There might be cars to drive on this job, some day."

He of the Inscrutable Eyes generously diverted the fire. " Would you require an agreement ? We had a man in view, but he stuck out for a year's agreement and we didn't feel justified in——"

" That's all right, sir. Agreements don't interest me. They cut both ways. I'm ready to take over and get my teeth right into the work. If I make good, I shall want more. If I don't, you can send me away. That's fair enough, isn't it ? "

" Yes, that seems fair. References ? "

Produced.

" I know that one," said Black Hair.

" And I know that one," said his colleague.

" Very well. Now we must see the other applicant. Wait outside, please."

" Thank you. Good day, gentlemen."

Was it also good-bye ? He hoped not.

The Shiny-Haired Acolyte was officiating once more. The Other One now going through it. Would he never come out ? The minutes were like hours. How was he getting on with the wretched tricycle that he owned and could ride ? Not quite fair, that ; give him his chance, and for goodness' sake do something, look at something, talk, and stop fidgeting !

Ah ! Here was the Other One, closing the door and coming back to the show-room.

The Jury were considering their verdict. Shiny Hair was acting as Usher.

To converse seemed puerile. What really *could* two men talk about while other men were settling their fate— when one's gain must mean the other's loss ?

Better to keep away, to look at a chassis—whatever that might be, while he looked at a limousine—whatever *that* might be, and thought of his tricycle.

Movement. Shiny Hair was going into the room— now coming out. Which would he approach ? Shiny Hair made straight for the Other One.

So that was all about it. It had gone. A chance in a lifetime. The tide in affairs had been turned by a motor-tricycle. Oh why ? And what *could* he say to Her ? " Care now, don't look cheap ; pull yourself together. Congratulate him ! Go on, it's all in the game ! "

He swallowed a lump and went across to the Other One.

" Best of luck to you. I did want the job, but we can't both win. Best of——"

" What are you talking about," said Shiny Hair. " I'm telling him he needn't wait. It's *you* they want. Come along ! "

The show-room seemed to flame.

A few dazed words to Other One, and then—the Committee.

Black Hair speaking.

" It's like this." (There it was again.) " We have carefully considered the applications and we have come to the conclusion that—that—anyhow, when can you start ? "

" Have I ? Is it ? When can I ? (Gulp.) I can start to-morrow."

" That's the stuff. We think you're going to be all right, and you start to-morrow."

The atmosphere softened. Handshakes and good wishes. Kindly-uttered nothings to cover the novitiate's embarrassment.

And so—" Good-night."

.   .   .   .   .   .

He was telling Her the great news.

" . . . And the funniest part of it all is that I know nothing about motoring. Twice in a car, that's all. A queer thing. They are all in the early thirties— except perhaps the Militia Colonel. Successful, too, and so entirely decent. The Black Haired one can't even be my age, and yet he's a famous racer. The one I went to see, you remember, with the Inscrutable Eyes, is a wonder. I've never seen a better turn-out. My dear ! spotless. Perhaps one day I may have clothes like his. And so *decent*. D'you know, to-day, for a moment, the blinds went up, and I could see him reading my mind.

" He read that I was bluffing about the pay being small, that actually I was aching for the chance. I know he did. I can read eyes too.

" He is going to lend us a typewriter. There isn't enough money to buy one, yet.

" The very office is to be lent, one small room in the offices of the lawyer chap who sat with the big crowd when first I paraded for inspection. He is so cute and clever, with an eye to the future. A sportsman.

" Dear, they're all good. Even the chap who sickened me with motor-tricycles isn't bad. Getting down to earth again, there are practically no funds. It's just a gamble on the future. Ninety members and a hundred pounds in the bank.

" It's up to me to make good on that. Black Hair displayed prevision—' all that is of the most optimist,' as a Frenchman would put it. ' If we go on as we hope to,' he said, ' I see no reason why one day we shouldn't have five thousand members.'

" He appeared to be in a minority of one.

" Good luck to that dream, anyway. They seem to be up against something or somebody. They seem to have grievances which we have got to voice in no uncertain manner, and fight about.

" I'm to go ' on the road,' whatever that may mean, on Saturdays and Sundays, and rest on Wednesdays. You can see me resting, eh ? I don't think.

" It will be a pinch. We can't live on the present pay, but think of the future ! Didn't you say, in the dark days, that somehow you could see me sitting in a secretarial chair, with others round a table passing resolutions and—passing resolutions ? Well, here's the tide in our affairs, to be taken at the flood.

" It's a week ago, almost to the minute, that I let the Highbury bus go by, and to-morrow——

" It's like this. (Oh, bother, now I've caught that expression.) We are both just on either side of thirty. That's young for these times. Who can tell ? Some day it may mean something quite big—to be——Hold my hand ! "

" To be what ? dear ! "

" Secretary . . . of the . . . Automobile Association."

THIS MOTORING

CHAPTER I

THE WHY OF IT

W HAT, really, had occurred to bind those shrewd business men of such varied interests into that essentially British institution, a Committee ?

What had inspired them to give money, to lend office-room and requisites, to foregather at call, no matter how inconvenient the day or hour, in order to " get things done " ? There could be no personal profit for them. Why did they do it ? There must have been a reason.

There was !

They had all come into the motor game at the start. Several had plodded to Brighton on Emancipation Day, 1896, when the Act came into force permitting motors to be driven on the high roads without being preceded by a man with a red flag. A few raced. A few wrote. Some—just motored. They belonged to Motor Clubs which governed the Sport, as it was termed. They went in for Hill-Climbs, and Tests and Trials, and Club Rallies, and all that. So far so good ; but when they went for a would-be enjoyable run at the week-end they got " trapped."

Persecution by the Police had been prevalent in the earlier days of cycling. Perhaps earlier still, in the mail-coach era. It blossomed into full flower with the advent of the motor car.

1

Whatever may be urged in favour of the Motor Car Act of 1903, it was bad in at least one instance—speed. Under one section, speed by itself was to be an offence, irrespective of danger.

Twenty miles an hour and no more! Never mind when or where. At four o'clock on a summer's morning, across a plain, with nobody and nothing to be troubled, twenty-one miles an hour meant breaking the law, with penalties in the way of fines, endorsement and even suspension of driving licence, for those who were caught in the act.

This Motoring had certainly startled English country life out of its usual calm. The roads were rich in dust, and passing cars churned it up over all and sundry, and the sufferers naturally cursed both driver and machine as a nuisance.

" This is awful," was the wail. " Why can't somebody do something about it ? "

Feeling ran high. Meetings were held. What should be done to be rid of this new plague ?

" Here ! What about that new Act with the speed limit, and fines, and things ? Get the Police to set traps and make the beggars pay. There's money in this ! "

There was !

A measured furlong on a nice, straight piece of road, safe and tempting to the motorist. Two policemen in plain clothes, one at each end, with stop-watches— hiding. A third in uniform, beyond the end of the measured distance. The scene was set.

Enter the victim. A boy. One of England's nicest. A bit of a mechanic, you know. Loved messing about with engines, and electric bells, and all that sort of thing. So Mother had bought him a car, and then wished she hadn't, because he might get into trouble. As if ? Silly, wasn't she ? Oh, the world was good to live in !

So here he was—on a glorious Saturday morning, full of the joy of Spring, full of pride in his two cylinders and ten horse-power. Happy lad !

2

He, had covered the first eighteen miles from home in just over two hours, including traffic. He had filtered considerately through the village, side-stepped the baker's cart with a friendly smile, evaded the suicidal tendencies of the inevitable village dog, struggled up the hill with a boiling radiator, and now—he took in a vista of broad wide road on the lens of a healthy eye. Happy lad. Good stuff, this. Good to be alive, eh ? " Come on, old girl—let's see what you can do. Open the throttle and off we go."

The scene was set. Law was lying in wait.

" Here he comes ! Steady now, wait for it ! Wait for it ! "

Into the trap. Click went the watch, click, and wave of the handkerchief. Now then—one, two, three, four. Second timekeeper, a sergeant, on the ball now. Click, one, two, three, four, five, six, and so on, up to . . . Yes ? No. Yes ! Wave now to the uniformed man. He's covered the distance in *less* than . . . That's over twenty miles an hour. Caught !

Uniform, getting the signal, stalked into the middle of the road, with upheld hand. Stop !

Happy Lad, feeling a little bit sick inside, slowed down and pulled up.

" What's the matter ? I haven't run over anyone."

" Wait for the Sergeant." Just that. No " Please," no idea of " Sir." Oh, no !

Here, indeed, was a changed man. For years prior to This Motoring his weather chart as a policeman had been " fair to warm, with occasional local disturbances in the shape of a poacher or two, a gipsy or two, or orchard raiders of tender years. Further outlook— settled." But now, humans proceeding on wheels, in chariots hitherto impelling deference and salutes on sight, and so on, were *his* ; his to hector, to command, and to intimidate, whatever that might mean. The Law had delivered them into his hands.

" Wait for the Sergeant ! "

3

" Ooh ! " What will Mother say ? Never mind ; light a cigarette and try to look unconcerned.

Arrived the Sergeant—unctuous, gloating over his catch. Here was this young fellow-my-lad, with sheep-skin coat and sheepy look. Make him shiver, make him squirm.

" H'm—h'm. What's your name ? Where do you live ? With your mother, eh ? H'm—h'm. It's my duty to inform you that you have been timed over a measured distance—h'm—and covered that measured distance in . . . seconds, which is equivalent to a speed of . . . an hour, thereby committing an offence against the Law, which same entails various penalties, and for which in due course—h'm—you will be called upon to stand your trial. Pass along."

Poor Happy Lad. If he was wise, he didn't argue. He just passed along, otherwise he feared every silly thing he had said would be taken down, altered, and used in evidence against him when the time came to stand in the local Police Court a few weeks later.

In due course he got the summons to attend at Blank, in the County of Blank, on the blank day of Blank, Blank, Blank, at 10.30 a.m.

He attended, and waited miserably with other sheep, sometimes for hours, until his turn arrived, and then——

" Charles Edward So-and-So ! Into the dock."

" Into the *what* ? Am I a common felon ? "

" Oh, very well ! Stand in front of it."

" Now, then ! You are charged with exceeding the speed limit at such and such on the morning of so and so, thereby committing an offence under Section 8 of the Motor Car Act of 1903. Do you plead Guilty or Not Guilty ? "

" Look here ! I say——"

" Do you ? "

" N'not guilty."

" Call Sergeant Slocum."

" Here, sir."

4

" Take the book." Mumble, mumble, mumble, " whole truth, and nothing but the truth, so help me God. Kiss the book."

" At Blank, on the Blank day of Blank, I took up a position on the Fairmile with two other police officers. I timed the prisoner——"

" Prisoner ? Here, I say, who are you calling a——"

" The defendant, then. As I was saying, I timed the defendant over a measured furlong which he covered in . . . and a quarter seconds, which is equal to a speed of twenty-one and three-fifth miles an hour. When stopped by the uniformed officer and in-in-terrogated (gulp) by me, the pris—the defendant—said, ' What the blazes is up now. I want my lunch—can't you find something better to do ? My aunt's house was burgled last week, why don't you arrest burglars instead of hiding yourself in a hedge to catch decent folk who pay rates to be protected instead of persecuted ? I don't know what the blazes this country's coming to. Your rotten old county is the unmentionable limit—I'll never give a bean to your rotten old athletic club again, and serve you jolly well right ! ' "

" Any questions ? " This from the Chairman of the Bench, who calls for a moment's notice.

The Bench system is typically English. The Great Unpaid. An extension of the beloved Committee system, five or six members present and voting, proud of the magic letters J.P. on their visiting cards. Kept gently in check, sometimes, by a sort of secretary, called a Clerk, paid, knowledgeable, trained lawyer, and competent. Sitting once a week dispensing justice, and for the most part doing it well. Albeit, sadly slow to absorb, and prejudiced against new ideas, reluctant to move with the times, and profoundly sensible of the dignity of their great office.

" Drest in a little brief authority." A hunting man or two, a tradesman or two, and the Chairman, portly, plethoric, waistcoat straining at its buttons, healthy red

5

face, watery blue eyes, generous supply of chins, thin grey hair, and white well-waxed moustache. A horseman. Yes, sir, a horseman! Woof! Damn this motoring, this rabble, with their confounded machines, snorty and evil-smelling. Blinding decent folk with dust, frightening his mare! He'd show 'em! What did they think they were, after all? What were they? Road Hogs! Progress? Development? The world must go on? Rot! What had been good enough for his grandfather was good enough for him. He'd show 'em. Woof!

Dear sporting Sir Somebody. He meant well. Honest and clean, he brooked no control but that of Emma, her Ladyship, at the door of whose morning room all might, majesty, dominion, and power accruing from his Chairmanship would be put aside as it were a cloak.

He meant well; but he could fine a young chap ten shillings and costs for wheeling, just wheeling, his bicycle from Mother's garden gate to the gutter, and when doing so sternly express the view that " these machines are dreadful, dangerous things, which should never be allowed on the road."

He meant well. Oh yes! but he could let off with a fine a brute who had beaten a pony nigh unto death, and at the same sitting order the birch, *the birch*, to a shivering pitiful boy for taking a few apples, and then go back to the ancestral home to play with a baby granddaughter.

Little did he realize that in twenty years or less that same granddaughter would be whisking him along the high road at a comfortable " fifty " in the family " shopping bus."

Hear him now, dealing with this case.

" Any questions to ask the witness? "

" Yes. No—that is—— Look here, your Honour, your Worship. What harm did I do to anybody? I *ask* you. There was no one about, nothing—not even a pig, except the police. I was quite safe. I could have pulled up in the length of this room. I *did*, when the uniformed man signalled. He'll tell you I did. What possible harm ? I *ask* you . . ."

" Woof ! Call the next witness."

Police Constable S.O.S.

" You swear, mumble, mumble, kiss the book." Evidence, the mixture as before. Confirmatory to the fraction of a second. Wonderful ! How did they do it ?

" Any questions ? "

" Oh, what's the use ? "

A glance towards brother Justices, two hunting men on his right, two tradesmen on his left. " The usual, eh ? Agreed ? "

Agreed.

" Five pounds and twelve and sixpence costs or one month."

" Five pounds or what ? Here, I say, hang it all, I've only got four pounds with me."

" Very well ; stay in custody till you get the balance. Next case. Woof ! "

So it went on. The high road had become a Tom Tiddler's ground, gold and silver to be picked up at will. " ' Emancipation Day,' " said the new Highwaymen. " Oh ! good joke, but that was nine years ago, and now we're doing some Emancipation for ourselves at your expense."

" Five pounds and costs—that's the stuff. Twenty, thirty, forty, fifty of you every Bench-day, come to the Sheep Pen at 10.30 sharp and be fleeced."

Was this really England ?

It was.

Was rural officialdom losing all its sense of proportion in a craving for motorists' money ?

It was.

Who would be bold enough to tackle this menace ? Who would arise and fight the battle of the Open Road ?

7

Those who were being bled cried FORWARD.
Governing bodies of the Sport cried BACK.
Something *had* to be done.

.   .   .   .   .   .

Two partners in a Motor Firm were talking it over.

" It's like this. If trapping doesn't dry up soon, our
business will. Everybody's furious. One of them said
to-day—' Fine turn of speed on the flat your car has, and
very nice too ! but at five pounds a measured furlong ?
No, thank you ; much more of it and back I go to horses !
He isn't alone in that. What were our people thinking
about when they agreed to an arbitrary limit on speed—
by itself ? They couldn't see beyond the bonnets of
their cars. But here we are, well in the soup. It seems
easier to make laws than to revoke or even amend them.
We may have this infernal Act round our necks for another
twenty years. Meanwhile, what shall we do ? "

" What shall we do ? Let's think ! "

Thinking. . . .

Thinking. . . .

Still thinking.

Then—

" Got it ! "

" Got what ? "

" An idea ! You saw that letter in the motor papers,
a couple of weeks ago, suggesting a scheme for fighting
police-traps ? "

" Yes, the writer must be a jolly good chap. Let's
find a copy."

" Here it is. . . . ' Form an Association . . . cyclists
. . . find out traps . . . warn motorists . . . subscrip-
tions a fiver per annum.' . . . A bit high, but still . . .
Here's a good line . . . ' wish to make no capital or
glorification out of this thing . . . after giving rough
outline . . . willing to withdraw and allow other people
. . . but prepared to devote . . . time and energy . . .
if required.' "

" Yes ! Good luck to him any way. Nothing seems to have happened, though."

" Very well, then. Let *us* take a hand. Let us sub-sidize a few keen bicycle riders, members of clubs or, even better, those fellows who sprint off from Fleet Street to Whitechapel or Ealing with the racing editions— All the Winners ! ' They can ride. They are cute. They like fresh air and a bit of sport. This will be both for them, with ten shillings for the week-end thrown in. They can string down the Brighton road, eight or ten of them, nose out the traps, and then——"

" Yes ! and then ? "

" And then, ride back a few hundred yards to the London side going down, or the Brighton side coming up, and warn the motorists, before they enter the trap. See ? "

" Yes ! but——"

" But me no buts ! It's easy. We give them a flag to wave—with our name on. (Business for us, there.) They wave, the driver slows a bit. ' Trap lower down, sir ! Go easy.' ' Thanks. Who are you ? ' ' We're from So and So, sir, doing this for the good of the cause.' Bright ! that,' says the driver, and goes easy, passes through the trap at a little under the odds, smiles at the uniformed officer, and—lets her out again. See ? "

" Yes ! But suppose the boys are found out, as they will be, and prosecuted, as they may be, for—how does it go ?—for obstructing the police in the execution of their duty."

" We can cross that bridge when we come to it. Any way, it's an idea."

CHAPTER II

WAR ON THE PORTSMOUTH ROAD

TEMPLE BAR. Committee sitting. Chairman—
known to favoured intimates as " Colonel "—is
speaking :

" Well ! gentlemen, here we are, all nice and——"

" Afternoon, Colonel ! Sorry I'm late—must work
sometimes ! What ? "

" That's all right, old man. Sit next to me. As I
was saying, gentlemen, here we are. Oh ! How do
you do, So-and-So. You missed our last meeting.
This is our new Secretary. Paid, you know. Mr.
Secretary, meet Mr. So-and-So ! As I was saying—
we are now established on a proper business footing. We
can get on with the good work. The sportsmen who
started the big Idea have handed it on to us to complete.
Thanks to our Solicitor—that's you, old man !—we
are a constituted body, with aims and objects and—
objects and aims, and all that."

" Hear ! Hear ! "

" Thank you, gentlemen. I will now call upon our
Secretary to read the minutes of our last meeting, and—
what ? Oh yes, thank you. On behalf of the Committee
of the Automobile Association I welcome him to his new
work. He may not know what lies he may have to—I
mean what lies before him. He may not visualize the
potentialities of the—of the possibilities. He may not—
but any way, read the minutes, please."

Minutes duly read.

" Shall I sign these minutes, gentlemen ? "

" Agreed."

" Thank you. Any correspondence ? "

" Yes, Mr. Chairman. A letter from a member complaining that he joined and paid his two guineas last Monday week, because he was saved from a trap on the Brighton road, and—then was caught on the Portsmouth road, last Sunday. He doesn't wish to appear grasping, but he's getting rather sick of spending all his time on one road, and when can we extend our activities ? "

" Um ! Any more ? "

" Member wants to know if we can give him a route from South Hampstead to Southampton, and where would we recommend him to stop for the night on the way, if he has to. Would somebody lend me a Contour Book, please ? I can get the hotels from a Railway Guide."

" Let's take the second one first. Any one got a Contour Book ? Yes ? Thank you. There you are, Mr. Secretary, and that's that. Now, about the Portsmouth road. Can we afford it ? What's our bank balance ? "

" We haf exsactly seventy-fife-four-six in de Bank."

Thus the Honorary Treasurer. An entirely lovable Anglo-German, more British than many British, living for forty years in England, marked out by fate for heartbreak and death within the first twelve months of the War.

" How many new members are there for election, Mr. Secretary ? "

" Fourteen, including our first lady member, a peeress—by marriage. She wishes to be registered under initials, in order not to embarrass her people."

" Ha ! That's a good one ! But never mind, it's another two guineas. Is it your pleasure, gentlemen, that these new members be duly elected ? Agreed—so be it. Now back to the Portsmouth road. Yes, Mr. Secretary ? "

" With great respect, Mr. Chairman, we ought to, we

must, and we can, extend to the Portsmouth road. It's by way of becoming a bigger scandal even than the Brighton road, and that's bad enough."

"Quite right!" broke in a Committee-man. "A friend of mine was caught twice on the same run—of forty miles. He swears that the policeman working the stop-watch didn't start clocking until several seconds after he entered the trap. It's disgraceful. Before the Bench a policeman's word goes for everything, and ours for nothing. We must either go on or go back."

"Hear! Hear! Go on—go on! That's the stuff."

"What do we do now?" This from the Colonel.

"It's quite all right, Mr. Chairman. The boys are keen. They love their week-ends' sport. They have friends eager to chime in. We can switch over one or two of the keenest from the Brighton road, as a kind of backbone."

"What about inspecting them?"

"Quite easy. The Trade are splendid. Helping us to help them, as they put it—taking it in turns to lend a car and driver, any Saturday or Sunday. We've only got to ask and there will be a chassis with an egg-box or a shop-soiled tonneau, for no payment. And they're sending us new members. Keen as mustard they are. It's splendid."

"That sounds good. Well, gentlemen! In for a penny in for a pound. We don't know where this may land us, and we don't mind, eh, what? Still we must not forget our finances. How long will the bank balance last at this rate?"

"Well, sir, our present expenditure is at the rate of nine pounds a week!" explained Mr. Secretary.

"All in?"

"That includes Patrols' pay and office salaries! The Portsmouth road will cost about a fiver more—for the present; and we are averaging ten new members a week."

12

" Very well, gentlemen. I put it to the meeting. Portsmouth road—those in favour—those against ? "

Carried unanimously.

" That's all for to-day." Meeting finished.

.   .   .   .   .   .

Thus did the War extend to another front. The cyclist scouts were adorned with yellow armlets, a simple and inexpensive equipment which could be and was removed when they were looking for traps, and assumed again when warning the motoring innocents.

So far none of these scouts had been prosecuted for obstruction, but cursing was loud and deep, and frequently a perspiring policeman would close in upon a scout and say :

" Here, you ! I want your name and address, and if you don't stop this game of hide-and-seek I'll lock you up. You, with your road-hog employers."

" Oh, will you ? Just try it on. Hedgehog ! Think you're everybody, but *I* know the Law as well as *you*. You can't ! See ? "

" We can't, eh ? Well, let me tell you. We'll have you one of these days, for something, somehow."

Relations were indeed strained.

.   .   .   .   .   .

" Bill ! " said one of the older scouts to his mate. " Ever read ' Sherlock Holmes ' ? "

" Rather ! What's the idea ? "

" Good. I'm him for a bit, and you're Watson. How does Sherlock open up ? Oh, yes. H'm, my dear Watson, what you want is de-de-duction—that's the word. I've discovered that there's only one stop-watch in this blessed village and it's on sale in the shop-window two doors from the police-sergeant's cottage. You know the one—with COUNTY POLICE over the porch.

" Now ' Watson,' it's quite a simple matter to deduct that the old Johnny who runs the shop lends out the stop-watch, because sometimes it's in the window and sometimes it's not. Who does he lend it to ? Ah ! Who-o-o ? Get me ? When the watch is on show, easy work for us—when it's not, we're in for a busy day."

"Marvellous ! You're wasting your young life. Go back to Aldgate and write detective stories."

．　．　．　．　．　．

Secretary was casting up the cash-book. Staff was putting on her hat to go home when—telephone began ringing——

"See who that is, please ! "

"It's Mr.—couldn't catch the name, but he lent us a car two Sundays ago, and he'll be round in five minutes. He seems a bit excited."

"Oh, very well ; don't wait. Good-night ! "

What on earth's up now ?

Five minutes elapsed.

"Hallo, sir ! "

"Hallo, yourself. Bit of luck to catch you in—here's a rum go ! It's like this. I've been caught—what ? No, there's nothing rum about that, but I think we've got 'em—got that chap who starts his blessed old stop-watch when he likes, and not when we're signalled. You know that bit of road called the Fairmile ? "

"I do."

"You know the rather stiff bit of hill before you get to it ? "

"I do. I've been up it backwards."

"Very well. I was going up it this morning on first speed—all alone, and, just when I had got her going again, the balloon went up."

"The *what* ? "

"I was caught, and for once I turned and bit the whole bunch of them ; called 'em everything under the sun. They were wrong—*wrong*. I couldn't have been doing twenty and they knew it, and I'd show 'em up, the—

14

the—never mind what I said. That doesn't matter, but what *does* matter is this. When I had ' passed along, please,' and pulled up to cool down, along came one of your scouts—that fair fellow with a hook nose—and said, ' Were you caught, sir ? ' I said, ' Was I—oh, don't try to be funny ! ' He said, ' I'm not, sir. I was behind you up the slope and through the trap, on my bicycle. On my bicycle, one man-power ! How *could* you be doing over twenty, if I could keep up with you, as I did ? ' "

" Ooh ! " The Secretary whistled.

" Ooh to you, twice ! I tell you we've *got* 'em ! Put your man forward as a witness when my case comes on and we'll flatten the lot out. It'll be great."

" All right ! I think we can promise to defend you free of charge—you're a good friend. But don't be too sure about our man going into the box. That requires thought. The Committee must decide. It might cut both ways, do more harm than good. Any way, I'll let you know in plenty of time."

Committee sitting, ordinary business disposed of. Chairman speaking :

" We've left the Fairmile Case to the last, gentlemen, so that every member could be here. I—er—don't want to—that is, there's no need to—er—get nervous at all ; but, well—it's a bit of a dangerous corner and we must drive with special caution. You've heard the details from our Secretary. The question is—shall we or shall we not let the scout give evidence. What do you think, Walter ? "

" My opinion is No, we shouldn't. Defend the driver, Yes ! And do it properly—put up our best. But if our man goes into the witness-box you never know what the other side may bully him into saying, nor what mess we might be landed into."

" Thank you ! Charles One " (there were three Committee-men named Charles), " what say you ?"

" I agree with Walter. We're skating on pretty thin

ice as it is. In the clubs they chip us about conspiracy to defeat the ends of Justice, and ask if the dock at the Central Criminal Court will be big enough to hold our Committee and the Secretary when the case against us is sufficiently complete for the Police to proceed. We don't mind that—better men than this little band of pioneers have gone to gaol for their opinions—but why should we precipitate the crisis? No! Colonel, I'd rather pay the chap's fine myself than run that risk just yet."

The Secretary was nervously tapping Morse on the table — dash-dot-dash-dot : They're right. They're right. He mustn't go.

" Now, Mr. Solicitor ! "

" Well, Mr. Chairman ! I've listened with great interest to our colleagues' remarks, and there is no doubt that there is much to be said for their opinions. Of course, if we win—if our scout's evidence upsets the case for the police—it will be a great triumph, and bring us a flood of new members. On the other hand, if we lose, it may hurt us considerably."

(Tap-tap. He mustn't go.)

" What I suggest, Mr. Chairman," continued Mr. Solicitor, " is to leave it to our Counsel. The scout can be at the police court, at call. When Counsel sees how the case is likely to go, he can decide whether or not to call our man. That's how these matters are usually handled—leave it to Counsel."

" Oh, very well ! We must follow precedent, I suppose, eh, gentlemen ? Agreed ? But remember, Mr. Solicitor, we'd rather not."

(Tap-tap. He mustn't go.)

.   .   .   .   .

In spite of that consensus of opinion he went.

Counsel are somewhat of a race apart. They are absolved from legal or financial responsibility if their advice or conduct of a case is wrong. The sufferer can only pay, curse, and swear " Never again."

Morning dawned on the Fairmile Case.

The Secretary was speaking to the Solicitor's clerk, who was off to the Court to spoon-feed Counsel. " I'm not usually timid, old man, but—I don't like it. I'm nervous. It means so much. You understand, don't you ? It has been left to Counsel to put our scout in the box if he sees fit. *Don't let him see fit.* He mustn't go. If only I could get to the Court, but I can't. The Staff must have her lunch, and there's no one else to mind the office. Oh ! *do* be careful."

" All right ! Don't get nervy. I'll do my best."

" Thanks ! Good luck, and give me a ring on the 'phone when it's over. I'm anxious."

A wretched day, until the telephone rang. " That you, old man ? " came a distant voice.

" Yes ! yes ! Go on."

" Sorry ! We've lost ! Five pounds and—you know the rest. But what's worse, our Counsel ignored all my urgings to the contrary and—put the scout in the box. Old man, it was *awful !* They browbeat the poor little beggar until he squirmed and contradicted himself, and then—you should have heard the Chairman of the Bench ! —' We accept the evidence of the police witness, and we do not accept that put forward by the defence. More may be heard about this. Defendant is fined five pounds and costs, or one month.' "

" Oh ! I was right then. Thanks all the same, jolly good of you. Good-bye."

What did he mean by " More may be heard about this " ?

Three weeks later. On a Monday evening. The Secretary was clearing up. The Staff was getting out her pennies for the bus fare.

" A letter has just come in," she said.

" Go and get it, please ! Thank you, that's all for to-day. Don't miss your bus. Good-night ! "

Must balance the cash first. Good ! Now ! Who's this from, I wonder ? Funny heading to start with, anyhow. *H.M. Prison, Brixton.* My goodness !

> To the Secretary. Dear Sir,—This is to inform you that when leaving my beat on the Portsmouth road last Saturday I was arrested on a warrant and detained at the local police-station until the morning, when I was brought here. I am to be taken before the Bench on Wednesday. I am charged with committing perjury in the Fairmile case.

Perjury ! Ooh ! A bit of a facer, that, and just as we were getting along so nicely. Wonder if our solicitor friends have gone for the day. Ring up. Thank goodness !

" Here, Frank ! read this. What do you make of it ? "

" H'm, nasty," was the reply.

" What can we do to help our man ? "

" Nothing in the way of getting him out on bail at this hour. Magistrates are not sitting until the morning. Arrest seems to have been cleverly timed so as to get him locked up for a few days at any rate, as they've often threatened. They're certainly ' one up ' at this hole, whatever may be the finish of the match. You might run over to Brixton and make sure he's all right. Leave half a sovereign with the warders for a few comforts— that's about all you can do."

" Very well, thanks ; the sooner the better. It's an awful blow ! If we don't beat 'em and he gets convicted it means the end. We'll never get a man to scout for us again. Oh ! why *did* they put him in the witness-box when all our instincts were against it ? "

" Cheer up ! No use crying over spilt milk. It's all in the day's work. Off with you to Brixton. Who knows ? Perhaps it isn't true, perhaps it's only a joke ! Good-night and good luck."

Only a joke, perhaps. But out there in the street,

where as usual the workers were swarming into buses for home and high-tea, the news-placards blazoned, in what seemed to be letters of fire :

MOTOR   SCOUT

ARRESTED.

ALL   THE   WINNERS

All the Winners ! !   Ooh ! !

CHAPTER III

IN THE DOCK

THE police-court, at the close of a hearing that had lasted two hours or more. Solicitor speaking : "He pleads not guilty and reserves his defence—and of course applies for bail."

"Bail ! Um—any objection, Inspector."

"No, your Worship."

"Very well ! "

To defendant : "You are committed for trial at the next Assizes, and will be released on bail in two sureties of fifty pounds each. Witnesses will be bound over to attend at the trial. The Court is adjourned."

"There was no alternative," said shrewd Solicitor, on the way out. "It would have been madness to expose our defence before that bunch—I mean Bench. As it stands, we know all they've got to say and they know practically nothing about us. At the Assizes we get another chance. We can turn their witnesses inside out by cross-examination, and put in plans and diagrams and photos and expert timekeepers as evidence against their testimony—and, last but not least, we shall have a Jury. Even if the Judge happens to hate This Motoring—though I hope not—we still have the Jury. Let's get some lunch. And, by the way, don't put the scout back on the road, on any road, until we know his fate—and ours. It means everything to the whole lot of us. We *must* get him off, and we *will*."

Same afternoon. Committee sitting, specially summoned. Chairman speaking :

"Well, gentlemen, here we are again! Thank you for coming at such short notice. This Fairmile business seems like making a bit of history—looks pretty black, too. Our man should never have been put in the box; but mind, gentlemen, no recriminations, please. No names, no pack-drill, as we used to say in the service— what? But there's one small point. Where's the money coming from to fight with? We can't do much on a two-figure bank-balance."

"Don't worry about that, Colonel—Mr. Chairman, I mean. It's not the first time we've had to dip into our pockets. Fight first, and square up after, eh, Walter?"

"Quite right, Charles! We all came in together and we'll stick together."

"And so say all of us, and so say all of us. For— or——"

"Splendid! gentlemen," resumed the Chairman when enthusiasm had subsided. "A perfectly proper spirit. What says Shakespeare? 'Come the three corners of the world in arms, And we shall shock them. Naught shall make us rue—if—if'—you know the rest."

"Oh! jolly good!"

"It is unanimously decided to fight the case to a finish and—damn the expense. Agreed? Agreed. That's all for the present. Thank you, gentlemen."

The Meeting finished.

. . . .

Now for some staff work, on a quite new kind of war-game.

The general idea was this: Motorist prosecuted for exceeding the limit. Swears that he didn't. Supported in his contention by motor scout, who swears that he followed the car up a long hill and through the trap on a pedal-bicycle, and that therefore the speed alleged was impossible in all the circumstances.

Police swear that the limit was exceeded—timed by

them over a measured furlong. As for the scout, by
a majority of three to one they swear that he could not
have followed the car, as they did not see him. They
did not see him, therefore he couldn't have been there,
and his evidence was untrue. Untrue evidence, given
on oath, is perjury punishable on conviction by imprisonment for a term not exceeding so many years. So much
for the general idea.

Special idea, that is tactics to be employed by the
opposing parties, identified respectively for the purpose
of this quite new war-game as Blue and Yellow.

Blue, having taken the offensive, sits tight, hoping for
the worst. " Convict him ! Put him away for a year
or two ! That'll smash up the whole crowd of busy-
bodies for good and all. We said we'd get one of them
some day, for something, somehow. Very well, then."

Yellow, very much on the defensive, can do anything
but sit tight. Yellow must get the finest advocate in
criminal practice, and must give him plenty to get his
teeth into. Mustn't lose a point, nor drop a stitch.

Mr. Solicitor was right. Plans of the road, to be duly
sworn to, showing the approach up the hill, with
gradients, and the trap itself, where the police hid or
stood ; photos taken from each hiding-place or position,
with a car appropriately placed, to demonstrate why
they might not have seen the scout on his cycle following
close behind—as they one and all swore was the fact.

Timekeepers, renowned in the world of motor trials
and tests, and of unblemished reputation and character,
to reconstruct the crime with stop-watches guaranteed
at Kew Observatory, to show His Majesty's Judge, and
His Majesty's Jury of twelve good men and true, what
a mere flash of time those seconds really were when it
came to it, and how feasible it was that a cyclist should
follow close behind a car while the police were trapping
the said car, with their attention concentrated upon it ;
and how feasible, again, that they should not have seen
the cyclist—if they didn't.

Staff work ? Yes, indeed—weeks of it. Not a point to be lost, not a stitch to be dropped. Ah ! Consider what it meant !

" Just got notice, Frank, we're in the list for next week. Who's the Judge, I wonder ? "

" Here we are. _The Times_ Law Sittings. This is our Circuit. Mr. Justice —— Oh ! that's nasty—he's a thorough sportsman but hates motors. We must look for his charge to the Grand Jury. I'll bet even money he ' goes ' for motor-scouting for all he's worth. One of the old school, you know—like old ' Woof Woof.' ' This Motoring, these road-hogs, rudely disturbing the countryside, frightening peaceful folk and slaughtering innocent chickens.' Oh, yes ; he'll rub it in. But there's one thing—he may allow his prejudice to take him too far, and then—we've always the Jury."

" Good, old man ? The Jury ! Let's hope some of 'em motor, and have been caught. That might help."

The day arrived.

" Better go down by train, eh ? They may be trapping, and that would put the jolly old lid on it. Where's the morning paper ? Ah, here we are—' Motor Scout Case, Charge to the Grand Jury.' Ooh ! ' In charging the Grand Jury Mr. Justice ——' Just what I told you ; he's let himself go—all out. ' This Motoring a menace. This organization, an outrage—illegal—attempting to defeat the ends of Justice—ought to be suppressed—calling for the sternest measures '—have a look for yourself."

" No, thanks—tear the darned thing up. We've quite enough to bear, without his Lordship's vapourings."

Here we are—what a crowd. Quite a red-letter day for the little county town. Cars lined up outside the Town Hall. People jostling each other and murmuring, and looking here and there—what for ?

" Make way. Stand back there, please. Stand back "—for His Majesty's Judge, resplendent and awe-inspiring in full-bottomed wig, ermine and scarlet, heralded by javelin men, handed, by a smaller wig and quiet gown, from a carriage and pair—not a motor car (bad omen that), passing grandly into the Court of Assize. Let's hope he had a good night's sleep. Every little helps.

"The Court's crowded, but come along—we'll get in somehow."

"No, thanks, old man ! You go. I'm staying outside, with my pipe for company. Don't think me too much of an idiot, but I simply *can't*. Our staff work is finished to the last button on the last gaiter. We can do no more. It's up to our Counsel now, and—I'm staying outside. See ? "

"All right, all right, keep your pecker up, and we'll meet later."

. . . .

The Court adjourned for lunch.

Half a dozen of the faithful band of Yellow forgathered. Mr. Solicitor, shrewd and brave as ever, speaking :

"I'm hanged if I know how it's going. The old gentleman—'scuse my irreverence—is dead against us. It's sticking out a yard, as the saying goes. Blue have finished their innings, and we opened the batting just before the adjournment. Our first witness, the chap who was trapped, made quite a good show. After all, he could only repeat what he said at the police court ; but the other side didn't shake him. He did very well— very well. You're the next wicket, Mr. Surveyor, with your plans ; and you next, with your photos. We'll spread 'em all over the Court till it looks like an art gallery, and impress the Jury. After the timekeepers we'll put the scout in the box—last wicket. He seems pretty cool, and we've always got the Jury."

"What are they like ? " asked the worried Secretary.

"Oh ! The proverbial curate's egg—tradesmen, and

a farmer or two. Four or five stand out as rather more our type—they look as though they could run a car if they liked."

" Let's hope so."

" There's one comfort ; our leading Counsel is a topper, earning every guinea on his brief—snapping at every bone in the Blue dish. He made a fine hash of the Inspector. Got him to admit that he had bought a cheap stop-watch with his own money—*with his own money*. No ill-will against motorists. Not vindictive. Oh no! Great fun ! A pity you missed it."

" Fun ! You call it FUN !! Ooh ! "

" We'd better be getting back. Coming ? No ? Well, have it your own way—two hours more and we should know the worst. So long."

Two hours. What was the scout thinking about, poor little beggar. What had he really done, any way, to be landed in such a pickle ? All for a miserable ten shillings every week-end, baked with the heat, or soaked with rain, to make a motorist's holiday. Pretty rough on him. Wonder if he realized the importance of the part he was playing in this drama of the road.

He had the centre of the stage. The outcome of those few minutes' toilful pedalling up the slope and along the Fairmile, and his subsequent evidence, honest and earnest though it had been, might bring him to disgrace and detention. A convict—dreadful word. And if—oh no ! please !—if that happened, it meant the end of a brave endeavour.

The Committee ? Who, in years to come, would spare a moment's thought for them ? They were doggedly championing a cause already regarded by some as lost, and by others as being of questionable dignity. Sportsmen all, to know them was to like them, yet their name was Ishmael, and frowns were their portion.

The Press breathed pessimism. If, that evening, the news-placards flamed with a tragic message—MOTOR SCOUT CASE, VERDICT and SENTENCE—how

easy to jeer—" We told you so." Hear them. Hear an
editor to the leader-writer, answering his call. " Come
in, George ! About that scout case, result's just in.
Convicted. Knock out about a quarter column, will
you ? eh ? Oh, better come down on the side of Law
and Order. Thanks ! "
And then—the next morning :

We have previously commented upon the curious
lack of foresight which appeared to prompt several
quite reputable and otherwise sane gentlemen to
combine to finance and prosecute a campaign against
an established law. Such conduct, however well
meant, is obviously contrary to our insular, one
might say instinctive, respect for and submission
to the Statutes of our country.
Without appearing in any way harsh, it must be
said that these gentlemen have shown a regrettable
lack of discretion. They have done those things
which ought not to have been done. This is now
evident from the conviction of one of their hirelings,
reported in a previous edition, for perjury.
While we sympathize, as we must, with the un-
fortunate victim of an ill-fated and foredoomed cause,
we can only express the hope that his well-meaning
but misguided employers will do their duty by him
when he comes out of prison, and then close down
the whole unhappy scheme.

Yes, indeed ! That was the sort of stuff to be
expected—if !
But the game wasn't lost yet. Light another pipe,
and hope on.
" Hallo, Mr. Expert ! Finished your evidence ? So
glad to see you. I was dreaming—might call it nightmare. How goes it ? "
" Oh ! so-so. My plans made quite a good show,

and now the photo-man is doing his bit. But the Judge!
He's a terror. After Blue Counsel had tried to tie me
up and failed, his Lordship had a go, and he couldn't.
He tried hard, too. He's got a grudge against the lot of
us, but we know our business. An Expert well in hand
is worth two on the Bench."

" Oh, yes ! "

" Just one cigarette and then I'm going back to see
our team finish the innings. Cheero ! "

Hope on.

This vigil was vaguely reminiscent—of what ?

Of course ! how alike.

Thousands of those about to become fathers were even
then experiencing much the same. They were being
ordered by an aproned autocrat to " Go for a walk ! not
too far, but go—we'll let you know how the poor soul is
getting on. Go ! you're doing no good—you're only
in the way ! "

Kindred spirits, they were—outside—walking up and
down, pulling at a pipe, and praying. One touch of
nature.

There appeared a face, familiar, and friendly.

" Ah ! Nurse—sorry, I mean Mr. Solicitor, how is
she ?—I mean, hang it all—I'm all muddled up. What's
the latest ? "

" That's all right, my boy, take it easy. Our innings
has closed—the Judge has summed up. Dead against
us. He'll give the poor chap two years if he gets a
chance. Our Counsel actually corrected him twice—a
thing unheard of before. Splendid. He 'bit' him,
actually. What a nerve ! The Jury have retired. Come
with me. That's the Jury room."

" Oh, yes ! "

" They're in there now."

" Oh, yes ! "

" You're talking too much, my boy. I'll leave you
for somebody quieter, and have a smoke."

Ten minutes—twenty, thirty. Solicitor returning.

" Here they are at last "—as he went back into Court—
" I must go too." He threw his cigarette away.

One minute, two, three, and then—What's that ?
Solicitor, rushing out—smiling !—smiling !

" NOT GUILTY ! Hurrah ! Not guilty. Now you
can say something more than ' Oh, yes ! eh ? ' "

" Rather ! Thank you a thousand times. You've
been wonderful. What a relief ! Shake hands—witnesses too ! Jolly good, old man ! you too."

Pats on the back for poor little scout. " Well
done, quite a little hero, isn't he ? A good supper for
you, and next week we put you on another road."

There was the Inspector. He didn't seem so big and
menacing as before. A word with him would not do
any harm.

" Evening, Inspector ! We've had a good fight, and
bear you no ill-will. What about shaking hands ? "

" Well, sir, if you put it that way—certainly. No ill-
will at all—you gentlemen give us a mighty lot of trouble,
but—well, well, it's all in the game."

Then for telegrams to the office and home.

" Come along ! What ? it's raining ? Never mind,
who cares for a drop of rain, when we've won ? "

In the train once more, nearing London. " If we had
a newspaper now, you wouldn't say ' Tear the darned
thing up,' eh ? " What a day !

" Here we are—pass along quietly ! No police
trap to stop us, and now let's all stick together and
celebrate."

Chorus every one—" We w-on't go home till——"

" No ! So sorry, dear good chaps—I'm immensely
grateful and all that, but please cut me out—let me off
just this once."

" Well, of all the— 'for goodness sake, why ? "

" Well, it's like this. You see, we're not on the
'phone at home yet, and I promised Her—that is, we
arranged—that is—oh hang it all, how shall I put it ?
Look here, you remember that old song—a bit gushy,

but rather sweet—it goes like this—' I know of two bright eyes, waiting for me ' ! "

" Yes, but——"

" Well ! They are—waiting—for me—at the Troc ! "

.   .   .   .   .   .

After the battle came the reckoning.

Committee sitting. The Chairman, beaming through his monocle, said : " How to find the money ? That's the question. We are overdrawn at the Bank. Any ideas will be gratefully considered—and don't all speak at once."

Charles Two said, " Let's have a dinner—that's a typically English idea—but why not ? "

" Why not ? So long as we hold it, and don't give it. That is, everybody pay for his ticket. A few leading lights of the Press, of course, must be honoured guests."

" Agreed ! Agreed ! "

" As soon as convenient after Christmas, eh, gentlemen ? Some time in January."

" Yes ! Colonel," said Charles One. " Not too large a room, then we can hope to fill it. And, here's an idea. Give 'em a nice light show afterwards. Variety turns—quite new that, eh ? and—Walter !—he will help—won't you, old man ? There's the value of having one of London's leading impresarios on our Committee."

" Certainly ! You arrange the dinner and leave the show to me," said Walter.

" Bravo ! Taken as read. Now about the money—the bill of costs. I believe you have a suggestion, Mr. Secretary ? "

" Yes, sir, and it's like—I mean—it's this. When they've all had plenty to—that is, after the coffee and liqueurs—the time will be ripe for a moving speech from the Chair, and if one may say so, nobody can do it better."

" Hear ! Hear ! "

" Thank you. Go on, please."

" Then, instead of passing the hat round, we'll have cards printed with the heading ' Fairmile Perjury Case,' or something like that, and worded :

> *I shall be pleased to give........pounds........*
> *shillings towards the expenses of the successful defence.*
> *Name ....*
> *Address ....*
> *Membership Number.....and date..............*

" You see what I mean, don't you ? When they've only to fill in a card, instead of paying up on the spot, they won't be so particular to a sovereign or two, and we can easily collect the money, by post."

" Good. So be it. Those in favour ? Agreed."

. . . . . .

A sub-Committee was formed to get on with the Dinner.

. . . . . .

Somewhere in London, somewhere about 9.30 p.m. Chairman speaking :

" And finally, gentlemen, this hardly-won fight has to be paid for. There was no other course : Ours not to reason why ! ours but to do and (but we didn't) die. Now we ask you to help us, in order that we may continue to help you. Our position is precarious but promising. We are patrolling four separate roads, and the membership has just reached three hundred. Our bank-balance is nebulous to the point of being negligible. The law costs are round about three hundred and fifty pounds. We want the money, gentlemen. The many famous variety artistes who are generously giving their services to our deserving cause, thanks to our distinguished colleague—that's you, Walter—(Hear, hear ! Jing ! Jing ! of glasses)—are eager to do so and get back to the Holborn Empire, the Tivoli, and the Oxford.

" Before we start, let me beg you to signify your appreciation of their kindness by filling up the card which lies in front of every one of you. Fill it up for as much as you can, or more than you can, afford, and then—enjoy the Show."

Loud cheers.

.   .   .   .

A great success. Everybody delighted.

" So unusual," said one ; " so—intimate. Who would believe there could be such a difference between sitting in a five-shilling stall at the Holborn or the Oxford, with yards of orchestra and footlights between Row D and the Sisters Sunflower, and the same dazzling pair on a foot-high piano platform almost within touching distance of our seats at the table ? And when they did their dance, old boy. Ooh ! wonderful ! "

" But the biggest hit was the Conjurer ! Poor chap, there was a big mirror behind him—you can guess the rest."

All over. " Time, gentlemen, please." Lights dimmed. Waiters coughing a requiem.

" Must count the cards before we go—just a few minutes, please."

" Magnificent—three hundred and sixty-two. That will clear the Bill of Costs, yes, and one quiet chap, a Scot, said as he gave in his card marked a fiver, ' If ye find ye're short o' the amoont, juist let me know and I'll send ye the balance.' Bless him, it makes one go all warm. Let's hope the dear man will live to see it in print, one day."

And so to bed.

CHAPTER IV

THE BADGE OF HONOUR

"WE must have a telegraphic address, please," said the Secretary. "It's only a guinea a year."

"Of course we must, eh, gentlemen?" said the gallant Chairman in Meeting.

"Agreed!"

"We'll leave that to you then, Mr. Secretary."

"Right, sir! I will try to get something which will work in 'Auto' or 'Ass,' or both." So he called at the G.P.O. with that intent.

But the G.P.O. said: "No! Sorry; we're full p with 'Autos' and 'Asses.' It can't be done!"

"Well," asked the Secretary, rather despairingly. "What can you suggest, please. All this is rather new to me. Very grateful for any help or advice."

The G.P.O. man smiled sympathetically. "All right! Here's a bunch of names we would accept. See if you can find a decent one. Take your time."

"Thanks very much indeed."

The bunch was a queer one. ANODYNE? No! BENIGHTEDLY? No! that was too long. Something crisp needed. AUDIFORM? DIALECTIC? ERYSIPELAS? Ugh!! nasty, but——

"I say, please! Here's one I think my people would accept. May I have a day's option on it? To put it forward?"

"Sorry!" said G.P.O. "No option. You must take

it or leave it, and it may be gone by this afternoon. Must keep to the rules, you know."

"Oh, very well, thanks. It sounds good. I'll risk it ! "

So Secretary paid over the guinea, with some trepidation, and walked away with FANUM.

"Fanum ! The word is inviting, but what does it mean ? " said someone at the next Committee meeting.

"Not a race-horse, but we hope it will be a winner ! Let's ask a learned friend, if we can find one."

He was found, and explained that Fanum is Latin for a Temple.

"Who knows ? " added the Learned One, getting poetic ; "it may be a good omen. A Temple of Motoring Freedom. A sanctuary for the oppressed. A——"

"Oh, thanks—that's enough ! Let's hope it proves a winner."

.   .   .   .   .   .

"Too many organizations," someone had written, "formed with similar objects." Yes ! maybe they were. Doing the same sort of work !

Perhaps, but one moment, please. Not entirely. Only one of the few was fighting the battle of the Open Road. The Trade Society knew that, and said so—nice people—and showed their appreciation in practical form.

"Cars ? Yes, we'll lend you some, until you can afford to buy one. Anything else ? " they had asked. "Oh yes ! of course, we'll let you have a little Stand at our Motor Show—free ! Then you can get more members ! "

Nice people.

Apart from the Road Campaign, the lines were certainly much the same. Well, that would have to sha e itself. Meanwhile, on with the good work, and don't worry too much about The Others.

Committee sitting, Chairman speaking.

"Members are coming in well, gentlemen ! More for

election to-day than last meeting, and it's been like that for the last six meetings. Fancy, thirty ! A record, eh ? "

" Yes ! Mr. Chairman, there are still a few good sportsmen left in the world, although——"

" Although what, Charles One ? "

" Well ! Colonel, it's the mean ones—the ones who don't join. Our men save them time and time again, and they just take it all as ' read.' "

" He's right ! " said Charles Two. " In the City this very day I tackled a chap who was bragging about having been warned, and how he had laughed at the police ; and when I asked him if he was a member he said No ! I said, ' Very well, give me your two guineas, and I'll fix you up this afternoon—I'm on the Committee.' ' The —— ' he said, ' why should I when I can get warned for nothing ? ' This is a long speech for me, Mr. Chairman, but it's nothing to what I told him—in front of everybody too ! A rank outsider ! "

Hear ! Hear ! Shame ! " That's the trouble. They can all get our protection and the good have to pay for the bad."

" Yes ! yes ! All right, gentlemen," broke in the Chairman. " Order, please ! Here's a fresh problem. Let's think it out."

" If I may suggest, Mr. Chairman ! " said the Secretary.

" By all means, out with it ! "

" We identify our men ; they wear an armlet and a red-and-white disc with a number on it."

" Well ? "

" Perhaps we can give them caps soon, and one day we'll have 'em in uniform—but that by the way. My idea, with all deference, is—identify our *members*. It has never been done before. Let's have a badge on the cars, nice and prominent, so that our men will see it easily."

" By Jove, that's good. Go on, please."

" We can charge a few shillings—as a fee, mind—

34

they mustn't buy them outright. So we shan't lose any money. Perhaps we can register the design so that no Others can copy it. And, what's more, our men can salute the Badge, and only the cars which carry it will get any help. The rest can go to——that is, they can look after themselves."

(Hear ! Hear ! That's the stuff !)

" One moment, please, gentlemen," from the calm and collected Chairman. " Yes, Walter ; you were saying——? "

" I was saying, it's a wonderful idea and we ought to adopt it at once. We shall be talking in thousands instead of hundreds when we've had it going a few months."

" Well ! that's settled. No need to put it to the vote, eh ? gentlemen—agreed ? Agreed. Good. That's *that*. Now a sub-committee to settle the design, and then— off we go. And—jolly good luck to THE BADGE ! "

" THE BADGE ! THE BADGE ! "

.   .   .   .   .   .

On the road, a few weeks after.

Great fun. The badge-maker—a member, of course— had put in noble work. All hand-cut, a slow process, but never mind—make a sport of it, early and late, and Saturday afternoons—get 'em out. And members, too, tumbling over each other to procure them. " An early number, please—heirloom for the family some day, perhaps—what ? "

Oh ! great fun.

" Look ! " said a member's wife. " There's a car in front with Our Badge on—he's being saluted by Our man. Nice, eh ? Our turn next. Ooh ! Here we are. Go on, return the salute. No ! not with your left hand, silly !—right hand—and take your cigar out of your mouth. Ahhh ! I'm going to like This Motoring. Is my hat on straight ? How many more shall we meet between now and lunch ? Oh, I say, here's another car coming towards us. What do we do now ? Must recognize

35

Our Badge. You'd better salute him. Yes, don't be
shy. Brotherhood of the road, you know. What!
you don't like to—oh, you are a—anyhow, I shall smile
at her, so there."

Oh! great fun, and even greater, coming back, to see
an indignant one pulled up and holding forth to Our
scout. Pull up too, near enough to listen!

The indignant one was saying, " What do you mean
by it—(splutter)—I was caught, just here, on the way
down this morning for the very first time on this road.
Why didn't you give me the——What do you mean
by it ? "

" Well, you see, sir " (very politely, according to
instructions), " you see, sir! it's like this! You're not
a member, are you ? "

" What's that got to do with it ? Any way, how do
you know ? "

" You haven't got Our Badge on, sir. I'm sorry, but
you see how it is, sir, don't you ? "

" Oh! "

And that was *that!*

.   .   .   .   .   .

" The Association has progressed by leaps and bounds,
the membership now being nine hundred and forty."

So ran the first Annual Report, issued in June, 1906.

The Balance Sheet showed figures of similar mag-
nitude.

Value of badges held by members . £28 2 6
  „   „ Patrols' field-glasses.....   3 11 3
  „   „ Office furniture........   4 14 6
Debit balance on the year's working .. £289 18 4

Other items of interest : " Gratitude to the Press for
their great sympathy and invaluable assistance . . . hardly
a week passing without one of the myriad persecutions
and anomalies to which motoring is subjected being
dealt with fearlessly and critically. Members of the

Press have been invited to witness the operations of the Association's Scouts, the expenses in connection therewith being borne by the Committee. . . . A scheme for guarding roads in such districts as are not yet patrolled has been inaugurated."

A scheme for guarding—pray, what did that mean? Oh yes, of course—the Agents' Pole.

It was this way.

Trapping of motorists had become a veritable epidemic, and was spreading. Newspapers carried the infection. Big hauls in motor fines at local Benches in the South of England, within easy distance of the Metropolis, fired other local Benches with the spirit of emulation.

"We can't expect to get the same amount of motor traffic in these remote parts," said the Mayor of Sloppington-on-Mud to his local Council, "but there's no harm in casting a line now and then—we may catch a few. Our police can take it in their stride, so to speak, as it were. Very well, then."

It was so easy.

Cleaning up the South African War was not very much more difficult than the task of this new organization, whose telegraphic address was officially FANUM, but more explicitly "Ishmael." Members paid their money to be protected. With pardonable forgetfulness at small mercies when they were saved, they cursed at being caught, and asked in no uncertain language *why?*

"Hang it all!" said Mr. Chairman, wiping his monocle. "We can't be everywhere all at once. We must walk before we can run. Scouts cost money. What the—that is to say—any suggestions?"

"If you please!"

"Certainly! Order, gentlemen! Carry on, Mr. Secretary."

"Thank you, sir. The Garage people, the small repair-shops, have hailed our advent into the fight. They look upon us as their saviours, and are willing to do anything and everything to help on the good work. As you know, we're linking them up by degrees as our Agents. A.A. Agents—with a sign, and all that. Brotherhood of the road means business for them. Each of them knows the local conditions, and especially the local police."

" Well ? "

" Why shouldn't they act as a kind of coast-guard, look-out, Lloyd's agent—never mind what it may be called so long as it fits our bill. It has been suggested that we provide them with a kind of barber's pole, with a ball and a lanyard, quite cheap. The ball, painted yellow, can be pulled up and down. When it's down— at rest, so to speak—it will mean nothing. When it's up—that is, at the end of the pole—it can mean, officially, ' A.A. member, stop here ! I may have a message for you.' What it *will* mean in fact is, ' Look out ! They're trapping up the road, just beyond my shop.' "

" But, can we trust them ? "

" Oh, yes—we can. They're keen and straight ! Their livelihood, and certainly their future, depends on our fighting this motor-trapping business to a finish. Do let us try it—only about five shillings for each pole."

" Very well. Gentlemen, shall we try this new idea ? "

" Let's ! "

" All right, then."

.   .   .   .

And then for some staff work with the friendly A.A. agent and repairer. He had to be attracted to the new idea.

" Get him interested," was the next item on the Agenda. So—the campaign started with something like the following line of talk.

" Good morning, Mr. A.A. Agent. Here is the scheme—and this is the pole. We, that is, we and you, depend upon each other. We want you and you want us. We're asking no favours that won't react to your benefit. Small beginnings, etc., etc.—you know the rest.

" What ? Oh, very well, it *does* look like a barber's pole, and you haven't taken to easy shaving yet. Good ! Ha ! Ha ! and all that, but listen ! This pole means business for you—as well as for us. It's another means by which this scourge of trapping can be fought."

" Yes, but how on earth ? "

" One minute, please. How often, I ask you, have you spotted the sergeant and his merry men riding by your shop on their way to an enticing measured distance ; and then, half an hour after, you've seen quite nice people in quite nice cars gliding by your window, all heedless of their impending doom, and you've said to yourself—you know you have—' If only I could stop them in time ' ? "

" Yes ! well ? "

" Well ! here it is—the way to stop them in time. And if we know our motorist, he'll buy something from you, if it is only a sparking-plug, out of common gratitude. See ? Of course you do. Very well then. Up with the jolly old pole, right here and now. Our members, you know, those with the Badge up, are going to be told all about it, and about YOU. When the yellow ball is down, it will mean ' I am here if you want me.' "

" And when it's up ? "

" It will mean ' Stop, please ! I have something to report.' You may have various things ! You see, you're in the family, as it were : you're one of US. Our members know that. We'll train 'em to know it, and to deal accordingly."

" Yes ! but what about when there isn't a trap ? "

" Oh ! do listen. Anyone would think we're trying to sell you something you don't need, instead of helping you, but one day, mark and learn, one day you'll see the point more clearly. Meanwhile, let's assume we are selling you something, and you're jolly well going to buy it, too ! Here's one of the ways in which the barber's pole will serve. Your little show is here, well up the Great

North Road. An A.A. Member, for example, left London to-day at 9.30 a.m. Say it's a Saturday and he's going to stay with cousins for the week-end. Married three months and never a cloud until this unhappy morning. The eggs were hard. He said so. Fatal error. She snapped out something short and biting. He resented it as a slur upon his mother's hitherto untarnished reputation as a housekeeper. Only one dignified course to take. Retire with dignity, and don't kiss her. ' I'm going now ! Good-bye ! ' Going now ! going—Gone.

" He cranks up the car—misses the gate-post by a millimetre, looks at the window, takes off his cap. She's not there—not there. Not a sign. After all he'd done to make that woman happy. That's life, and damn the eggs. He goes on his way, miserable. She ran to the window to cry out, ' Come back, George dear. Darling, I'm sorry ! The eggs *were* hard,' but too late—he's gone ! "

" What then ! "

" I knew you'd be interested. Now ! Just wait. What does she do ? Ah ! ! Woman of resource, worthy mother-to-be of budding motorists. She turns up the Great North Road in the A.A. Handbook, finds *your* shop, and telephone number, and gets *you*. She says, ' Oh, please, Mr. A.A. Agent, do signal " Stop " to car numbered A101, and tell George—that is the gentleman driving—he's all alone—to telephone me, his wife, at once.'

" You say ' certainly, madam ! ' And you put the jolly old ball out, and he sees it—he's been looking for it, aching for it—pulls up dead, and you tell him the tale, and he shuts you out of your own office while he speaks to her. When he comes out his eyes are shining, and though he doesn't really need an extra tyre—you know, a nice big fat expensive one—he buys it. And that's where you get off—see ? Even without the traps. Now, will you put the pole up ? "

" That settles it. I surely will."

And he did.

CHAPTER V

ROAD SERVICE

AS time went on motoring ceased to be confined to week-end runs, and in consequence scouting became a whole-time job.

In 1906 the number of permanent patrols approached forty, swollen at week-ends to approximately a hundred, and the work of supervising the men entailed, in that one year, travelling over twelve thousand miles in a motor car purchased for this special duty—single cylinder 6 h.p.—cost £100.

A membership of three thousand made this possible. The Staff, by now augmented, needed elbow-room. Ticking at a typewriter on a window-sill was not efficient. The friendly atmosphere of Temple Bar had to be left for somewhere further West. A pity, but there it was.

All concerned were sad, everybody in those dry old law offices had been so sympathetic, so decent. Still, friendship could remain, and there was always the telephone—so, cheer up and get on with the moving.

Four rooms, on one floor, quite near Piccadilly Circus. Space to expand, to grow. Splendid ! To get ahead and keep there, that was the problem.

· · · · · · ·

A friendly scribe put the query : " When the police traps cease from troubling and the stop-watch is at rest, what will the A.A. do then ? "

What, indeed ?

It had been suggested in quite a nice way that but for

this motor-trapping there was neither need nor reason for a new organization. Never mind, there must be room, and there would just have to be.

Others were butting in. New journals were being published, as had been the case with cycling. Survival of the fittest, that was the fair way. No inherited monopolies. No Divine Right to this or that precedence. Efficiency must be the deciding factor. Who could gainsay that ? What did a year or two of seniority matter in this new era of unknown portent ?

Very well, then ! On with the good work, and ' De'il tak' the hindmost.' A place in the Sun, to be earned and kept.

One of those keen Committee-men put the case succinctly.

" Initiate ! That's what we'll do, Mr. Chairman ; and let those who care to, Imitate ! The motoring public will understand. They'll sift the wheat from the chaff. Don't let us forget, *we* put out the Big Idea —to fight the motor-trap and show it up in all its—in all its—Un-Englishness. A heavy word, but you see what I mean, don't you ? "

" Yes ! And while we are initiating, we've a perfect right to chip in on any work that isn't original to motoring."

" Of course we have. Our conscience can be easy. Road signs ? No freehold in them. We used to say ' thank you, Cyclists' Touring Club ' for a warning that This Hill Is Dangerous, when we rode Penny-Farthings— you know, a 54-inch wheel with a 12-inch one keeping up. And Foreign Touring ! Is that a motoring patent ? I should say not. The jolly old C.T.C.—still running, and good luck to 'em—they introduced International Touring facilities. That's rather a mouthful, but it meant that with a C.T.C. member's card we could take our bicycles into France and Germany, and so on, as tourists—without messing about with Customs and depositing duty, or anything like that. But I'm talking too much ! "

" Not at all. Go on, it's valuable."

" Right ! Legislation's on about the same level, and—lots of other things. Let's stick to our principles —to initiate but never imitate. Oh, yes ! We'll not copy any other motoring body, but ideas from the pre-motoring era are a legacy common to us all, and the freehold of none, eh ? "

" Hear ! Hear ! Absolutely right ! What shall we do next ? Any ideas, Mr. Secretary ? "

" Yes, please. In the papers recently it was stated that postmasters in villages are being asked if they will kindly paint the name of their village over the post office window, so that motorists, when in unfamiliar country, can see where they are. Quite good in theory, if it's done and done quickly ; but, in practice—well, we know our dear, slow, old England. And again, that's not enough. We can give them more. Our idea is Village Signs—circular enamelled iron plates in black and yellow—showing the Badge—our name, of course. Name of the Village boldly across the middle, distance from London at the bottom, and the name with the distance of the nearest Village or Town going or coming."

" That seems good, but what about the cost, and how to get them put up ? "

" The cost is smaller than one would expect. For a fair supply, about twelve or fifteen shillings each— carriage included ; and they'll last for years and years."

To get them up ? That was rather a problem until the next brain-wave came—A.A. agents. Knights of the Pole and good friends all.

" We can work out the names and distances from maps, send a rough drawing to the Agent, so that he can check the mileage, deliver them direct, and leave the rest to him. That for a start, anyway."

" Um—what say you, gentlemen—do you like it ? "

" Rather ! And here's another brain-wave. Let's do it NOW. Let's pick a good village near London, up with a couple of signs—hand-painted to save time, replace 'em afterwards—then get one photographed and reproduced in the papers. They'll take it like a shot —something quite new ; and it will stake out our claim, see ? "

" Splendid ! Agreed, gentlemen ? " Agreed.

So within a hectic ten days came another bit of " rather good fun."

Out on the Great North Road. Snowing, but what matter ? A.A. Agent, Knight of the Pole, pleased as could be, and his esquires, complete with a handful of waste and the inevitable " fag," grinning their interest in this new ceremony—quite an Investiture. Ladders borrowed from the builder—a brace-and-bit performs its function, and——

" Clap hands, everybody ! "

The first village sign was UP.

" What's this ? " said the Editor of a very leading motor journal, looking at a photo before reading the story. " They're at it again, Arthur ! Something new, too ! Can you make room for the picture and cut the story to a four-line par underneath ? Tell the Master Printer to hold up for an hour. You can scrap that short article about Sparking-Plugs on page ten—leave it till next week—then we'll get the first show. Three days before the Other journal comes out. Twig ? Right ! Get on with it. After all, these people are on their toes, eh ? They do get things done."

. . . .

Whatever the world might think of this rather cheeky young organization, it had at any rate struck one clear and unmistakable note—that of Service, immediate and personal.

Give the member something for his money, and keep on giving him more—that was the idea.

Service, immediate and personal. On the road ? Yes, that was going well.

Where else ? And how else ?

Thinking. Thinking. Thinking.

Then ! Committee sitting. Chairman speaking.

" We've a new proposal to consider, and this one, gentlemen, is somewhat of a tall order. Let's listen ! Go on, please, Mr. Secretary."

" Thank you, sir ! You know, for a long time to come we can't expect to patrol every road on which our members travel ; and even, when we do we can't protect them all, from everything."

" Agreed ! "

" They are being either trapped or held up for minor offences, such as licence left at home, or back light gone out ; and in each event they are getting the inevitable summons."

" Agreed ! "

" Thank you. We know that a summons means that one, that is you, that is we, are enjoined to appear on a certain day, at a certain hour, at a certain police court, to, etc., etc., ' wherefore fail not at your peril,' or words to that effect."

" Agreed ! "

" We know that according to British law—Mr. Solicitor has confirmed this—attendance by the defendant is admitted to be sufficient if a Solicitor attends in his stead. You know what a blesséd—that is to say, how inconvenient it may be when one of our members, living, let us say, in Brighton (Sussex), gets stopped in Buckden (Huntingdonshire), a hundred a twenty-odd miles away, for something or other no more dreadful really than selling a penny stamp to a friend without having a licence to do so ; and then, according to the inevitable summons, must fag all the way from Brighton to Buckden on a certain day, or run the risk of being arrested—mark you, arrested—and taken to Buckden or thereabouts, like a common felon. We know this has actually happened, and it's awful, isn't it ? "

" Hear ! Hear ! He's right."

" Order, please, gentlemen. Go on," enjoined the Chairman. " Thank you."

" It may be never mind how inconvenient and expensive. A wasted day, or even two. A loss of business. His only alternative is to engage a solicitor, a local one, to appear for him. That's all very well, but whom shall he engage ? In any case a complete stranger. And what will it cost him ? He doesn't know, poor chap. Bear with me, please. I had to lead up to it.

" It's like—beg pardon—the big idea is this. Let our next Service, direct, immediate and personal, be that of Legal Defence—FREE Legal Defence. Oh, don't jump. Mr. Chairman and gentlemen, it's *feasible*. We've talked it over with our good friend the Solicitor. He will undertake to link up a connection of legal luminaries throughout the country, and make them agents of his arm, so that in strict accordance with the rather meticulous etiquette of the legal profession, they will handle our members' cases for a special, and moderate, fee, doing their best in each instance, and relying on the perfectly reasonable hope that what they lose on the swings they may gain on the roundabouts. I hope this is clear. And another thing. This will help to keep our members as well as to get them ; because, you see, like an insurance policy, if they haven't paid their sub. promptly and it's overdue at the time they get into trouble and need Legal Defence, they can't have it free because they're not covered."

" Yes, of course—eh, gentlemen ? "

" Hear ! Hear ! "

" But what is our risk ? "

" That's the chief point, Mr. Chairman. We don't know. No one *can* know, but it can't be too dreadful. We faced a worse risk with the perjury case. Fire insurance of private property might give us a lead. Let it be remembered that our members are not really looking for trouble. They don't *want* to be caught or held up and summoned. They have to pay the fine whatever it is, and that's a deterrent. Reasonable that, eh ? What is more, our Solicitor—good luck to him—is prepared to take the risk, until such time as we can take it. We shall know where we are, but he won't. A step in the dark, it may be termed, but——"

" Yes, I agree ! " broke in the Chairman. " We all agree, don't we, gentlemen ? Our very inception was a step in the dark, and why not another, and others, when they turn up ? "

" The suggestion, gentlemen, is—we pay a flat rate of so much a head, that's our risk—and—and—how does it go ? We give Free Legal Defence to every car member and his paid driver, and to every motor-cycle member in any proceedings under the Motor Car Act in Courts of Summary Jurisdiction in the United Kingdom. How's that ? "

" Not out ! Bravo ! "

.   .   .   .   .   .

So here was yet another Service—direct, immediate, personal. While all the motoring world wondered.

.   .   .   .   .   .

In view of—of—oh, well ! everything, it may not be unfitting to record a certain regrettable incident of very early days of This Motoring.

A member of the staff (at that time numbering four in all) of the Youngest Organization—defaulted.

The Committee received the Secretary's report with gravity proportionate to the disaster.

The monocle of the gallant Chairman seemed to reflect menace. The distressed Secretary wished people would not wear monocles.

" I blame myself entirely," said he. " The boy came to us with quite good references, and worked hard. I suppose I shouldn't have trusted him, but you know how one gets inclined to leave a bit more and yet a bit more to willing people. It does them good—and— it seemed reasonable to let him fetch the money orders

C*   47

from the post office for the scouts' weekly pay, and then to let him make up the pay-roll and address the envelopes and—and—complete the job.

" All went well until last week, when letters arrived from the scouts asking for their pay, which hadn't arrived. And that very morning—last Wednesday— when I called for an explanation, the wretched fellow who *could* explain, smelling trouble as I suppose, slipped out of the office and hasn't been seen since."

" What did you do then ? " menaced the Monocle.

" I went round to his home directly we had finished work, and his father said he hadn't turned up and that he was worried, too. And on Thursday I got a letter —here it is—expressing all kinds of sorrow and shame, and saying he had got first into bad company and then into debt, and the temptation was too great to be resisted, and—he had joined a cavalry regiment, and would we please not prosecute him."

" Um—hah," said the gallant Chairman. " Joined the Army, eh ? " and the menace in his monocle seemed changed into something resembling a twinkle. " What do you say, gentlemen ? Will you leave it to me, an old soldier ? "

" Certainly—we leave it to you, Colonel ! "

" Well ! It looks as though we have lost a servant whom we shall not miss, and the Army may have gained a promising recruit. He won't go wrong again. The Army will knock a lot of nonsense out of him. Shall we do the gracious thing and leave it at that ? "

" Agreed ! Agreed ! "

" Before we leave this matter, Mr. Chairman, may I ask how much money was involved ? "

" Quite right, Walter," said a member, " you always think of everything. How much was it, Mr. Secretary ? "

" The week's pay roll for our scouts, sir," replied the worried one, " at present amounts to EIGHT POUNDS, TWELVE AND SIX."

The Youngest Organization was going ahead " like one o'clock," whatever that may mean ; and a happy Committee, not very long after, hailed the Treasurer's report with joy.

" We can now afford to put the Brighton road and the Portsmouth road scouts on full time, gentlemen," beamed the Chairman. " Isn't that splendid ? And better still, a great idea has been submitted to me, for your approval. We can afford that, too ! Now wait for it ! Wait for it ! as my Sergeant-Major used to say. Let us put our men in uniform——"

" Ooh ! "

" Khaki——"

" Ooh—that's fine ! "

" I thought you would like it, gentlemen. After all, our men, good though they are, every one of them, do look rather rag-tag and bob-tail in their civilian kit with only an armlet and badge. Now, with a tunic and breeches, and leggings, and cap complete with badge—how's that ? "

" And we'll have one of our smartest men photographed ! " said a member.

" And get plenty of pictures into the papers," said Charles One. " Nothing like publicity, you know ! "

" Splendid ! " came from the Chair. " This is, if I may say so, an epoch—another epoch in our history. We—er—are now acquiring a status—a—an atmosphere, if I may say so, which will—er——"

" Let me finish it for you, Colonel," broke in Charles Two. " It isn't my joke—I saw it in *Punch*, and it's this : ' Uniform will give tone to what otherwise might be regarded as a mere vulgar brawl.' Ha ! Ha ! That's a good one, eh, Walter ? "

Joking apart, the effect on all concerned was excellent. The A.A. men acquired a new dignity. The members conceived an increased respect ; the salute gave an additional value.

.   .   .   .   .   .

49

This military touch to a hitherto somewhat irregular
—or even guerilla—force, led the minds of those who
ran it to other bright ideas.

" What about when it rains ? "

" Oilskins ! Let us issue our men with oilskin coats,
and overalls," suggested one.

" And cap-covers to match," said another.

" And let 'em be yellow, to go with the khaki," said
a third.

" Splendid ! " said all—and it was done.

The military touch was not yet finished.

" What does a sentry do when it rains ? Where does
he go ?

" Into his sentry-box, of course."

" Happy thought. Why shouldn't we put up sentry-
boxes for our men ? Just a few to start. You know
what I mean, Mr. Chairman," said the author of the
suggestion. " Paint them black with large yellow A.A.
badges. There's publicity for you—all day and every
day."

" Jolly good ! But we shall have to get permission,
and we are not very popular."

" We must do a bit of wangling, sir. Pull a few
strings," said a member. " I'm on our local Council,
and I will influence permission for one or two in my
district. It's not so difficult as it looks."

" Yes ! " said another, " and there is still such a
thing as private property. I will gladly have the hedge
cut in a corner of my land on the main Banstead-Reigate
road, to make room for one. Authority can't stop me."

" Splendid ! " cried all—and *that* was done.

Authority was rather surprisingly sympathetic to
the new development, and A.A. sentry-boxes were
graciously permitted, to the credit of Authority and, as
it proved, to the public interest.

The best idea of all came from the young and fertile
brain of the Assistant Secretary who broached the subject
to his chief.

" I say, sir, about these sentry-boxes. Do you think you could get the Committee to spring some money for a brain-wave ? "

" Yes, of course—whose is it—and what is it ? "

" It's mine," said the younger one, " and it's this. Why shouldn't we link up our sentry-boxes by telephone ? What do you think ? "

" I think it's wonderful," said his Chief. " A pat on the back for you—but, frankly, the possible outlay frightens me. Let us get estimates and work it out."

This was done, in accordance with the best traditions of This Motoring, which meant " immediately, if not sooner."

The Committee acclaimed the idea with loud and prolonged applause—and—*that* was done.

It took time, naturally, but His Majesty's Postmaster-General and staff behaved admirably. At first amused, as they were, at the very impudence of it, they drowned official reticence in a sea of enthusiasm, and got on with the job. All credit to a far-too-often and unjustly maligned Government Department.

The sun smiled broadly when, for the first time, an A.A. sentry-box proudly displayed a sign—A.A. TELEPHONE.

" Here, Mary," cried John, whose Badge numbered merely one hundred something. " The jolly old A.A. is at it again. Telephone ! Let's pull up and have twopennyworth."

" Yes, sir," said the beaming khaki-clad patrol. " It's *ours*—beg pardon, sir, I mean it's yours. Only connected up this morning. What number do you want ! "

" What numbers have you," grinned one of his umpteen hundred employers. " Sorry, that joke is worn out. Just for fun give me my home—Ripley 313, and how much is it ? "

" No charge for local calls, sir—you're only five miles out, so you pay nothing."

" Nothing ? "

" That's right, sir, and soon we will be on trunks
—long-distance as they call 'em in America—and then
you will be able to 'phone as far as to York if you like,
or Inverness if we can."

" But what about the cost of a trunk call ?   How shall
we pay ? "

" Don't know, sir," replied the patrol.   " Head Office
will settle that—like it does most things."

There was another difficulty to be settled by Head
Office.

A.A. men were on duty all day—night-service was
not then possible. Night-driving was. So, another
happy thought came. The doors on the roadside
telephone-boxes were cut into two—borrowing an idea
from horse-boxes. A specially-cut key was issued to
every member, with directions to the effect that the
telephone-box could be opened and the telephone used
at any hour of the day and night—for local calls, free !

In the case of trunk or long-distance calls, a notice
was posted under the eye of the member, asking her
or him—when no patrol was in attendance—kindly to
enter name, membership number, etc., also the exchange
and number called, in the book provided, and to place
the fee for the call in the box fixed to the table. This
for the purpose of checking the Post Office accounts.

It was left to the honour of the member. Let it,
then, be recorded to the credit of This Motoring that
in any year since this benefit of membership of the
A.A. was introduced, the debit incurred by error,
omission, or commission, has never amounted to more
than two or three pounds for the whole service.

.   .   .   .   .   .

Over a chop one day a friend said, " Take it from
me, old man ; the show can't always be run from
London. If you mean to grow you must branch out.
You know the saying—old as the hills, ' What Lancashire

thinks to-day England will think to-morrow.' My advice is, open a branch office in Manchester—never mind how small. It will soon grow, and it's the first step to becoming National instead of Metropolitan. Those hard-headed, warm-hearted folk will like it, something belonging to them, serving them where they live."

" Thank you, George. We could just about manage it on our funds. We could put a North-countryman in charge, and get a small Patrol Committee to advise and—you know—take an interest and talk about it, and make the thing go."

" Rather ! And after a bit have a dinner there, and fix up a show afterwards, and cut the speeches short, and get 'em all cheerful and enthusiastic and—and— oh ! it's easy. There's the idea. Get on with it, and good luck to you."

Committee's approval unanimous. Chairman's offer, to run down in his car and help to select the office, accepted with thanks. Welcome from those who counted for much, cordial and sincere.

" Come right in, we've been waiting for you," said the hard-headed, warm-hearted folk of Manchester. " We thought you'd soon find that London isn't the only place under the sun. Help ? Of course we'll help. Lend you a car to get round the district, give you names of customers to circularize, make our friends join—we'll show you, lad ! When it comes to work, London isn't in it with Manchester ! "

Hard-headed and warm-hearted, oh, yes ! Slow perhaps to make friends, but sure when it came to keeping them. Every one was as good as his word, and within a few breathless weeks the Northern Area Office was going full steam ahead, never to look back.

And at the Motor Show, Olympia, that very autumn the five thousandth member was enrolled, and he a Peer of the Realm.

CHAPTER VI

FRIENDLY RIVALS

PALATIAL offices (four rooms), village name-signs, a Northern Branch, and the bold gamble of Free Legal Defence might cause a glow of pride, but the high road to the stars was notoriously difficult to climb, and the precocious A.A.—remembering that every great movement has to fight its way up—took the kicks, as they came, with the ha'pence.

Two organizations already held the field—and two being company, three were not. Feeling ran high at the insistent progress of young upstart Number Three, which was doing such original—and some said, illegal—things to open the road to the motor car.

In fact, and in due course, there was a regular row—in which the papers revelled, as papers will. Even the members, in a team spirit, enjoyed the little war—possibly as a counter-irritant to that waged by and against Law and Order around the twenty-mile-an-hour speed limit.

As history showed, it was not so much a war as the growing pains of the A.A. Perhaps, then, it was inevitable—this row—but all the same it was a pity.

The grievances of the Motor Union were not difficult to understand. It was an essentially democratic body, run by a Committee, Secretary, and Staff, all animated by the highest principles, and working whole-heartedly for the cause.

It might, with justification, have followed the devices

and desires of an indignant tobacconist who, when his trade was prejudiced by a flamboyant multiple shop opened next door, appealed to his vacillating customers by means of a bold sign stating :

I WAS HERE FIRST.

For the Motor Union could claim priority of tenure by at least a couple of years.

"That's all jolly fine," said an A.A. Committee-man in meeting one day, when this argument was advanced by one of his colleagues who belonged to both organizations. "But they have copied our Badge—you can't get away from that."

"Quite true, Mr. Chairman," said another. "And mark my words, if we don't look out they will be putting men on the road in M.U. uniform, modelled on our scouts—pinching our birthright."

"Don't make our flesh creep," pleaded the Chairman. "Surely they wouldn't go so far as that."

"Why not ? " said He who Belonged to Both. "Who is to stop them ? We haven't bought the blooming road, as Albert Chevalier used to sing ! "

"No ! But we've fought for the blooming road," said Charles One, " while the others looked on ; and if after all our struggle and strife, just as we are getting along nicely, another crowd is calmly going to step in and share our success, while we—well—it's a damned shame, that's what it is, and we ought to fight 'em ! "

"That's the stuff ! " cried Charles Two. " Fight 'em ! Put me down for a tenner, as a start ! "

"ME TOO ! ME TOO ! Fight 'em—that's the stuff ! " chimed in the others.

The meeting was getting a little out of hand. The gallant Chairman, for once quite perturbed, polished his monocle.

"Gentlemen! Gentlemen! Now really, I say, this is most unlike you. Walter!" he appealed, "do help me to get the boys quiet—say something, please! They always listen to you."

"Well, Colonel, that's very kind of you," said a quiet voice, "and I'm sure we all agree with the two Charleses that something ought to be done. But we are sensible men, and we don't fight shadows. We must wait until they *do* put men on the road."

"That seems fair," said another. "But what about their copying our Badge? You can't tell it from ours at a short distance."

"All right! We can try, if the meeting feels like it. But let us go slow—a polite letter or two to stake out our claim. Yet I would still rather tackle the two things together—if the second ever does arise: make one bite at the two, and bite hard."

"Thank you, Walter," breathed the Chairman. "He's right, eh, gentlemen? We will keep our foot off the accelerator for the time being. Agreed?"

"Agreed."

"Just one more bit of news," said He who Belonged to Both. "It's this. The Motor Union people are going to form their own Insurance Company in order to bring down the present far too high rates of premium. That's their own idea, not ours, and I think a very praiseworthy one."

"It certainly is," said the Chairman, "and good luck to them."

Chorus of "Hear! Hear!"

"I'm glad you all like it," said H.W.B.B. "The scheme was put up to them by a very bright young insurance man, who is to be General Manager of the new Company. He will be the youngest ever of his rank, and looks like going far. Good luck to him, too; but, as Walter said just now, we are sensible men. I don't often talk so much, and if I——"

"Not at all, old man; carry on, do!"

" Thank you. I mean just this. Let us make a row, and have a good scrap by all means—it keeps interest alive—but, take it from me, there will be only one end to that scrap, there can be only one practicable end——"

" Which is ? "

" Which is, Mr. Chairman, that in a few years' time, if not sooner, we shall all get together and live happily ever after. I tell you, I know that crowd, and they're good. They have the same aspirations and principles as we have. Personally, they—oh ! I hardly know how to put it, but if we who sit round this table were to find ourselves mixed up with them at dinner, like the crews on boat-race night, it would be difficult to tell an M.U. man from an A.A. man—that's all ! "

" You don't say so ! " said Charles Two. " Why ! I have heard that one of them is a Parson."

" Yes ! " was the reply ; " and he is a pioneer motor-cyclist, and a sportsman."

" Anyway," said the Chairman, " our job at the moment is to get on with the polite letter-writing."

The meeting was adjourned.

.   .   .   .   .   .

During the month following, the exchange of cor-respondence dragged on without either side getting any further. Then, suddenly, Motor Union road agents appeared on one or two principal highways. Negotiations were suspended, diplomatic relations severed, and the Committee summoned by telephone and telegram.

" Now, gentlemen," said the Chairman, with a twinkle that no monocle could hide, " for by no means the first time in a short but hectic career together, we find ourselves up against a stiff proposition, which may seriously threaten our future. Never mind, threatened men live long. Any ideas, please ? This is where we bite hard, as Walter put it."

" Bite hard ! That suggests an idea, sir."

" Go on, Mr. Secretary."

" Let us give a lunch—a Press lunch, and tell the boys all about it."

" Lunch ! Give 'em lunch ! That's the stuff," said Charles Two. " Put me down for a tenner."

" Thank you ! And just a moment, Mr. Chairman, please. We might get a Cartoonist—that idea is quite new to us. We know a real ' topper,' he draws for a sporting weekly, over a long name beginning with J."

" The very man for us," said a member. " I know him. He will treat the subject lightly, and get there just the same."

" Splendid ! " from the Chair. " Agreed, gentle-man ? "

" Rather ! and not a day to lose."

The luncheon was fixed for five days thence. Tele-phone and telegram to function immediately.

As an American poet has shrewdly sung :

> *Thrice armed is he who hath his quarrel just,*
> *But four times he who gets his blow in fust.*

The meal was a cheery affair—the flower of motoring journalism attended. They heard the case stated for the plaintiffs, asked many pertinent questions, and a few tendered valuable advice.

The results were immediate and far-reaching. Apart, perhaps, from the cartoons, a few of which erred on the side of cruelty, the tone of the dispute remained high. The wave of reasoned criticism found its reflex in many well-balanced minds to the extent that both sides gave a little, and within two months the quarrel was closed, never to be reopened.

" They have met the issue like good sportsmen," said the Chairman. " The M.U. badge will be altered beyond danger of confusion with ours. Their road agents will be gradually withdrawn. On our part, we are making concessions in certain work and spheres of influence which satisfy them, and—although it was a short row and a merry one—it's over, and it must never happen again, eh ? "

" Agreed ! Agreed ! Well done, everybody ! "

" Before we break up, Mr. Chairman," quietly said He Who belonged to Both, " remember what I told the Committee only ten weeks ago. The matter won't end here. It may take a year, or two, or three, but we shall have to get together. Somebody just called me ' Old Moore's Almanack,' but I don't mind."

" No offence, old chap ; we hope you're right."

" Time will show."

The meeting broke up with everyone in high good humour, and peace reigned in Coventry Street.

.   .   .   .   .   .

The ink on the last polite letter was hardly dry when the Motor Union found another quarrel on its hands —this time with its parent organization, oldest of the three, then called the Automobile Club of Great Britain and Ireland, later to be known as the Royal Automobile Club.

Precisely what happened, and how it happened, did not transpire, but again there was a real " dust-up."

" Not our business this time, thank goodness," said the A.A. leaders. " We must get on with our own good work."

It was Motor Show time, and like an Indian bazaar Olympia buzzed with rumour.

One very leading writer grabbed the A.A. Secretary by the arm and said, " I've just taken a great risk, and I'm in an awful funk about it. The two Other Organizations have definitely and finally parted, so I'm told, this very day, and I have burnt my boats—I've sent the news to my paper. It will be a wonderful scoop for us and me if it's true ; but if it isn't—I'll be a broken man. Do help me ! "

" Of course, gladly ; but how ? "

" Find out for me if it *is* true. You can—they won't

mind telling you ; then, if it is all right, you need not say a word to anyone, even to me, and no one will be a penny the worse, and I shall be able to sleep to-night. On the other hand, if my news is wrong, you can tell me without any danger of bad faith, and I shall be saved from a dreadful blunder—and will never forget the good turn."

" All right. If you don't hear from me by nine o'clock, you can sleep this night."

The news *was* correct. Not a word passed, and the very leading writer slept in peace and never forgot. Indeed, he paid back seventy times seven to This Motoring, like a true knight of the fountain-pen.

. . . . . .

The Youngest Organization was interested, of course.

" Stout fellows, the M.U., eh, gentlemen ? " said the Chairman, at the next committee meeting. " They have gone off with tails well up to new offices, with all their individual members, and about half of the affiliated clubs. Can't help admiring their courage. What price ' Old Moore's Almanack ' now ? "

That quiet oracle replied : " You may chip me as much as you like, Colonel, and the other fellows too, but—it will come."

" What will come ? "

" Amalgamation ! "

" Ooh ! "

" I think he's right, Mr. Chairman," said another quiet one, " but we must have patience. I've pulled off one or two big ones in my business. They take time."

" All right, Walter, have it your own way. But candidly I can't see it coming off in my day."

Poor fellow ! He was dreadfully right, in a way no one could then foresee.

CHAPTER VII

SCOTLAND CALLING

SCOTLAND called—clearly and insistently—for motor scouts.

With galling thoroughness, local authorities were administering the Motor Car Act to the letter, or rather, the furlong. Moreover, Section 9 provided for a special limit of ten miles an hour in certain populated places, marked at either end by slender iron posts bearing the warning prescribed by Law. None of these could be installed without an inquiry first being held, at which those not in favour could state their arguments against the restriction.

In England the opposition was steady and strong. It was taken as part of the day's work. Rivalry was forgotten in the common cause. The very slightly older organization had from the outset boldly challenged every fresh restriction as soon as due notice was published according to the Statute, and its chief paid official acquired well-deserved fame for the way in which he gathered together witnesses for the opposition and fought each case, tooth and nail, at inquiries held by Local Government Board Inspectors.

Better still, when the Youngest and Cheekiest Organization wanted to join in the fight, its help was welcomed.

In Scotland, the national motoring body fought gallantly, but despite that, the far too familiar 10 m.p.h. posts sprang up, as it were, like unpalatable mushrooms, all over the country.

61

It seemed as if old Sir Somebody had hundreds of prototypes across the Border, who, having uttered the Caledonian equivalent of " Damn these motorists— we'll show 'em ! " applied for a 10-mile speed limit, and got it. The situation became acute. The fungoid growth spread.

Scotland called. That is to say, a Scotsman called one morning at the four-roomed headquarters of the Youngest Organization, and said :

" I'm a member of you ; I carry your Badge on my car, and so do my brothers and many friends. We like your work and we wish you well. We pay two guineas a year and get practically nothing in return, except when we tour in England, which is seldom."

" That's quite true," said the Secretary ; " and we're grateful to you. We appreciate keenly your generous support, your resentment of persecution, your sympathy with the oppressed, your determination to —to——" He paused for breath, and the Scotsman chimed in.

" When you've quite finished, just listen to me. What you have said is all very well, but there's a limit to our generosity, and we are nearing it. I'm Scotch, and I'm a business man. I haven't called to-day to exchange compliments. We can do that at lunch—and I'm taking you—but meanwhile—I'm telling you—the A.A. must come to Scotland ! "

" Ooh ! "

" There's nothing else for it," he went on. " I like your idea—and you have my money to prove it. I like your Committee—great boys they are. One of them is my friend, in the same line of business. Shipping. Charles Two they call him, don't they ? "

" Yes ! "

" He's a great boy—not quite Scotch—but the Tyne's no' so far from the Clyde, and we're almost neighbours. Talk to him, my boy, he'll understand. And remember !

We've all got something to learn, even the youngest. I'm looking at you when I say that ! "

" Thank you ! I'm always ready to learn ! "

" All right ! Now, listen to me. I'm Scotch, and I'm a—never mind that. Although Charles Two is my friend, I come to you ! "

" Why ? "

" Because it's for you to propose and for him and the Committee to dispose. Do you understand ? "

Did the Secretary understand ? Oh, didn't he ? And his heart warmed to this keen, kindly man, who, speaking as from the bridge of a battleship to that of a motor launch, did so as " from one ship's Captain to another."

Scotland was still calling.

" Your people have already found out that London alone isn't England. That is why you have opened up in Manchester. Well ! London and Manchester are England, but England isn't Great Britain. Trade follows the flag. Fly the A.A. flag in Scotland, and we'll give you the trade. Is that clear ? "

" Indeed it is," was the reply ; " and there isn't much doubt of our Committee's decision, granted that our funds will permit of the development. There's one thing, though."

" What's that ? "

" We can't afford to open an office—yet ! We must walk before we run."

" You can leave the office for the time being," said he. " It's scouts we want. Take my own case. I'm a keen motorist. I'm not married. I live with my sister and a few brothers about twenty miles from our shipyards on the Clyde. We each have a car, and we drive ourselves because we like it. We go through six or eight of these confounded ten-mile limits with our hearts in our mouths and our feet on the brakes. We might just as well walk. What's the good of the A.A. to us if it can't do something ? Come to Glasgow and talk it over. You will ? Next week ? Good. That will do for the present. It's nearly one o'clock, and time we were away to lunch. We'll go to Romano's."

.   .   .   .   .   .

In Glasgow's principal hotel, the following week, seven men sat round a table, waiting for the crumbs to be brushed away.

"That's all ! Close the door—we'll ring if we want anything more," said the Moving Spirit, addressing the head waiter.

"Very good, sir ! "

"NOW ! To business ! "

It did not take long. Scotland wanted the A.A. and must have it. The only question was how ? The men could be chosen, trained, equipped, and put on their beats, but supervision presented difficulties. A handful of scouts, hundreds of miles from their base —an outpost in fact—might run to seed and discredit, if they were not looked after properly. And there were not enough members in Scotland to justify even the most modest office and staff.

The visitor from London put this to the meeting with all diffidence, but with no beating about the bush.

"I know ! I know ! " said the Moving Spirit. "A foreman can't run our business. There must be a head to everything. How would it be if we form a Committee ? "

"What kind of Committee, and what will it do ? "

"We will be the Committee, and we'll run the show for you. There's you, Willy—that's my brother—and you, Sam, and Bob (his brother was a Scottish Law Lord), and Peter, and you, H.D. (who was English). You're not a Christian name to us yet ! We'll take it in turns to inspect the scouts, and we'll do it thoroughly. What about that ? "

"Ye can cut me out, John ! " said brother Willy.

" One madman's enough in our family." So Willy
was cut out.

The scheme was put up to the Committee in London,
supported heartily by Charles Two, and cordially
approved.

In consequence, a very thin line of A.A. patrols
appeared on the roads of Caledonia, and made the
police and magistrates " stern and wild."

However well-intentioned, this system could not
last—and it didn't. What was everybody's business
soon became nobody's business. Those who were
not paid could not be kicked.

When a week-end simply asked for golf, there was
none to supervise. When it did not, there were too
many. On those occasions the harassed patrol-inspector
—a Londoner—scratched his head and said to his
Scotch sergeant : " Blimey ! Jock, how many more
blooming bosses shall we get to-day ? I wish I was
back on the Brighton road with only the Super to
please."

So Scotland called once more. That is to say, the
Moving Spirit went again to Fanum, London, on the
way to Romano's, and made speech.

" It's this way," said he. " We've done fine, and
we're doing fine. New members are coming in, as
you know ! but—if we keep on this supervising job
much longer, Sam and Peter and Bob and I, to say
nothing of that English fellow, will be fighting. You.
people have been awfully good. You've done well.
You'll go a long way yet. Now, dont' tell me you can't
go a bit further ! Just open an A.A. office in Glasgow,
and put a good man in charge—he must be Scotch,
mind. Do this, and you'll never look back. Don't
say you can't. Talk with Charles Two. He will
understand. He'll help it through your Committee.
Mind ! I'm telling you, this is Scotland calling ! It's
a big thing for us to ask you English to come into our
country. What, after all, are the English, compared

with us ? Take it as the highest compliment that we
—We ! ask you to come to Us."

His quiet smile, while saying this, belied the spoken
boast, and, seeing that smile and behind it, the English-
born, who might have felt annoyed, said to himself :
" Bless his heart, he doesn't really mean to be insulting,"
and let it go at that.

Charles Two was duly talked with. He proved a
sterling advocate. His colleagues got quite excited, and
before the lovable German-born—more British than
many British—Honorary Treasurer could attract the
Committee's attention to the question, " What is it
going to cost ? " it was proposed, seconded and carried
unanimously—that an office be opened in Glasgow—
and—hang the expense.

The last bit of advice from Scotland had been, " What
ever happens, the man placed in charge must be of our
race—none other will do. Our people are very
particular."

Very fortunately, the chief clerk at Fanum, Manchester, was a Scot. He had ventured south from Edinburgh to seek his fortune, and was making the most
of his chances. When offered this new one, he chuckled.

" Where is the joke, please ? " asked his chief.

" I was thinking," he replied, " that it's funny for
a Scotsman to go back when he has once left his native
country, unless it's to fetch his brother ! It's not done.
Anyway, sir, I'm deeply grateful, and if I can keep
quiet the fact that I'm an Edinboro' man, maybe I'll
get along all right."

Everyone was kind. The traditional gap between
Scotland's capital and the Empire's second City was
gently bridged. The national motor paper welcomed the
invading organization in the cause of road freedom, and
many warm and lasting friendships were formed, notably
with Jimmy, the Editor, whose personal charm was
great, and knowledge infinite.

The Club, too, already firmly established as the

national motoring institution in Scotland, with head-quarters in Glasgow, was not unfriendly. With charac-teristic honesty its chief executive official allayed the fears of his Committee with the broad-minded argument that " Somebody has got to do this trap-fighting work ; *we* don't feel inclined—therefore, why play dog in the manger ? "

That view was statesmanlike. It found its reaction in the exercise of meticulous care by the new-comers to stick to their job of serving, and leaving the Club to govern.

In due time, by a friendly and economical agreement, the complete A.A. patrol organization in Scotland was made available to members of the Club—the R.S.A.C., and that famous and most competent organizer of motor car trials and tests, who was known through This Motoring as " R.J.," quoted with a smile one line from the " Jackdaw of Rheims " :

" *Nobody seemed a penny the worse.*"

Scotland had called for motor scouts. She got them.

CHAPTER VIII

THE CHANNEL CROSSING

WITH a lull on the Home Front, there was time to look around—to look abroad, to indulge in a mental flight from Glasgow to Paris. Here the Others had still a decided pull. They could supply Foreign Touring facilities ; not so the A.A.—yet. A year or so of establishment had made all the difference. They were, so to speak, in on the ground floor. " Stay at home and join what you will," ran their fiat, " but if you want to go abroad on most-favoured-nation terms you must belong to US. We have a monopoly. We're Federated and Recognized." Thus said the Other Organizations with pardonable pride and conviction— so long as it might last.

Here was a problem, what to do about it ? Members were friendly but candid. As one put it : " You see, old man, I'm getting splendid value for my sub. and your show is perfectly topping and all that, and I don't want to belong to anything else—but what am I to do ? I promised the Missis to take her to France in the car, and give her a run into Belgium and so on. You know what women are. It's got to be done, and I want those jolly old triptyque papers that pass you through the Customs without having to plank down a bunch of money at the port and then hang about for hours on some beastly frontier trying to get it back. Surely you can fix it up for me ? There can't be any blessed patent about a simple thing like that ! "

" Er—yes, that is—No ! of course not. What you
don't see in the window just ask for, and we'll get it.
When do you propose to leave ? "

" Oh, not for a month. Summer holiday, you
know."

" Very well ! We're grateful for the idea really.
Jolly sporting of you to come so frankly to us ; add to
that kindness by sitting tight for a week or two, and
give us a chance to get something done—eh ? "

" Certainly."

" Thank you."

Lucky chap that Aladdin ! Only had to rub a lamp
for the genie to appear, and then order him to get things
done. Not much good rubbing the telephone-receiver !
Efficient but unresponsive. Unresp— " What ? Someone calling. Goodness, that's funny—hallo, hallo ?
Yes—oh, very well, thanks ; how are you ? Got an
idea ? Why, certainly, come right along now ; we're
simply gasping for ideas."

" Curiously enough this idea has to do with Foreign
Touring," said the man who was invited to come along.

He was quite a character. Tall, dark, cosmopolitan—
salesman, dealer, diplomat, everything by turns and
nothing for long.

" Look here ! " said he. " You want the triptyque.
The Other Organizations have got it, and your crowd
haven't."

" You're a thought-reader. Well ? "

" If I put you in the way of getting all you need, what's
it worth ? "

" Do you really mean that you can ? "

" I do ! I can put you in the way."

" Goodness, the telephone *was* an Aladdin's lamp,
after all."

" Speak in a whisper, please ; our bargain mustn't get
into print."

" Agreed ! Right ; now speak up ! "

" It is as simple as falling off a log. The Other

Organizations think they've got a monopoly ; but they're *wrong*, my boy, they're *wrong*. They've forgotten——"

"What ? "

" The Touring Club of France ! of Belgium ! of Holland, Switzerland, Germany, and of sometimes X and Y, as we used to say at school. Twig ? "

" Yes, but where can *we* come in ? "

" It's easy ! These Clubs exchange triptyques between themselves, following on the bicycle permits. You are not in their ring yet, but—here's my big idea. Off with you to Paris. I'll fix the appointment. I know everybody—it's my business to know everybody. There is nothing to prevent the Touring Club of France making members in any country. They want them, and the sub. is trifling ; six francs a year—five bob in English money—nothing. The T.C.F. is a great concern. It is democratic, so are we. It moves with the times, as we do. The idea of a British contingent of members will ' flame.' France wants foreign visitors, the more the merrier. Off with you to Paris."

" Right ! It shall be—next week-end. It must be a week-end because the office can't be left too long. Get busy with the introductions, and many thanks for everything."

. . . . . .

The Headquarters of the Touring Club de France in the Avenue de la Grande Armée are majestic. They caused the Pilgrim from A.A., London, on a cold grey Saturday morning, to shiver slightly.

He asked himself how would the bearded patriarchs in this palace of granite, with floors of polished teak, regard the proposition ? The T.C.F. boasted ninety thousand members, as against the A.A.'s eight. It seemed such awful cheek.

But, once inside a well-warmed room, talking to portly genial gentlemen, the atmosphere materially improved. Wonderful T.C.F., to grasp the idea so quickly. Clever, to see the possibilities—more members

quickly. Clever, to see the possibilities—more members
for them, more visitors, more business, more and more
money for France. Shrewd! Oh, yes, very, to ask
for a substantial deposit, even from respected Britain,
" only as a matter of prudence, you know, just in case
there might be trouble "—a British car allowed in on a
triptyque as a touring car, but sold there instead of
being taken out again. Triptyques were for tourists,
not for traders, and one never knew !

" How much ? Oh, say, fifty thousand francs ! It
would be just as safe with the T.C.F. as with the Bank
of England."

" Of course it would—yes ! " and so on.

But " Ooh," thought the Pilgrim, " here's a how-
d'you-do. Where are *we* going to find such a colossal
sum. Anyway, buck up ! Smile ! Don't let them see
the difficulty."

" Very well, gentlemen, you shall hear from our
Committee in due course."

.   .   .   .   .   .

Now for details, supplies of membership cards on
sale or return, supplies of triptyques printed by T.C.F.,
rubber-stamped A.A., a simply-drawn agreement, in-
vitations to lunch. All smiles and friendly compliments
which good Frenchmen pay so well, and then—the sun
shone out its blessing on the *entente cordiale*. Back to
London " with the goods."

Then followed an incursion into the realm of finance.
The deposit of £2,000 was " wangled " through the
bank with the help of kind Committee members, without
whose backing it could not have been done. Then the
shipping problem loomed. Until that time the South
Eastern Railway of England, which owned the Channel
services between Folkestone and Boulogne, Dover and
Calais, had no motor-car traffic. Mainly, the few
hundred motoring tourists crossed from Southampton
to Havre, on the South Western Railway service.

Here was a chance not to be missed. Rivalry was keen ; each of these Companies, now grouped together in the Southern Railway, was then going " all out " to get business against the other.

Nice people, the South Eastern, steeped in steam and rails and refreshment rooms. Oh, yes, and rather dubious about This Motoring, what it all meant and might mean—more rivalry perhaps. But still, they were nice people and quite ready to listen.

The Continental Traffic Manager played absently with his paper-weight, a model engine, while he listened to the proposals. " But," he said, " you don't seriously suggest we should carry your members' cars on our passenger-boats ? Whatever would the passengers say, let alone our Directors ? "

" It's the only way to encourage the new traffic," was the reply. " Our people drive their own machines, and won't be parted from them. Treat 'em as baggage, like bassinettes ; there's big business in it."

Oh, very nice people, the South Eastern, in all directions giving help which was so much needed. Transhipment of motor cars, with all its complications, was a problem to which the slender A.A. staff had not up to that time been introduced.

" Don't get nervous, it will pan out all right," said the good railway folk. " We know our business. Our agents shall be your agents, and our staff your staff. If the A.A. can boom our Folkestone-Boulogne crossing, we will do the rest."

Boom it ! There was an idea. Sweet indeed are the uses of—advertisement. " Suppose, when everything is tuned up and running, we work what the newspapers call a ' scoop '—that is ' wangle ' a car through the French Customs in record time, and take a few Press men over to see it done—you know the method, free passes, train and boat, costing your Company nothing much, and a bite of lunch over there in the Gare Maritime Restaurant—we'll pay for that. How about it ? "

" Excellent idea—certainly ! You find the car and people while we pull the wires at Folkestone and Boulogne. We're beginning to like this motor-car stuff," said the railway folk.

Everything went gaily according to plan, and the scoop duly came off. How it happened can best be gathered from the following very slightly expurgated account that appeared in the motor papers, early in 1908, from the pen of the present writer.

THE MOTORIST'S GATE TO THE CONTINENT

Through Boulogne Customs with Motor Car in Four Minutes

" Hello ! He-e-e-l-l-o ! That the A.A. ? That the Secretary ?—Mr. X, a member, speaking ! Say, you're shouting a good deal about this Touring Department of yours, and I am inclined to see what it really can do. This is Tuesday morning—I leave the Motor Club, London, on Thursday morning after breakfast, catch the midday boat from Folkestone, cross to Boulogne, and reach the Franco-Italian frontier at—never mind.

" I shall drive a four-cylinder dual ignition, 40 h.p. car. For further particulars see small bills. I want a triptyque, a *permis de circulation*, eighty litres of petrol, tickets, a deck-cabin facing south, and twenty pounds in French money. And I want a hole cut in the tariff wall of France big enough for me to drive through with a maximum of ease and a minimum of delay. Now if the A.A. Touring Department is all you say, let it establish a record, let it spread iself ! I send you a cheque to cover deposits of duty, etc., and you do the rest. Now make things hum ! Good-bye."

73

THE A.A. CHAPERONS THE TOURIST

Be it explained here, for the edification of those who do not go down to the sea in motors, that foreign countries abound in tariffs. This is to say that you cannot sell an English or other strange motor car in France without first paying a duty of about a sovereign sterling per hundredweight " all in."

And in order that the tourist shall not go behind this protection by means of specious explanations, every car, good, bad or indifferent, is mulct in certain deposits, not necessarily for publication, but as a guarantee of good faith, the said deposits being returnable as, and when, the car shall leave the shores of France.

The principle is not combated, but the practice is so intricate, so strangled with red tape, that one may, with reason, put the number of unattached touring motorists, i.e., those who do not seek the assistance of such societies as the A.A. nor subscribe to its funds—at a decimal point per centum.

The motoring societies make motoring and touring easy. Instead of shivering in a cold bleak *douane*, signing mysterious papers, and paying over mystical amounts in French coinage, with an irritating impression of having been " had " over the rate of exchange, to say nothing of the haunting fear that some breach of circumlocutory law may involve entire loss of the money, the A.A. member in search of sunshine finds every difficulty smoothed.

He wants to go to Bordeaux, and Biarritz, via Boulogne ? Very well. Forms, printed in plain simple language, are ready for him to sign. Deposits are taken at the offices in Coventry Street, tickets issued, seats engaged, petrol commandeered ; in fact, he and his car are carried about with every possible directness, and without the unpleasant " school treat " feeling engendered by the ordinary touring bureau. He waves his A.A. permits in the face of humbled frontier officials, and goes on his way rejoicing.

How a Record was Achieved

The system being almost perfect, all that remained was to beat every other system in the way of application ; in short, to add to the million and one odd records, for everything under the sun, that of " clearing " a motor car through Boulogne, timed by a stop-watch, and this is how it was done.

Copy of telegram from the Secretary of the Automobile Association to the Marine Superintendent, South-Eastern and Chatham Railway Company, Folkestone :

> "Reserve space Mr. X car A.A. 6000 first service Boulogne April 2nd. Arrives 11.30 leaves 11.55 deck cabin south aspect self and friends. Move."

Reply to " Fanum," London :

> " Right."

From Secretary, Automobile Association to Chef de la Gare Maritime, Boulogne :

> "Mr. X and car A.A. 6000 arrive Boulogne first service April 2 en route Italy wants clearance permis circulation but no licence, make violent love French customs, establish record, want eighty litres essence."

Reply to " Fanum," London :

> " Right."

FRILLS, FLOUNCES, AND GOLD LACE

Thus did it come to pass that on Thursday, shortly after noon, as the S.E. and C.R. turbine steamer *Queen* rocked lazily by Folkestone Quay, within twenty minutes of her scheduled starting time, Mr. X's " Forty " drifted quietly between coal trucks and empty baskets on to a neat contrivance called a " stage." She was attacked by four deck hands, who lashed the wheels to corner rings, while two others drained the petrol tank by means of rather incongruous wash-hand basins. A derrick then neatly swung the car aboard.

Gold-laced officials looked on with complacence ; they had nothing else to do. Once on deck, the car was made snug—French numbers replaced English ones, and polite officers showed the way to the deck cabin, facing south—one of the only two aboard. Here were daily papers, motor papers, cigarettes, soda water, and other necessaries of civilization. So much for Folkestone.

At about 1.20 English time, a small army of baggy-trousered democrats stood watching on Boulogne landing stage as the nose of the turbine cut a long white moustache in the sea two miles away.

At 1.33 her steam ladyship nestled comfortably by the landing stage. Thence time was measured by fifths of seconds.

BOULOGNE, TOULON, AND THE " CONTINONG "

Before Mr. X had passed down the gangway, the car was deposited on the Quay. Men clad in blue overalls rushed to the petrol tank with cans of *essence* and a wide-necked funnel. Gold-laced prototypes of Folkestone fluttered about with papers, gesticulated, advanced, retired and set to partners. The A.A. official ran here and there, persuading the petroliers, coaxing the customs, making himself generally indispensable.

Amid all the bustle stood the Chef de la Gare Maritime, spick and span and imperturbable the personification of " Bond Street " in Boulogne.

Thanks to his admirable engineering, the hole in France's tariff wall had been widened to pass an English car through, complete with certified papers, signed permit, and fuel for nearly 400 miles, in record time. Mr. X waved " good-bye " and headed due south at 1.37, " exactly four minutes from the moment the boat stopped."

It is no exaggeration to say that this record will not, and cannot, be beaten at any other Continental port. The completeness of the A.A. touring facilities and the whole-hearted attention of the South Eastern staff combine to remove practically every difficulty which motorists in search of sunshine have hitherto encountered.

There is only one gate to the Continent.

The countersign for passing the guard is " A.A."

.   .   .   .   .   .

The lunch " over there " had been well and truly earned, and was equally well enjoyed. All concerned agreed that thereafter the Folkestone-Boulogne crossing for motor-car traffic would never look back.

Naturally, not everybody could feel pleased, particularly the rival services. A few complaints rolled up in due course.

" It's all jolly fine, don't you know, for you to have got so-and-so through the French Customs in four minutes ; but what about us ! We had to cool our heels for over an hour."

" Very sorry, sir ; don't be too angry, please. The A.A. is young yet, and it must be kept before the public ; don't be too——"

" Oh, very well ! we won't, and," smiling now, " it was a topping ' scoop,' hanged if it wasn't."

CHAPTER IX

FOREIGN RELATIONS

" WHAT about *us* ? "
        The member's question had to be answered.
Yesterday's scoop must become to-morrow's routine.
The dress rehearsal had been acclaimed perfect—but
much more was needed to give the play a long run.

The triptyque was the key to the Continent—the Magic
Carpet—Aladdin's Lamp—Open Sesame—and so on.
But it was not enough to unlock a gate, sit on a carpet,
rub a lamp, or murmur " Sesame " with Oriental
fatalism ! Going abroad with a car was now practicable.
When abroad the going must be made so too.

John Bull is a world-traveller. He packs carefully,
marks his luggage clearly, constructs a time-table and
tours according to schedule. The explorer plunges
into the unknown ; not so the tourist. This Motoring
on foreign soil was strange to him ; an unaccustomed
business.

" We drive to the left," said he ; " and foreigners
drive to the right. Are accidents inevitable ? "

" Not a bit, sir—you learn it in five minutes."

" But how do I find my way ? "

" The A.A. will supply maps and routes."

" What about petrol ? "

" There is no difficulty if you use our garage list—
and avoid calling it ' petrol,' which is French for paraffin.
You must call it ' essence.' "

Language ? Easy. Currency ? Quite simple.

And so on.

Demands for foreign touring came in thick and fast. There was no speed-limit. There were no gendarmes, complete with stop-watches, lurking behind hedges.

And as the member assumed that the A.A., having shouted loud enough, knew all about it, it was up to the A.A. to develop the technique for foreign touring. The member *must* be served.

There was no time to waste. Arrangements had to be made for issuing tickets and car-vouchers for the steamers. Those hotels and garages had to be looked up, verified, told of the coming tide of British motorists, appointed, and issued with signs to reveal their identity.

There must be an office in Paris too—for the Innocent Abroad whose spring was broken or luck otherwise out.

Nothing must be left to chance.

The tide southward across the Channel grew, and Boulogne was full of the comings and goings of members—members, all complete with goggles and white coats—for dust still lay thick on the long, white ways to the sun.

Members carried two and three spare tyres strapped on the foot-board—this being years before the time of five-figured tyre mileage. They carried, too, a jumble of spare parts in the locker, with sparking plugs and the French phrase-book.

Going abroad, away from the tyranny of the speed-limit, had become a vogue.

The triptyque system was an avowed success, but it solved only the Customs difficulty—there remained drivers' licences and car registration.

The car could land on foreign soil, but circulation was impeded because most countries refused recognition of their neighbours' domestic licences, which were in a foreign tongue and could not be verified. Complaints flowed in of delays at this or that frontier, of driving-tests imposed—irritating, though quite necessary, perhaps, from the point of view of Authority.

Representations to Governments followed. The great ones listened, and in due course assembled in Paris—a veritable Motoring League of Nations.

The question before the meeting was : " Can we recognize each other's licences ? If so, what machinery must we devise ? "

Agreed : each Government to be responsible to the rest for the fitness and suitability of every car and driver intending to tour in any country which ratified the agreement.

Agreed : that a standard form of International Pass be printed, polygot in language to make it understandable by police of no matter what nationality.

It remained only to implement this simple solution of a vexed and vexing problem.

" We shall leave the issuing of the Pass to our Police," said France.

" Good idea," said another nation.

" Why not entrust the work to the National motoring bodies and Touring Clubs—seeing that they already issue the triptyque ? " a delegate asked.

Agreed : that this was a purely domestic question—for the discretion of each nation.

And so the conference shook hands and went home.

Apparently to bed—for nothing happened for six months, and then—

One evening, rather late, the telephone bell rang and a quiet voice said :

" Is that the A.A., please ? Can I speak to the Secretary ? You *are* the Secretary ? That's good ! I'm a member, and also a Government official. Keep my name to yourself for the moment, and—could you come round to see me for a few minutes, here ? Keep that quiet, too, please."

" Oh, rather ! sir. Thank you very much. What is it about ? "

" Well, I can't tell you over the phone, but it might

80

be ' something to your advantage,' as the legal notices word it."

" When, sir ? "

" Now, if you like."

" Now, if you like," and " something to your advantage," sounded promising. Sign the letters, wash quickly, grab hat and gloves, and race along.

This friend at Court was all that fancy painted. Quiet, genial and business-like. He came to the point at once.

" I am taking rather an unusual step, but never mind that. It's about motoring abroad."

" Oh ! "

" You probably have heard that there was an International Conference last year ; but it may be news to you that the Convention has at last been ratified, and the scheme is about to start."

" That certainly is news to us."

" I thought so—that's why I called you. You see, our Government is going to leave the job of examining the cars and drivers, and issuing the licence-papers, to responsible organizations."

" What—motoring organizations ? "

" Yes—and——"

" Excuse the interruption," exclaimed his visitor, " why can't *we* do it ?—but I suppose we are not respectable enough ! The police will queer our pitch. Of course, we can't very well blame them. We've queered theirs often enough, when they've been executing their duty. Yes, the A.A. has been rather outside the pale—and the other organizations are so very well behaved. They have not been threatened with prosecution for conspiracy to defeat the ends of justice—as we have—although one day the world will laugh at our so-called illegalities—and acclaim us for securing the freedom of the road."

" As a Government official," said the friend, " I can't comment on that ; but I see your trouble, and that is why I want to help you."

" Thank you very much."

" They—never mind names," he went on, " are going to be given this plum without the A.A. getting a taste of it ; but cheer up, the game is not lost yet. You have the right to issue triptyques—why not these new circulation-passes ? You have a sporting chance."

" Do you mean that ? You are good, really. What can we do ? This is all new to me."

" All right," said the friend, " a little help is worth more than a lot of pity. Now, first ! What's your membership ? "

" Just over twelve thousand."

" Income ? "

" Twelve thousand times two guineas."

" Good—and the Others ? "

" One of them has about eight thousand at *one* guinea. They used to be part of the other crowd, but there was a big row and they broke away."

" The other ? "

" I don't know."

" At any rate, you're well in front of one of the elect," said the friend. " Secondly, have you any big names on your membership register ? You know, people in high places, even in the Cabinet ? "

" Yes, rather—several. We keep 'em in a special index."

" Good again," said the friend. " Just what we want. You must send a formal letter to the Cabinet Minister, couched in strictly official language, beginning ' Sir, I beg most respectfully,' etc., etc., and so on, and ending " I have the honour to be,' etc., etc., setting out your claim for national recognition in its most convincing form. I will gladly help you with that."

" Thank you very much. It may seem silly to you, but we have never yet been in touch with Government authority, except across the well of a police court and the Assizes."

" All right. You must then pick out the most influential people, send a touching appeal to them, explaining why you have as much right to national recognition and international status as the other people, and beg them as members—don't forget—as members of the A.A. to bring friendly pressure to bear upon the Cabinet Minister who is dealing with the matter. His name is not for publication, but I will give it to you. He may also be a member—perhaps *not*."

" Thank you ! And then ? "

" Do all you can to time the arrival of that friendly pressure so that it will synchronize with the delivery of your official letter to the great man. That is most important."

" I understand ! "

" Splendid ! Now let us sketch out the official letter—you mustn't lose an hour. I have reason to know that a meeting is fixed for Wednesday next week, in the Minister's private room."

Ten minutes later this genial, gentle member of His Majesty's Civil Service cut short his visitor's stammered thanks and sent him on his way rejoicing.

Back to the office with all speed. Good luck ! Most of the staff were still there, and of course the faithful Second-in-Command.

" Thank goodness you waited, Francis," said his Chief. " I have some wonderful news, but first of all beg the typists to wait, and then get out our special index of Big People ! "

After the story had been told, and applauded, the work began.

The senior lady typist took charge of the official letter, and then—

" Now for our Big People ; we only want a dozen— members of the Government preferred. One, two, three, four—pretty good for us, eh ? Now for a few Leaders of the Opposition—the Front Benchers are quite nice to each other, sometimes, and here's a good one, in what they call ' another place.' *That* is a name worth while. The First Sportsman in England, they call him, since King Edward died, and a good friend to us and to all deserving people. That makes up the list of probable starters for this race. Now for the letters."

By ten o'clock that night all of them were typed and sent to the railway stations for dispatch. The tired typists were thanked and sent home under escort, and there remained little to do but wait and hope.

Hope was justified. The Big People responded, almost to a man.

Big in mind as well as in position, they did not consider the A.A. in the light of an Ishmael, but as a live organization to be smiled upon and supported.

" Rather fun, fighting these silly police traps," they had thought. " The twenty-mile speed-limit is absurd, and the law ought to be altered." And when their private secretaries said to them, " Here's a rather touching appeal from the A.A. people about foreign touring ; they are being left out in the cold," etc., etc., " and will you please write to Mr. X about it, personally," some of them answered, " Certainly—take this down, please." And a few said, better still, " I'll write the letter myself," and began it " My dear Mr. ——" or " Dear John."

On the following Wednesday morning the Second-in-Command of the A.A. staff burst into his Chief's room with an envelope marked " O.H.M.S. Private, by Messenger."

" I say ! Here's something important. Thought you would like to open it yourself."

" Thanks ! Ooh ! it can't be income tax. Perhaps it's—yes ! it is—the very letter we've been working for. Listen——"

I am directed by —————— to request the Chairman of the Automobile Association to attend a meeting in his private room on Wednesday, the —————— at eleven o'clock.

" That's to-day ! Pretty short notice, but never mind. But here's a mess : the Chairman is laid up with a bad cold. What are we to do ? "

" Only one thing for it," said the Second-in-Command. " You must go yourself."

" All right—that's better than telephoning an explanation ; they might tell me not to trouble to go. But what about kit ? "

" Kit ? "

" Yes. What's the correct attire in which to wait upon one of His Majesty's Ministers ? Surely morning coats and top-hats. I'm wearing a brown suit—with bowler. Ooh ! "

" Don't worry about that—risk it. This particular Minister wears blue, with a bowler, always."

" Good man. That's a comfort anyway," and away he went.

.   .   .   .   .   .

The representative of This Motoring's youngest organization felt very young and subdued when ushered for the first time on record into the private room of the head of a great Government Department ; and still more subdued to notice two other visitors, apparently from the Other Organizations, beautifully dressed, with top-hats complete.

" Good morning, sir ! I—I—you sent for our Chairman, but he's laid up with a cold, and we only got your letter this morning, and there was no time to do anything, so—I—I've come in his place, please, sir ! "

" Sit down."

He bowed to the Others and sat down.

" Now, gentlemen," said the Great One, briskly. " You know why you are here, and we've got to settle the matter this morning. What have you to say ? "

Then followed two perfectly-phrased speeches by the owners of the top-hats, which put their respective

claims for national recognition in a way which left no
doubt of the result.

" Thank you," in each case, from the Great One.
Then—

" And you, sir ! " rather fiercely, to Brown Suit.
" What have you to say for yourself ? "

Did the Great One really mean to be menacing, or
was there a twinkle under those bushy eyebrows ?
Anyway, now for it !

" Well, sir, I respectfully urge you not to leave the
A.A. out. It wouldn't be just. We have over twelve
thousand members, and they have a right to be as fully
cared for as the—as the members of the other two
organizations."

" Oh, have they ? " was the startling reply. " Let
me tell you this, young man ! If I had my way "—he
shook his sturdy fist—" if I had my way, you would be
languishing in gaol. Illegal work, yours is, obstructing
the police in the execution of their lawful duty—that's
what your Association does. In gaol, that's where you
would be if I had my way ! "

" Ooh ! " That was a facer. Should he reply ? There
was a reply—and a good one. Yes ? No ? No !
Better sit tight and look humble.

Perhaps there was a twinkle in the Great One's eye,
because after this outburst, which rather surprised the
gentlemen from the Other Organizations, the Great One
sprang another surprise, on them as well as on Brown
Suit.

" Well, gentlemen," he said, " I've heard all you have
had to say, and we can't stay here all the morning, for
I have more important work waiting to be done. I've
thought the matter over and I don't see any other
course to take than "—

(Now for it. Heads we've won, and tails we've lost.)
" than to—treat you all three alike. I shall give to
each of you the authority to examine and certify the
fitness of motor cars and drivers to tour abroad, on behalf

of His Majesty's Government, and the names of your associations will be included in the Order in Council which will be published in due course."

" Oh ! " Treat all three alike—*all three !*

Bless his great heart, there *had* been a twinkle under those bushy eyebrows, after all. Brown suits didn't matter—fighting police-traps didn't matter. Justice mattered. Bless him ! People didn't mistake when they called him " Honest John."

A few well-chosen words of appreciation by the Others, a joyful " Thank you very much indeed, sir. We'll take all you said about the A.A. to heart," from Brown Suit, and the meeting was over.

While the Others walked slowly along the corridor, in close conversation, Brown Suit slipped by unnoticed, raced down the stairs and took a taxi to another Government Department, breathlessly to ask a messenger :

" Would you send my card up, please ? It's very important. I'm sure he'll see me for a moment." This referred to the Friend at Court.

" Come this way, sir, please."

" Hello ! my friend, how did you get on ? There's no need to ask—I can see."

" Yes, sir ! it's ' heads '—we've won. I've come straight to thank you—you've been wonderful. I'll never forget you—never ! "

" That's all right ! Fill your pipe—try some of my tobacco, and sit down. What did the great man say to you ? "

" What didn't he say ? He shook his fist and said I ought to be in gaol, and that if he had the power to do so he would put me there."

" What did you reply ? "

" Nothing. I just sat still. Was that right ? "

" Quite."

" Thank you. Of course I had a perfect answer— a crusher. I could have said, ' Sir, greater men than

I can ever hope to be '—looking him straight in the eye—' have gone to gaol for their opinions.' "

" Ha ! ha ! "

" That would have tickled him up, eh ! remembering Tower Hill and political liveliness in the 'nineties, but I'm jolly glad I held my tongue. You see, the Others were there. If only we had been alone, I would have risked it—he's so—human—he has a sense of humour, and a heart."

" Good ! Now finish the story."

Story finished.

" Did the Others speak to you ? " he asked.

" No, Sir ! As the Americans say. They were courtesy itself, befitting men of high degree as they are, but—between us—I think Honest John's decision—to treat all three of us alike—gave them a nasty shock ! "

" Splendid ! " said the friend. " We needn't waste much sympathy on them. Our concern is with the A.A., of which I am a member, and which, from now henceforth and, let us hope, for ever, will enjoy official recognition as a national institution. Don't get too respectable though, or I shall resign. Ha ! ha ! "

" I can never thank you enough."

" Oh ! do stop that," said the genial and gentle one. " I've enjoyed every move in the game. It was quite simple. ' They ' hoped that the A.A. would be kept out. I got to know, and it didn't seem to me that you were being treated fairly, so—but now you really must excuse me. Let me know whenever there is anything else I can do for you. Good-bye ! "

88

CHAPTER X

THE GUARDS TO HASTINGS

THE editor of Britain's brightest ha'penny paper looked down his well-formed nose, and then said, " No ! "

" I'm sorry," he continued ; " it's quite a good idea in its way, and it would be a fine scoop for motoring, but there's nothing much in it for my paper, and I must think of that first."

" I know," said the visitor. " But please don't turn us down completely ; perhaps there is another way."

" All right ! Let us run over your idea again. You propose to demonstrate the potentialities of motoring by conveying one issue of my paper to every important town in Great Britain, in motor cars driven by members of your organization."

" Yes, sir, ' free, gratis, and for nothing.' "

" Quite so, but what does it teach the world ? What does it amount to ? "

" It amounts to—this. Suppose, one evening, there were declared a transport strike—no trains to run and no vehicles to work. Your paper has been put to bed, the machines are turning copies out by the ten thousand every minute, and there you are—helpless."

" Well ? "

" Then, you telephone us—the A.A. We say, ' Certainly ! ' and get busy with our 'phones."

" Yes ? "

" Oh ! we have it all worked out, it has taken weeks, but everyone would be ready to the last sparking-plug. Twenty powerful cars would parade at your delivery yard within an hour or two. They would take in large stacks of your issue, race through the early morning to twenty centres, where more cars would be waiting to take in their shares and race along to twenty more centres and shed their supplies to others, until—until—well, we have figured it out that Inverness would get its morning paper in the evening of that day, and Penzance before afternoon tea. It would be really a good scoop, now wouldn't it ? "

" Yes, my boy," smiled the editor, " a very good scoop—congratulations. But, as I said before, good principally for your bright young Association, and not quite good enough for us. We will deal with transport strikes when they come, but meanwhile we can't monkey with our distribution, even for the benefit of This Motoring. Our special train must leave Euston for Manchester at 2 a.m. until further notice, and that is all about it. Now, let us think of something else—don't be down-hearted."

" Thank you, but it's a disappointment. We had it all planned out so nicely, on the map, like a splendid tree, out to the tiniest branch—twenty powerful cars in your delivery yard, twenty more at—Ooh ! "

The editor looked down his well-shaped nose, heritage of a great tragedian father, and then said—" Yes ! "

" Yes ! you mean you will ? "

" Not quite that, my boy, but I have an idea of something better—for you. Why not troops ? Why not move some troops ? "

" By jove ! sir ! That's worth something ! Suppose we were to shift a whole battalion, at war strength, from, say, London to the sea, all by ourselves, would you back us up in your paper ? "

" Of course we will, and ' other papers please copy,' and pictures, too—and cinemas. Get on with it, and good luck to you, and while you're about it, get a well-known Regiment if you can."

" Thank you very much ; we will start at the very top : we'll try to get The Guards ! "

.   .   .   .

The new idea was received and adopted by the Committee with acclamation.

" ' Now we shan't be long,' " said the Chairman, quoting a music-hall ditty. " As an old soldier, gentlemen, I—er, ahem ! my heart yearns for the fray—I mean the day. The Guards, eh ! Walter ! think of it—the Youngest Motoring Organization, only four years old, and we're going to give the world a lesson in transport of troops."

" And war material, too ! sir ; don't let us forget that."

" Quite right, Mr. Secretary ! Gentlemen, I was nearly forgetting my early training. Of course—a battalion of Infantry at war strength—what is termed a tactical unit—is, let me see, yes ! a thousand and fifty officers and men, complete with machine-guns, small-arm ammunition, entrenching tools, cooking utensils, stretchers, and goodness knows what else."

" That's rather a mouthful, colonel ! " said someone. " We can't very well pack a machine-gun into a thousand-guinea limousine. Our members would object ! "

" And I emphatically decline to carry pickaxes and spades," said another.

" Or ambulance stretchers ! "

" Or boxes of ammunition ! "

" Or shoes and ships and sealing-wax ! "

" Or cabbages and Kings ! "

This in a chorus.

" May I speak, if you please, Mr. Chairman ? "

" Quiet, gentlemen, please ! Now Mr. Secretary."

" It seems rather cheek, but, really, these difficulties, although great, are small by comparison with—— "

" With what ? "

" With getting the Guards ! How are we going to get the Guards ? You know what the Grenadiers and Scots and Irish and Coldstreams " (there weren't any Welsh in 1909) " think of themselves. Salt of the earth, bless 'em, and quite right too. Machine-guns and stretchers and pickaxes and spades and all that— oh, yes, difficult enough—but when I try to visualize the flower of the British Army, in all its pomp and panoply, crushed like geraniums into five- or four-seater touring cars, I go cold down the back—and yet it must be done, somehow ! Think ! What a fine lesson to the world."

" Yes, what a lesson ! "

" And," said a quiet one, " what a gorgeous advertisement for the A.A."

" Don't be funny, Charles One," said the Chairman. " This is a solemn moment."

" Let us—think ! "

A hand shot up. " I've got an idea."

(He's got an idea ! He's got an idea ! He's——)

" Shut up, sir, and you, too—or I'll put you both under arrest. That is—er—I—forgive me, gentlemen," said the gallant Chairman, polishing his monocle, " I forgot myself, I thought I was back in my orderly-room. Now, gentlemen ! please ! "

" My idea, sir, is to get hold of an M.P.—a Member of Parliament—interest him in the scheme, pledge him to secrecy, and get him to approach the Secretary of State for War personally, and tell him the tale. You all know him. He has put our Territorial Army on its legs—and wheels—and he isn't strangled by red tape. He is the man for us."

" Splendid idea. Approved and adopted, eh ! gentlemen ! "

" Agreed ! Bravo ! "

" Good," said the Chairman ; " now for the M.P. Who knows one ? "

" What price so-and-so ? "

" No takers. His constituency is inland. We want one by the sea—near London preferred."

A hand shot up—again. " Got it, sir—the very one— luck of the A.A. His constituency is Hastings, ideal for us. His Christian name is Arthur—he's a regular Knight of the Round Table, too, because whenever you meet him you meet three or four brothers as well— wonderful family, and—pioneers of This Motoring, every one of 'em. Cycling, too, but that by the way."

" I back that, Colonel ! " said Charles One. " The very man for us. They are all close friends of mine, and two of the boys run London's second largest taxi-cab company. Who said machine-guns and pickaxes and spades ? "

" Bravo, Charles—splendid ! And so say all of us, eh, gentlemen ? "

" All of us ! "

Meeting finished.

.   .   .   .   .   .

His Majesty's Secretary of State for War looked thoughtfully at his visitor, and then, with a kindly twinkle, admitted that the idea was attractive, and likely to be instructive. " But why must you have Guards ? " he asked.

" I don't quite know," frankly admitted the A.A. ambassador, " except that it's a matter of atmosphere ! This is a big job, you know, and it's going to be done at no cost to the State—all voluntary help, from sporting motorists. We must have something to catch their imagination, and—well ! Hastings, my constituency, where the Normans landed years ago—and no un-friendly power shall ever land again ! It will sound so well, and look so well, don't you agree ? The Guards to Hastings—come now ! nothing is impossible, to you."

" Oh ! very well ! I'll see what we can do ! "

Coming from that high-minded and large-hearted man this meant " Yes ! "

And it was so.

.   .   .   .   .   .

So resilient was the spirit that the circular inviting A.A. members to join in the Guards' dash to Hastings met with a full response. In Company parlance the issue was over-subscribed.

Away with the good news to the Round Table, where the chief Knight sat with a few of his many brothers.

" It's most encouraging, so far. We have more than enough cars promised for the troops—as troops—and they will all turn out for certain—bar accidents—and the date is fixed. The 17th of March—St. Patrick's Day. How's that for an omen—remembering where you gentlemen were born."

" Foine ! "

" And more—the Mayor and Council of Hastings are simply tumbling over each other in their delight and anxiety to help. They are going to feed the whole battalion, at the expense of the town."

" Foine ! "

" Yes, and when the Commanding Officer said his men must have a hot meal—not sandwiches or bread and cheese—the Mayor agreed, and guess what they're going to give them ! Irish stew ! "

" Well, I'll be——"

" Quiet, George ! please."

" Sorry ! "

" Now, gentlemen ! " said the Secretary of the Youngest Motoring Organization. " We're well into the wood, but not half through it yet. These machine-guns and pickaxes and other impedimenta are becoming a perfect nightmare—almost our biggest problem. We were wondering if by any chance you could help, please."

Six feet and an inch or two of brother George unfolded, and he spoke :

" See here now," said he. " We've all got a warm corner in our hearts for this A.A., and the men who run it are our pals. They've given us many a hand. Now it's the family's turn. How many light lorries will be needed, do you think ? "

" To take the guns and ammunition and pickaxes and everything ? At a rough calculation, thirty," replied the Secretary.

" Oh ! a large order, that," said George. " Anyway, come over here in the corner, Willie, and let's figure it out."

Left figuring, then—

" See here now, Mr. A.A., you can go back to your Committee and say that the family—our family—are with you lock, stock and barrel in this enterprise, and we will shift all the stuff."

" That's wonderful, and thank you immensely ; but— please—how ? "

" My son ! Sleep in your bed, and leave that to Uncle Willie and Uncle George—we have spoken."

" Oh ! but *do* give me just an inkling. I must tell our people something."

" Well ! just to satisfy you, but keep it dark, mind ! London for about three days, including that of our family's Patron Saint, will be deprived of the use of thirty taxis, because we'll rip the bodies off, replace 'em with platforms, and lash all the guns and pickaxes, etc., to 'em—and there you are ! "

" George, you're wonderful ! "

" I know it," said he modestly. And that was that !

.   .   .   .   .

St. Patrick's Day was drawing nearer. The Committee met frequently at short notice, good ideas followed one upon another.

" How can we be sure the members will turn out ? " was an ever-worrying thought.

" Let's promise them lunch ! " ventured one.

" Hastings is feeding the troops. Surely we can spare the money to feed our crowd—if not, we'll have a whip round the Committee."

" Put me down for a tenner," said Charles Two.

" He's right," said the Chairman. " This is going to be our brightest scoop, and we mustn't leave anything to chance. How can we fix it up ? Any ideas, please ? "

" You can safely leave that to us, sir," said the Secretary. " We'll billet them in groups at each of our appointed Hotels—and that will please the Hotels as well as the members. If I may say so, it's a gorgeous idea—it will make it a regular family party, and relieve the members from a very natural anxiety."

.   .   .   .   .   .

With the final instructions as to where and at what time, " precisely, please," to parade with their cars, there was conveyed a cordial invitation to each member or driver to be guests of the Association to lunch at the so-and-so Hotel, Hastings, after having disembarked their respective contingents of His Majesty's Guards. " Members or drivers to stand by their cars for the return journey not later than 2 p.m., please."

The Secretary of State for War had lived up to his great reputation, and the Army Authorities were A.A. in their enthusiasm.

At that season of the year London enjoyed the presence of three battalions of Guards, quartered at Wellington Barracks, Chelsea, and the Tower, so it was decided to draw from each and make up a composite unit of Grenadiers, Coldstreamers and Scots.

Entraining (or embarking) would be easy at the two former barracks, but at the Tower—not so simple. Interference with traffic in the City of London was bad for business, and therefore to be avoided.

" Happy thought," said the Commanding Officer. " We'll march our fellers to the Thames Embankment, where there is plenty of room for you to pick 'em up."

" Blessings on the man who invented the card index system," said the A.A. workers, who were toiling to fit every car into the scheme of picking up. Three separate starting-points complicated a task already intricate enough.

" One thing is very important," said a senior. " Our members must be dealt with according to their residence, so that in military parlance they can proceed by the shortest way to their place in the alignment, ahem ! It's no good bringing people from Bermondsey to Chelsea, when they can slip over Blackfriars Bridge to the Embankment, and vice versa."

The cards were a boon. Each showed the member's name, address, make of car, seating capacity, extra driver, if any, and so on. With the aid of a large-scale map, and personal knowledge of streets and squares, three sets were eventually completed, indicating the cars most conveniently situated for each point, albeit not without a few anomalies.

" What shall I do ? " wailed he in charge of the Embankment. " I'm twenty-five cars short."

" And I have thirty too many," said Chelsea.

" Oh ! use your wits for goodness' sake," said the harassed senior. " Pick out some who live Westminster way—that's a fair dividing line, and you, Wellington— Barracks I mean, not the Duke—give him a few of yours from Hampstead and Highgate ; they can cut down Caledonian Road from Holloway and across Holborn—that won't make much difference to the morning traffic."

" Please ! "

" Well ? "

" What are we going to do if some of the cars don't turn up on, say, the Embankment—broken down or something, and yet Wellington or Chelsea may have more than they need."

Chorus of " Pessimist ! "

" Not at all," said the Secretary ; " he's entirely

right, and shows vision. A pat on the back for him.
Now let us think. The problem is—what are we going
to do if they *don't* turn up, and how are we going to
know ? Telephones are out of the question. Marconi's
can't help. There's only one way. Some of our best
hard-riding patrols must be brought into this—the
chaps who used to ' blind ' from Fleet Street through
the maze of City traffic with the early evening papers.
You know : ' Two-thirty winner-r-r '—full of cheek,
and bearing a charmed life. They're the boys we need.
Four at each point, at most, under the very nose of each
of you in charge. Dispatch-riders we'll call them.
Every five minutes you will send one off like a carrier-
pigeon to us at Wellington, with the latest news from
your particular front, and we will let you know how we
stand, through them."

" There is another possibility," said the Second-in-
Command. " One of our points may be short, and
the other two unable to spare any."

" Quite right, Francis ! " was the reply. " I hate
to spoil a patriotic voluntary enterprise, but—if the
worst happens—we must hire."

" Ooh ! that would be an anti-climax, after all the
work and the wonderful help of the St. Patrick people.
Can't we try the hiring-firms as well ? Why shouldn't
they be patriotic ? "

" No harm in trying ! Certainly we'll go along and
talk to them as pretty as can be."

The hiring-firms responded nobly. Each of them
promised to have four big cars tuned up, waiting like
fire-engines for the A.A. " S O S " if ever it should
come to that.

" And we will do it for nothing ! " said they in unity,
if not in unison.

One more river had been crossed.

The next contingency in this carefully prepared
impromptu was that of traffic.

Hitherto the police had been regarded by This

Motoring with respect not entirely unmixed with distrust. " P.C. 49 " was still very much on his dignity, scornful of a thousand-guinea limousine the while he would positively pander to a governess-cart drawn by an overfed pony.

When, therefore, in pursuance of polite requests by the Army, through the proper channels, instructions were issued that His Majesty's Guards, dashing to Hastings in motor cars provided by a certain organization, were to be afforded all reasonable facilities, his surprise was great.

When those instructions took the shape of a special order for St. Patrick's Day, prescribing extra duty for all ranks, and co-operation with the A.A. patrols when and wherever possible for the success of the experiment, he scratched his head and gave it up.

As for the police-inspectors, kings of their respective castles, dotted along the London-Hastings road, speech, for the moment, failed them.

" William ! " gasped one of them to his sergeant ; " read this while I get my breath."

" Blimey ! " said William, ". . . all reasonable facilities, battalion of Guards . . . night-duty men to work overtime . . . co-operate with the A.A. patrols . . . co-operate . . . and I nearly pinched one of 'em last week for smashing up our ' trap ' at the foot of River-hill. It can't be true, Inspector ! "

" It is, William, and you may as well put away your stop-watch, for that isn't all. Read on."

" Afford facilities for the distribution of handbills, which are being printed by the A.A.—copy attached."

This historic document may possibly merit reproduction—anyhow, it is shown overleaf :

" All I can say is," said the Inspector, having got his breath, " I hope it snows ! "

" Oh, really ! " said William, himself an old Cold-streamer, " you don't mean it. After all, you know, sir, the Guards are—the Guards ! "

" You're quite right, and I'm wrong, and I'm sorry, and I take it back. I hope it won't snow, and that it will be a fine day. After all, William, we're sportsmen first and policemen a good second." So saying, this very human inspector shut the office and went home to his tea.

.   .   .   .   .   .

Curiously enough, it *did* snow. The inspector's particular and personal bad fairy must have been a minute or two late for her tea, and, in consequence, heard what she should not—because just two days before the great adventure materialized a telephone carried to Fanum, London, the disquieting news that an inch of snow lay on the dreaded Riverhill.

" Oh ! Oh ! " wailed the overwrought A.A. staff. " This is the unmentionable limit. Let's give up motoring and go back to greengrocery, where we belong."

" Why ? " said a reporter of Britain's leading ha'penny—who had been told off by the editor to write the thing up and do it well.

" Why ? Can't even *you* see ? Try ! Just imagine Riverhill with a coating of ice over an inch of snow, and all our beautiful cars with the beautiful Guards skidding and sliding into one another, and all of them messed up together at the foot, with possibly a few bones cracked, and everybody cursing the A.A., and the Irish Stew getting cold, and——"

" Oh ! do dry up ! " said the newspaper man. " You need a tonic. This is England, don't forget. To-morrow the sun may shine. Let us dig out a car and go over the course."

" Right ! " A car was dug out and the course gone over, on March 16. The snow had ceased, for which relief much thanks. The good fairy of the A.A. had evidently gone on duty in time to hear the inspector's recantations, for during that day the sun, with a wink at

Wednesday, March **17**th, 1909.

(St. PATRICK'S DAY)

A BATTALION

OF HIS MAJESTY'S GUARDS

WITH TRANSPORT

Will pass along the **Hastings Road TO-DAY**

returning to London in the afternoon.

IT IS BEING CONVEYED IN SEVERAL HUNDRED

MOTOR CARS.

Will all Drivers, Cyclists, & Pedestrians

Kindly keep as closely as possible to the near side of the road as the Cars go by.

THE AUTOMOBILE ASSOCIATION,

PRINCES BUILDINGS,
COVENTRY STREET,
LONDON, W.

her and a friendly nod to St. Patrick, worked overtime, and—the road was adjudged safe.

. . . . . .

The Committee had met and adjourned. The last card had been placed in its pack. The last word had been spoken to a tired staff except :

"Thank you all again—whichever way it may go to-morrow. There's nothing we have left undone—nothing more we can do. The rest is in the lap of—St. Patrick ! Come on, boys, let's drink to St. Patrick —in his native beverage, and not too much soda."

"St. Patrick ! St. Patrick ! "

"If only the cars turn up."

"If only it doesn't snow ! "

"Good night ! "

"Good luck ! "

. . . . . .

While a dog-tired staff slept, while a police inspector mumbled drowsily in his bed, "Sorry, I take it back, and hope it'll be fine," and his sergeant, ex-Coldstreamer, dreamed of his beloved regiment, the A.A.'s good fairy tuned in to St. Patrick's own particular wave-length, and spoke with clarity and conviction.

St. Patrick, always a little gentleman, told her to "slape in pace and lave it to him."

At precisely a quarter to six the next morning, one of the most concerned of the youthful A.A. staff kissed his wife good-bye, and boarded a friendly milk-cart for a lift down Highgate Hill to the Tube station, on the way to Fanum, London, Wellington Barracks, and—with luck—Hastings.

Already they had looked out of the window together, and danced with glee.

The sun was shining—the sky was blue. "Oh ! what luck ! eh—just as it was when we were married."

" If only the cars turn up," said he.

" Don't be silly," said she. " Of course they'll turn up, and it isn't snowing. Now run along and don't miss your train."

.   .   .   .   .   .

The remainder of this story is difficult to frame, and not easy to credit, but—it is true.

The snow had gone—the sun beamed. The staff were on duty to the minute, and at the spot. Everyone knew his job and did it.

Every A.A. member who had promised to help turned up to the minute or so at his or her appointed place, with the sole and quite honourable exception of two—who started, but broke down on the way.

The flying-squad of A.A. patrols " blinded " to and fro between the Embankment and Chelsea and Wellington Barracks in their best " all the winners " style, carrying news monotonously good. All present and correct. No complaints. No requirements.

Drivers of the hired cars so generously promised— in case !—sulked unwanted in their garages, but not forgotten—oh, no ! Beer and cigarettes and warm thanks were forthcoming to those who also served by sitting and waiting.

The transport, machine-guns, and pickaxes, and— need we go over it all again ?—Of course it was all present and correct—trust Arthur and his round table of brothers for that.

" The Guards ? "

Oh, don't be foolish. They stepped into their various five-seaters, with packs and rifles complete, just as gently as they would sit down—like the gentlemen they were— in their Company Commander's lady's drawing-room. And not a car was a penny the worse for the trip, bless them one and all.

It had been ordered that the three sections, plus

transport, should proceed independently from their respective starting-points and converge into one tactical unit at cross-roads near the Crystal Palace.

They proceeded, converged, and formed an imposing column of route between two lines of delighted cheering people, astonished police, and smiling A.A. patrols, all the sixty odd miles to Hastings, to get a vociferous welcome—a speech from the Mayor—and—a dinner of Irish stew.

Everyone was happy.

The Press were splendid. He of the well-shaped nose especially.

Lessons to be learnt ? Oh, rather !

" The very first time it had been done."

" Quite so—and the A.A. did it."

" No doubt other countries would be interested."

They were. Germany, in particular, published full accounts, with maps and illustrations.

When the excitement abated somewhat, a cynical friend, possibly with memories of a school recitation—
" The Battle of Blenheim," said, " Now—joking apart—what really *did* the Army learn from the Guards' dash to Hastings ? "

" Any amount of things, but certainly one."

" And what was that ? "

" Chin-straps ! "

" Chin what ? "

" Chin-straps ! You see, it's like this. What they called the Brodrick service cap was only made to stick on the head by itself. It wasn't meant to be worn in a motor car. When we took the Guards to Hastings many of the troops—and even some officers—had to tie their caps on with their handkerchiefs to prevent them being blown away. So, in future, all caps will be fitted with chin-straps."

" And the A.A. did *that* ! "

" Ooh ! "

Not so many years later, in August, '14, a column of
London General Omnibuses—somewhere in France—
was proceeding to the front line with the Guards.

On the back seat of one of them a sergeant mused
over his responsibilities, and then hailed his corporal.

" What does this remind you of, Bill ? "

" What does what remind me of, Sergeant ? "

" Riding in a motor in full marching order. You
remember the last time we were doing it—I was a
lance-jack and you a rookey. Surely you remember—
we were in a regular Crystal Palace on wheels—all glass
and shiny wood and cushions—didn't know where to
put our feet—on the road to Hastings ! "

" Yes ! and we had Irish Stew for dinner, and beer."
The corporal wiped his mouth.

" We were only playing at it then. Who'd have
thought that—that——"

" Yes, who'd have thought it——"

" Lummy ! "

CHAPTER XI

CEAD MILE FAILTE

THE Guards were not to monopolize the Irish Stew. The A.A. was soon to be invited to share that appetizing dish. A beckoning finger was wagged to this effect at an early Olympia Motor Show by a famous Irish motorist, known to favoured intimates as Jimmy, and seconded by his partner Arjay. With names so very similar to those of motoring celebrities in Scotland, it seemed the finger of fate, and yet—why ?

" Listen while I tell you," said the famous one. " It cuts me to the heart to have to admit it, but our country is woefully behind the times. In the matter of roads, and signposts, and hotels, and garages, the same sad tale must be told. Just think now," he went on. " We have only now begun to use steam-rollers—there can't be half a dozen between Derry and Killarney ; and our signposts—they're a joke ! As for tarring, it's unknown ! Am I not right, Arjay ? "

His partner indicated assent. He didn't talk much.

" But what has all this to do with the A.A.," seemed a reasonable question. " You have your National Club. You own the leading Irish motor journal. Won't representations by the one and propaganda by the other get things altered ? "

" Perhaps," said Jimmy ; " but not soon enough. Our people rail at the English as a nation, but they like them personally. We want the English, with their cars, and their custom. It's the truth I'm telling you. We love our beautiful Emerald Isle. We want it to prosper. The Club and our journal are doing all that is possible, but the A.A. is wanted, too. Come over and help us to ginger things up."

They were two good men. Jimmy was an inveterate punster, teller of tales, sportsman, patriot, and a born salesman. He had the features and build of Napoleon, and loved to be told so. Later on, great work in the war earned him a knighthood. Arjay was another fine character, somewhat of a mystic, who always slept out of doors, and had written a book about it. Both have now " passed over."

Without doubt, the invitation was a compliment not to be despised ; but the extension could not be expected to pay for many years, and finance was an ever-recurring problem.

When this point was put to them, Jimmy said : " That's the worst of you English, always thinking in pounds, shillings and pence. How much does an A.A. patrol cost ? "

" Well over a hundred pounds a year, including his uniform and equipment," was the reply.

" All right, then. If you don't have any patrols— say a hundred for Ireland—that's a saving of over ten thousand pounds a year, for a start ! There's finance for you ! "

What could be done but laugh, and agree to think it over, and put the idea up to the Committee, and take a chance, in accordance with the light-hearted traditions of the A.A. ?

But before that :

" There's one thing, though, where you must help— and now——"

" An' phwhat's that ? " asked Jimmy.

" The man to run Ireland for us must be Irish. Your people wouldn't tolerate an Englishman. That much we do know."

Then Arjay, his quiet and deliberate partner, said, " I think I have the very one for you."

" Good ! Where ? "

" Here ! In this very Olympia Show. Irish born, raised in New Zealand. He's going round the stands writing up exhibits for our paper."

" Is he a journalist ? "

" Not until yesterday," was the reply. " But he can write, and he can drive a car. He took a sporting chance. Said he'd work for just his expenses to get a start."

" Very well," said the A.A. man ; " let's have a look at him. But before that—seriously now—does Ireland *really* want us, the A.A. ? Your ideas of finance are like your Irish signposts—a joke. Ours are not. It means a big risk to open another office—in Dublin—and maybe also in Belfast, and later on in Cork. Still ! if you can show that it's our duty to do it, we will try."

In reply, the great little Irish counterpart of Napoleon let himself go. With that eloquence which even then had made him a star turn at every public dinner on either side of the Irish Sea, he demonstrated that two plus two would make five. He scouted any idea of a loss. With silver tongue he portrayed his beloved country with good roads conveying the motoring pilgrim from one beauty spot to another—from Derry to Killarney, guided by A.A. signs. He acclaimed the merits of the personal touch which, he said, " has made the A.A. what it is and is going to be."

" Look at our hotels ! " he continued. " They're all right for us, because we don't expect too much. We get a hearty welcome from the landlord, a smile from the waiter, and a twinkle from the chambermaid, and we shut our eyes to such trifles as a mouldy door-mat, or the stains of yesterday's claret on this morning's breakfast-table cloth, or the sheets that should have been changed but were not. Their hearts are warm, and the food is hot, and the wine is good, and that's all we care about. But you English are so exacting.

" Mind ! I'm not saying you're wrong. Come to

Ireland and help us put all this straight. Writing letters won't do it. Bullying the hotel people won't do it. They're Irish, and they're proud. The personal touch *will* do it. Your bright young Road Managers— I've seen them—who call on the landlord, and handle him gently, get him on the right side, in the right mood, by means of peaceful persuasion instead of dictation ; *they* can do it, and work like that will bring its own reward. Good roads ! Signs everywhere ! Well-run hotels and garages, and an appreciative public giving liberal support ! There's a picture for you ! "

Arjay indicated assent.

They were right. Their man was the right man, and though it took nearly two decades, the magic was duly wrought, thanks mainly to these two good souls who loved their country.

CHAPTER XII

IN THE MATTER OF SALUTES

WHILE chin-straps engaged the attention of His Majesty's Army Clothing Department, and long before they adorned the chins of His Majesty's forces, a certain young and healthy Organization was learning that progress towards maturity was not all amusement and birthday gifts. There must be bumps and ailments, too. Scouts and set-backs had all to be taken in the stride and not dwelt upon too lightly or too heavily.

But the shadow of impending legal strife was distinctly heavy. Another battle had yet to be joined in this great war for road freedom, and the outcome of it could not yet be foreseen. The highways of Britain were still for the greater part dusty, giving bitter annoyance to wheeler and walker. Tar-spraying was taking a long time to materialize and resentment a longer time to die out. Speed—even low speed—raised dust, and dust raised an outcry. Thus began a particularly annoying ailment of This Motoring—a persecution which, born of dust but carried on out of sheer cupidity, spread like a plague through the country.

To make this clearer, let it be remembered that in one week one county bench alone, in free enlightened England, took one thousand pounds sterling from This Motoring, in the shape of fines for exceeding the speed-limit and other quite venial offences.

Yes, Cupidity was the only word to describe that. Naturally this record was regarded as a scoop and boomed as such by some newspapers. Inevitably, too, it added envy to the latent hatred and uncharitableness.

" Have you seen it ? " said one to another at the Council Meeting. " A thousand pounds in one week ! *A thousand*—Oh ! If Blankshire can do it, why shouldn't we ? No harm in trying, eh ? Let's put on more Police Traps."

" Yes, let's ! "

In that way, as with a stone flung into a pool, the circle widened and widened, and trapping became what the theatrical world would call a star turn on the programme of rural Bumbledom.

It had been borne in upon the simple mind of the average police constable that the road to promotion was paved with motoring convictions. Burglary, setting fire to a barn, or a punched head, had, like the poor, been always with them, but motor traps ! Oh, splendid ! A bunch of fivers every bench day, booked to their credit, growing in volume and likely to grow, except for this interfering Organization which made bold to combat their activities and, what was worse, bade fair to prosper thereby.

" Awful cheek ! " said those good men. " What a pity it was that the Fairmile Perjury Case went the wrong way—that the scout was not convicted. That would have finished the whole show."

And to crown it all, the Pharisees were flaunting a Badge on their cars ! " Awful cheek ! The badge of the law-breaker—that's all it was. Ought to be ashamed of themselves, but never mind, they shouldn't have it all their own way. As old Sir Somebody had said, ' We'll show 'em ! Woof ! ' " A few shots were left in their locker. Perjury, of course, was a wash-out. They wouldn't be caught like *that* again ; but obstruction of the police in the execution of their duty—that sounded good. Worth trying, anyhow. Perhaps the clerk of the bench, a lawyer, could advise how to set about it.

Better put the matter up for consideration by the Powers that be.

The Watch Committee—Powers that be—sitting.

Chief Constable attending as a matter of course, and learned clerk to the bench by request.

His Worship the Mayor speaking.

" Gentlemen ! . . . wish . . . convey . . . your behalf . . . appreciation . . . presence . . . learned clerk . . . this meeting . . . benefit . . . great experience . . . legal knowledge on this—on this—what I mean to say is we were getting on very nicely with This Motoring, and—let 'em break the law if they're fools enough to do it, and be caught by our police, and pour out their money in fines. Quite good. We'd never had such a time, until they, sort of—got together—and sort of—turned round—and sort of—kicked back ! That's it—kicked back ! They're laughing at us. Flaunting their confounded Badge at us. Law and Order. Laughing—Oh ! Mr. Clerk, what can we do ? "

" May it please your Worship, that is, Mr. Chairman, as the Law stands you can't stop anyone from preventing anyone from committing an offence, before it is committed. I hope I make myself clear. It's like— I mean—if Bill Sikes talks airily of ' doing a job ' it is no illegality for a friend—the parson, perhaps—to seek to dissuade him from a moral lapse. Indeed, it's the friend's duty to steer him off the road to ruin. That's not obstruction within the meaning of the Act, but——"

" But what, Mr. Clerk ? "

" But if Bill has marked down a couple of—shall we say stop-watches in Councillor Biggs's shop-window, and is actually on the job, the friend mustn't scout and warn him when P.C. 49 is coming round the corner. That's obstructing the police. It would prevent them getting evidence of an actual crime."

" Well ! what's that got to do with——"

" Just a minute, please. It means that if a motor scout, outside the trap, stops a car and tells the driver that there is a trap working, we can't very well get him for obstruction, *but*—if he is in the trap, between our police, at the time he warns a car to stop, that car may be exceeding the speed-limit at the time, thus committing an offence under the Act—and the position is in line with that of the thief breaking Councillor Biggs's shop-window."

"I see ; thank you, Mr. Clerk ; and I think we all do, eh ? Oh ! just a moment. The Chief Constable wants to speak. Go on, Chief ! "

"Thank you, sir ! I would like to say a few words. The learned clerk to the bench has told us what we can do, and it's for the Watch Committee to say if we shall do it. Mind you, sir, I'm not sure that I like the idea. I was a soldier before I became a policeman, and although of course duty is duty, and motor-trapping is now part of our duty, I can't help feeling a little sympathy for the other side. You know what I mean, I hope—that is I'm sure you do—British Army, er—little of it goes a darned long way—old song, you know, but, er—er—always fights fair. That's it, fights *fair*. Never stabs in the back. And this seems rather like stabbing in the back. I don't like it, but if it must be—it must."

"Very well, Chief ! We can't, of course, dictate to you. We can only suggest, and—thank you ! "

So in due course, on the open road, the new idea was tried out.

The police sergeant speaking :

"George ! ! Here's one of those motor scouts. Now, you know what to do ! We've got one trap here and another furlong measured out further up the road. Let him see us all settled nice and comfortable here, and then, away we go to our other pitch, so that he is in the middle of the trap instead of outside it."

"All right, Sergeant. It shall be done ! "

Then a car—with the A.A. Badge—slowed up by a scout's salute, and a wave—"Look out, sir ; trap just ahead."

"Thanks ! Cheerio ! That's worth a year's sub., what ? "

" Yes, sir ! Good day, sir. Good—Ooh ! Afternoon, Sergeant ! Nice day ! I thought you were
lower down the road."

" Nice day ? Yes, but not for you, young fellow my
lad ! We were *not* lower down the road, and we've
caught you ! You and your illegal Association. Slowed
down one of your members, did you ? Exceeding the
limit, was he ? Oh, yes, he was. Stopped him in the
very act, and in this very trap. We timed him doing a
fraction over twenty an hour. Three of us, and only
one of you. Now then, give me your name and address—
sharp about it, and you're going to be summonsed for
obstructing us, the Police, in the execution of our duty."

And that was that ! A summons, attendance at the
police court, and trial.

The sequel was forty shillings and costs, or in default
one month.

The new campaign had quite a good run. What
Surrey thought to-day, Sussex would think to-morrow,
and Hampshire and Huntingdonshire and other Shires
would take up the scent and follow it.

They did. Summons followed summons. Scout after
scout was fined, until the brows of those who sat on the
Committee and ran the show were puckered indeed.

" Oh, dear ! we're up against it again," said the Chairman. " Rather fatiguing, what ! How many more
prosecutions can we stand before throwing our hand in ?
The Press were getting sympathetic—now they're not so
quite, if you understand me. They're asking what we're
going to do about it. Walter ! what do you think ? "

" Well, Colonel—I mean Mr. Chairman—we started
by fighting, let's keep on fighting, and go down fighting,
if we *must* go down ! Let's appeal. I don't know to
whom, but the Solicitor can tell us. Let's take the very
next case and fight it out."

" Bravo ! Agreed, gentlemen ? "

Agreed.

" Very well, then. The very next case we get of one

of our men being prosecuted and fined, we—how do you put it—oh, yes, thanks—we apply for a Case to be Stated, and then the—the—oh, yes, thank you—the Divisional Court of Appeal will settle the question once and for all."

" Settle what ? "

" It will settle, we hope, the question whether warning a motorist of a police-trap is or is not illegal—and when, and why, and how ! "

Eminently business-like, this Committee, if one might so put it. No ssing about. No shivering. Fighters all.

" Agreed ! Get on with it." And that was that.

Refreshing to note the surprise of the Bench at the Something-ford Court of Summary Jurisdiction, when for the *n*th time a motor scout in the employ of a certain Association was, almost as a matter of course, convicted and fined—but the Solicitor for the defence sprang a mine by saying, " May it please your Worship, we apply for a Case to be Stated, with a view to an Appeal."

" Appeal ? Did you ever ? What awful cheek ! "

It might be, but the situation was critical, and something simply had to be done.

Here again This Motoring found itself at the parting of the ways.

Authority had unlimited means. It could pursue a policy of attrition. Prosecute and get them fined. Wear them out. That was the stuff. Prosecutions. Fines. Wear them out. Woof !

Yes—but ! Curious people, the English. So obstinate ! Never know when they're beaten. Keep on bobbing up for more. Silly ! eh ? Oh, yes. Back in the Committee-room they talked it over.

" Sink or swim, gentlemen. Agreed ? "

Agreed.

" Splendid ! And this time we needn't grudge a pound or two. Eight thousand members. Eight thousand, and

only three years and a quarter since we went all out.
Splendid ! Settle the question once and for all, get the
finest lawyers, put up the best case, and—and—Damned
be he who dares cry Hold ! enough !—eh ? "

" Hear, Hear ! We'll go down fighting ! and we'll
all go down together."

" And mind you, gentlemen," said the Chairman,
" our fight will come before the Divisional Court of
Appeal, at the Royal Courts of Justice, Temple Bar,
just opposite to the place where we started our great
adventure. That's a good augury, eh—who knows ?
We may win ! "

(Hear, hear ! We may win !)

" Yes, we may indeed, gentlemen, but just a moment.
Why are you so quiet, Mr. Secretary ? "

" Oh ! nothing in particular, sir, thank you ; except—
except—what are we going to do if we *lose* ? "

" If we lose. If we—by jove ! you're right. We may
lose, and if so—what ? "

" We must take that possibility into account. In the
Army, you know, tactics and strategy and all that, always
provide a retreat—what ? "

" Well, go on ! "

" Thank you, sir. It's like this. Oh, please don't
mind—it just slipped out. Some of our members are
getting nervy. They're talking about taking the Badge
off—dreadful idea. They say that the police have a
particular ' down ' on cars which display our Badge.
That they single them out for special—how shall I put
it ?—inquisition. That attitude of mind presages a kind
of rot which must be stopped, or it will break us. If we
had lost the Fairmile Case, which, thanks be, we didn't,
it would have been the end. We know that. If we
were to lose this Appeal, it might again be the end
—but it may not. Forgive my putting it so bluntly,
but—never mind about our winning ! What are we
going to do if we *lose ?* There must be some way
round."

" Quite right ! Quite right ; there must be a way round, and we must find it."

There was a way, and it was found.

Lawyers, great ones, Genii of the Lamp of Evasion, were retained and conjured to apply themselves to the problem of what to do if the Appeal was lost, if Authority was right, and the A.A. was wrong.

" Spare neither money nor pains. This is a fight to a finish." Thus said all concerned.

While the laborious business of building up a case for appeal progressed, and briefs, evidence, and ideas for special pleading were being prepared against the fateful day of the appeal, the Genii took counsel together and exuded wisdom.

The fateful day dawned, as fateful days will. The case of Rex *versus* Never-Mind-Whom stood first on the list, and the array of Counsel in wig and gown was excelled only by the resplendence of His Majesty's Judges on the Bench—three in number—speaking of each other as Learned Brother, and looking every inch of the part.

Said the Lord Chief Justice—now lamented and always loved as a great English sportsman, " I think I ought to mention that I am, in fact, a member of this wicked Association."

" I believe I am, too ! " said a Learned Brother.

" I most certainly am not," said the third Eminence, who was an amiable and noted rider to hounds.

" Does it matter ? "

" Not at all, M'Lord," said the Leading Counsel. " Our case stands on its merits and—may it please your Lordship, it is this "—and so on for half an hour, punctuated by a few pertinent questions, put in the kindliest way.

Leading counsel for the appellants finished and sitting down. A pause. A rustle of silk gown on the part of Leading Counsel for Authority, ready to plunge into argument.

" Thank you, Mr. Blank, we need not trouble you."
" Oh ! "

Cold shivers. That meant that it was over and the appeal lost !

It was even so. Judgment was delivered in a few well-chosen sentences, with a twinkle or two, and a genial discrimination between " organized warnings " and what His Lordship termed a " friendly wave " by one driver to another. Appeal dismissed. The legal battle was all over in forty-five minutes, and it had cost eight hundred pounds.

Back to the Committee-room. All present. Chairman speaking.

" Well, gentlemen, we've lost. The Learned Judge's ruling amounts to this :

" Our scout was doing something—showing his red disc, and signalling to our member when he was actually in the trap and being timed. That's the case in a nutshell. He was warned at the very time—mark that—at the very time he was breaking the law—this absurd law—by driving at twenty-two point one miles an hour, on a perfectly safe open road. Goodness ! how everyone will smile at that in a few years to come. Meanwhile—we—What's that, Mr. Secretary ? "

" There's a Press-man on the telephone, sir, wanting our views. May the call be put through here, please ? "

" By all means ! Carry on. Let me speak to them. Hallo ! hallo ! You're the News Agency ? Good afternoon ! What about our appeal ? Yes, it's lost. We all know that. Are we going to close down ? No, we are not, we are going on. We have no intention of withdrawing our patrols or weakening the system. Instead of spending less money we shall probably spend more. What's that you say ? ' Well, you'll be——' Oh, what language, but we're quite serious. Yes, certainly you can publish something on those lines. Those who live longest will see most. Thank you ! Good-bye ! "

" Thank you too, Mr. Chairman," from the Secretary.
" That will keep the ball rolling, and now——"

" Yes, gentlemen. Now we may hark back to our
previous Meeting at which we agreed to find a way round.
That, too, is in a nutshell. Our case has failed because
our man was doing something—something positive.
I've said that before, but let it pass. Suppose, in certain
special circumstances, our men were to do *nothing*.
Just stand still ? See ? Of course you see. Thanks
to our Solicitor's sound guidance, and the best possible
advising counsel, we have put in some good hard staff
work, so to speak, behind the firing-line.

" As we stand, or might be standing, our members
will open their morning papers at breakfast to-morrow,
and turn straight to the Case. You can imagine umpteen
of them saying, ' What ? Scout Appeal lost ? That
looks like the end, and I've only just renewed my sub.
I'd better write that item off as a bad debt.' But, gentlemen, it isn't going to be a bad debt. They may severally
and collectively eat their bacon in peace, because——"

" Because why ? "

The answer to that rather inartistic but quite human
query was on the morrow to be furnished by the local
postman.

For some time prior to The Day a devoted little band
of clerks had been sweating away, addressing envelopes,
folding, inserting, and gumming down a personal com-
munication for every one of the eight thousand-odd
individual members of what the Learned President of
the Court of Appeal—himself a member—had humor-
ously termed " this wicked Association."

And now—the Committee Meeting over—all hands
to the pump for sticking on penny stamps, and bundling
sack after sack to the post.

So did it happen on the morrow that side by side
with the morning paper, lying in accordance with
tradition exactly one inch to the right of father's table-
napkin, there lay also an envelope in flaming yellow,

bearing a no-longer strange device, and containing a notice in equally flaming yellow, which read :

TO (AA) MEMBERS.

WHEN A PATROL

DOES NOT SALUTE

STOP

AND ASK THE REASON

" Now what may that mean ? " said one to another. " We've lost the Appeal and that should put an end to motor scouting ; yet there must be some reason in this notice. Let's give it a trial run next week-end."

Out on the road in due course the new instruction was put to the test. This Motoring was still rather fun, don't you know, and anything new added zest to the day's enjoyment.

Where, hitherto, A.A. Patrols' salutes were looked for, especially by Mrs. Member, here was a new game. ' We've passed four of our men, George, since Kingston, and they all saluted," said the lady passenger. " I want one who doesn't, just to see—Hallo ! look out, there's another at the bend. Well, fancy that !—he stood stock still and didn't take the slightest notice of us. And you've gone right by him, silly ! Oh, do pull up and let's go back."

" All right, my dear, but mind, leave this to me ; I'm the member, not you."

Then : " Good morning ! "

" Good morning, sir ! "

" Good—er-m ! When a patrol does not salute stop and—that's it—why *didn't* you ? "

" It's quite all right, sir. Lucky you did stop, you were doing a comfortable thirty, and "—whispering— " they're at it half a mile ahead, sir."

" They're——"

" Yes, sir, trapping ! Caught seven already they have, but none of Ours."

" Ooh ! Thanks awfully, jolly fine ! Good luck to the A.A. Badge ! "

" Yes, sir, but remember, *you must stop.* We can't tell you anything unless you stop—see ? "

.   .   .   .   .   .

It stood out plainly that the latest piece of impertinence displayed by " this illegal Association " would not for long go unchallenged.

In the House of Commons about that time a Member's question had drawn from the Home Secretary the reply that " there could be no doubt that the scouts employed by the Automobile Association as road patrols hampered the police in carrying out the duties which Parliament had imposed upon them, and that if the evil continued it might become necessary for Parliament to intervene for their protection."

Commenting upon this, a leading daily newspaper suggested that the Home Secretary " might be well advised to study a list of members of the Automobile Association and see from it the opinion many of his colleagues in the Cabinet and Judges of the High Court hold of its necessity and usefulness by the fact of subscribing to its funds and its tenets. Its roll of members embraces most of the best known names in the country."

" Now for it ! " said a bold, bad Committee-man, when this was read at the next Meeting. " I bet an even fiver that we get another summons for obstruction by one of our men before the year's out."

Nobody took the bet, which he would have won with

a month to spare, because there we were again with a perfectly good prosecution for obstructing the police in the execution of their duty, and all the rigmarole incidental thereto. Same old labour of getting up the case for the defence, selection of advocate (must be good), preparation of brief. Same old everything, even perhaps the result, but—No ! on the contrary, three loud cheers. For the very first time in A.A. history, the case was dismissed.

In this connexion the following comments appeared in *Truth* :

> The Automobile Association has scored in its latest scout case, though it is not too clear from the brief published reports exactly how they managed to do it. It appears, however, that in this instance the scout was stationed within a two-mile trap, and the Magistrates seem to have decided in his favour on the ground that the car which he warned was not proved to have been exceeding the limit at the time, although the police contended that if it had not been warned it would have been found to have done so at the end of the two-mile stretch. In the recent case in the Divisional Court, when the decision went against the scout, the Lord Chief Justice laid special stress, it will be remembered, on the fact that the car was, in the opinion of the police, exceeding the limit before the trap was entered, and presumably the Dartford Magistrates had this point in mind in giving their more recent decision. From this it would seem to follow, therefore, that to get a conviction against a scout for obstructing, in future the police must tell off a man to shadow the enemy in order to be able to testify as to the speed of the car at the moment of warning.

Rather fun This Motoring, eh ?

CHAPTER XIII

AMALGAMATION

THE Chancellor of the Exchequer was busy with his Budget.

The progress of This Motoring could not be overlooked, and drastic changes in the method of taxing motor cars were to be introduced.

The old-time carriage duties of a guinea or two would give place to a scale ranging from two to forty guineas per car per annum, according to horse-power.

This had been decided after having consulted the recognized motoring organizations with the accent on the word recognized. The horse-power formula had been prepared by an expert Committee of the R.A.C. and—it had stood the test of time.

Increased taxation was a bitter pill, however skilfully gilded by Celtic oratory ; it would not have been swallowed but for a definite undertaking given by the Government that " the proceeds of this special taxation would be devoted to the work of improving the roads."

" Not a bad idea," said those who bore the burden ; " but how is it going to be done ? Are we really going to save on the roundabouts—meaning wear and tear of our tyres and springs—what we shall lose on the swings under this new scale of taxation ? "

" The Government will create a Central Road Authority," said a Right Honourable Gentleman in reply. " All motor-car taxation revenue shall be passed to IT and spent by IT *on* the road, *for* the road, and for *nothing but* the road."

"Not too bad, if we get the right men to handle the money, and get the work done," was the general feeling. "Much depends on that—we want workers rather than politicians." The Government agreed.

The new Authority was to be called the Road Board, with a paid Chairman and Secretary, and half a dozen unpaid members, all gentlemen of standing and wide experience in road and motoring problems.

The Chairman was appointed first.

He was a railway man.

"He is a splendid fellow, and all that," said one of those keenly interested ; " but why do they pick upon a *railway* man, however good ? Surely this is a *motoring* matter ? "

"Anyway, we must see to it that the Secretary's post is filled by one of us," said another. " Let us do something before it is too l te."

Luckily it was not too late. The Press proved a friend indeed. Inspired by a trenchant article in a leading British daily, written by one of motoring's brightest literary men, the daily, provincial and technical journals roused public opinion and kept it awake to the fact that the Road Board secretaryship called for a man with highway and motoring knowledge of the highest order, and no one else would do.

"And what is more," declared the bolder writers, "we know the very man."

.   .   .   .   .   .

But much was to happen before the journalistic tipsters could claim to have spotted a winner, and no one can guess how events would have shaped had the Good Fairy of the A.A. been temporarily indisposed.

.   .   .   .   .   .

One day the Bright Young General Manager of This Motoring's Insurance Company came for a bite of food and a bit of business to follow. Prolific of ideas, he

had hailed with satisfaction the friendly relations that
had followed the fuss with the Motor Union. As its
official company he now hoped he might serve the A.A.
Hence the luncheon.

The A.A. staff liked his cheery optimism and breadth
of idea, his rather taking lisp and responsiveness. He
breathed progress.

Recollection of their own struggles impelled a fellow-
feeling for this David-like concern, whose puny strength
was being pitted against the wealth and power of mighty
Insurance Corporations, "Established A.D. 1814—
reserve capital umpteen millions sterling," and all that.
No doubt, some of these were saying, "Give it six
months, or a year at latest. The thing can't succeed—
it must fail." Quite a lot of clever people had said
the same when the first thin line of A.A. patrols stretched
out along the Brighton road. Very well, then.

.   .   .   .   .

With the coffee came the business—and the happy
smile of the B.Y.G.M. became rather faint. "It isn't
your fault," he was being told, "but, all the same, our
people are very angry with your people, and that is bad
for everybody."

"What have they done now?"

"They have copied our Free Legal Defence scheme.
It's disgraceful. First the A.A. Badge copied; then the
road scouts copied. One is modified and the other
withdrawn after a regular row. Peace is achieved,
everyone nice and friendly, and then your people copy
us again, put the clock back—and spoil everything."

"I know!" said he, rather dolefully. "It's dis-
heartening. Never mind who is to blame—it wouldn't
be fair to say—the mischief is done, and I suppose there
will be another awful row."

"No! The A.A. won't start one. We shall sit tight
and let others judge the case on its demerits."

" There's only one way to stop this nonsense," said the B.Y.G.M.

" And that is ? "

" Amalgamation ! "

" Oho ! ' Old Moore's Almanack ' again ! "

" What do you mean ? "

" On the A.A. Committee we have a lovable chap who belongs to both the M.U. and the A.A. Over two years ago, when the row was on, he prophesied amalgamation, and his colleagues rather chipped him. He was wonderfully patient under the chipping, but he stood—and still stands—firm. ' It must and will come,' he says."

" Good chap ! If only he were right. What can we do to give Fate a gentle push ? "

" Not a thing, only carry on and hope that something will turn up."

" Afraid you are right," said the B.Y.G.M. as he rose to leave. " By the way, concerning the Road Board Secretary ; did you notice that some of the leading papers hint that they can name the very man for the job ? "

" Yes—and it sets me wondering if——"

" Me too, because if they mean the man I mean——"

" And I also ! "

" That would ease things considerably, eh ? "

" It would ! "

This talk was rather cryptic, but it meant quite a lot.

.   .   .   .   .   .

At the next A.A. Committee meeting there was bad news.

" Gentlemen ! " said the Vice-Chairman, " our poor friend, the Colonel, is dreadfully ill, and unlikely ever to be better. He was sitting in this very chair polishing his monocle only last month, and now—it's awful, really—his doctor says we must not expect to see him back."

The members present passed a resolution of heartfelt

regret and sympathy, and adjourned as a mark of respect to their friend, a brave and tireless fighter.

The gallant Chairman's place was kept vacant, and a Noble Earl, in deed as well as in name, consented to be elected in his stead. This was duly proposed, seconded and carried with acclamation.

. . . . . .

Then Fate gave another spin to her wheel. One morning there appeared headlines rather startling—

ROAD BOARD SECRETARY
FAMOUS MOTORING LEADER APPOINTED

The Press campaign had succeeded ; the Government had kept faith ; the prophets had been right. Mixed with a pardonable amount of " we told you so's " were compliments to the Right Honourable Gentleman who had piloted the Road Bill through the Commons, and warm praise for the Motor Union, whose executive had " placed patriotism before personal interest, by allowing their gifted chief-paid official to accept the responsible and difficult post of Secretary to the Road Board, without regard to the effect which the loss of a man of his exceptional ability might have upon the welfare and future of their own organization."

" I say ! " cried the Assistant Secretary of the A.A. that morning ; " of course you have seen the papers ? "

" Oh yes ! "

" All about the Road Board and your opposite number who has been offered the job. Wonderful, eh ? What will the M.U. do now ? "

" What the A.A. is going to do is more to the point," was the reply. " First a letter of congratulation to my opposite number, to be sent round by hand. Then— to-day, Friday, is going to be our busy day. Mail-day as they call it in the City. Take it that the mail-day card is hung up in the front office. We are not at home."

" If you would let me in to the big idea, please, I might be more useful ! "

" Of course, how silly of me. I beg pardon, and let us have a meeting at once. Race round for the others. Five heads are better than two. We'll imagine we're taking another lot of Guards to Hastings. Meanwhile I'll 'phone to our young Insurance Manager friend, and beg him to drop everything he's doing and come along. He has ideas ! "

In less than half an hour six devotees to the cause of This Motoring were gathered together, eager as terriers waiting for the ball to be thrown.

" Gentlemen ! " said the Secretary, their senior by a few months. " We are in sight of big developments, and thank you very much, Jack, for answering the wolf-call ! " (This to him of the happy smile and taking lisp—the B.Y.G.M.) " It isn't altogether your pigeon, but——"

" That's all right, old chap, very pleased."

" Thank you again ! You've seen the papers about the great appointment ? "

" Of course ! "

" Suppose we could induce *our* Committee to hold out the olive branch to *your* people, and invite them to a friendly exchange of views on the subject of amalgamation ; would they accept ? "

" Yes, I feel sure they would—and——"

" What then ? "

" Take my tip and strike while the iron is hot. Don't lose a day."

" We won't lose an hour. Gentlemen, workers all ! This is where we must take risks, even on a Friday. Keep your seats, please. I, who have never before dared to do such a thing, am going to convene a meeting of the A.A. Committee, and—hang the consequences ! "

" To-morrow is Saturday. Most of our very sporting Committee-men will be doing something. It must be Sunday."

" Sunday ! ! " gasped one. " Well, of all the cheek ! Sorry, sir. How are you going to meet, and wh re ? "

" Somebody's house ? " ventured another.

" Bravo ! That's a brain-wave. Listen, you fellows ! We have many friends, but our best one—my best one—who put up money and lent his typewriter until we could afford to buy one, and backed the A.A. through thick and thin—mostly thin, bless his heart—lives about fifteen miles out, on the Brighton road. That's an omen ! We started our great adventure on the jolly old Brighton road, less than five short years ago, and now ! Oh !—I'll ask him to entertain the Committee to tea and—other comforts, and he'll say ' Yes ! ' He'll say ' Yes ' right enough. Get his office on the 'phone, Francis, and then pass it to me."

Telephone instrument duly passed.

" That the—— ? A.A. Secretary here. Can I speak to—— ? Oh ! is it you, sir ? What luck ! Look here ! Please don't mind. I'm all out of breath ! Something big is in the wind, and we want your help. It's like this."

The story was told.

" And, you see ! " he concluded, " if only I can tell the Committee that you will be glad to welcome them, they will turn up ! You will ? Oh, thank you ! At four o'clock, then, on Sunday, and you'll put a flag out so that they don't go blinding by your lodge-gates, eh ? Thank you again—I can never really——" but the great one had already rung off.

Accordingly, in response to telephone and telegram, the unselfish and rather bewildered Committee turned up to time on the Sunday at their colleague's house, exchanged greetings, and asked, " Without wishing to be inquisitive, you know, what the blazes is up now ? "

" Tea, or anything stronger if you like, first," said their host, " and then, the big idea. Take the chair, Archie ! " This to the Vice-Chairman.

Chair duly taken.

" Now, Mr. Secretary ! "

" It is awful cheek of me, sir and gentlemen, to upset your week-end like this, and I don't know how I had the nerve to do it, but—well, there is a faint chance of this Sunday being historical. It's like this. The Road Board have found the best possible man. The M.U. lose him. We have lost the Colonel, and his noble successor has not yet formally taken his place as Chairman of our Committee. I hope you see where this is leading ? "

" Don't we just, eh, Walter ? And you, Charles One, and ' Old Moore's Almanack '—why, he's actually blushing ! "

" All right ! " said the last named, " I won't say I told you so—yet ! Ha ! Ha ! "

" Ha ! Ha ! " That was a good start—whatever the finish might be.

" So I thought," continued the Secretary, " we might strike while the iron is hot, as a good friend of the A.A. suggested, and, more cheek of me—sorry, please—here is a draft letter which you, sir, might sign as Vice-Chairman, when it has been cut about and improved, and we might send it round by hand to the Chairman of the M.U."

" What is the gist of it ? "

" Well, first, it congratulates his organization upon the high compliment which the appointment by the Government of their chief-paid official implies ; then it sympathizes with him and his committee in their great loss, unselfishly borne in the general interest of motoring ; and then—and then——"

" Go on ! Let's have it ! "

" Then—this is the difficult part—we, in a measure, swallow our past grievances and hope that they will, as we do, consider this a peculiarly appropriate time for both Committees to meet, frankly to discuss the possibilities of closer working. That is as high as it need be put to start, and—that's all, sir."

There was a pause, while the idea was digested.

" First of all," said the host generously, " our Secretary did quite right, I think, to get us here to-day. It is a big idea and it may make history."

" Agreed ! Walter is right," said many of those present ; and the Secretary sighed with relief and smiled for the first time that afternoon.

" Shall we send a letter ? " asked the Vice-Chairman.

" Agreed ! Agreed ! "

" Splendid ! Very well, then. It isn't much use for sixteen of us to mess about with the wording. Let's leave it to a Sub-Committee of Charles One, Walter, Charles Two, and of course you, Mr. Solicitor, please ! with the Secretary. Come on all the rest—let's have a look at Walter's garden while they get on with it. Whistle for us when you're ready," he said. And out they went.

The letter was completed in half an hour, and when the Jury returned—that is, when the Committee re-assembled—it was approved and signed for delivery on the following morning.

" Before we part, Archie—beg pardon, Mr. Chairman, I mean," said Charles Two, " I have a suggestion to make, and it's this. We must get to know their Committee-men. We are all friends here ; we've worked, and joked, and worried, and—yes !—suffered together. How shall we get on with the other crowd, and how can we find out ? "

" You're quite right, old man ! It's as serious as taking a partner," said a colleague.

" Or getting married," said another.

" And they may not like us," remarked a third.

" Glad you agree," said Charles Two. " Therefore, if they like our letter, if the ' conversations ' develop—let's ask 'em to dinner ! "

" Bravo ! The very thing," said he who was affectionately called Old Moore. " I spoke of something like that when the row was on. You know !

Boatrace night—crews dining—one Cambridge between two Oxfords. One A.A. between two M.U.s—all round the table ! ”

“ And put me next to the Parson ! ” said Charles Two. “ That will be a test, if you like.”

“ And put Charles down for a tenner,” said his neighbour ; “ he seems to like it ! ”

“ It remains now to pass a very cordial vote of thanks to Walter for his hospitality,” said the Vice-Chairman. Carried with acclamation.

After a final drink the unpaid devotees of This Motoring drove away to their respective homes invigorated by the feeling that something attempted something done had earned a night's repose.

. . . . . .

The dinner clinched it. Although quite a lot had taken place, a charmingly-worded reply had been received to the A.A. invitation ; although the Chairman of the M.U. had, with characteristic foresight, declared himself boldly in favour of an alliance—on equal terms ; although sub-committees had been formed and had met to discuss details, and reported back, and met again ; although all this had happened, Charles Two and Old Moore between them had made success assured with their idea of the dinner—which clinched it.

It was held at the Imperial, better known as “ Oddys,” and the proceedings were designedly informal. No speeches—just talk, and the opinions expressed on all sides were in effect—“ Nice men ! Pity we didn't know them earlier. What on earth led us to row with each other ? ” and so on.

Equality in numbers on the Committee. Mutual trust from the word “ Go.” That's the idea. Officers too ! as far as possible. The permanent officials presented no difficulty in the matter of their distribution. The head of the M.U. was a famous Parliamentarian and future Statesman. Obviously the best possible choice for Chairman of the combined organizations.

" But," said an anxious worker in the cause of peace at an A.A. Committee Meeting, " what about our own Chairman ? The Noble Earl ! "

" Um ! that's rather a snag ! He is such a fine sports-man, he's been so good-natured about the whole thing. We mustn't hurt his feelings. Any suggestions ? " said the Vice-Chairman.

" I have an idea, please."

" Silence for the Secretary ! Go on, let's hear you ! "

" We can tell him the truth ! That will appeal to him. He won't stand in the way, and—why not ask him to be President—we haven't a President. What better man could we have as President of a sporting show like ours than the First Sportsman in Britain, as he is, since King Edward passed away ? "

" He's right—absolutely right, Archie ! Beg pardon, Mr. Chairman, I mean," cried Charles One.

" Hear ! Hear ! " said Charles Two. " That's an-other fence cleared in this Grand National. We're nearly on the straight for the winning-post."

" Not so fast ! " said a quiet voice. " A lot depends upon the way we put it to him."

" Quite right, Walter. Shall we form a sub-committee to draft a letter ? "

" No ! In my humble opinion, Mr. Chairman, it ought not to be done that way. There's too much to explain. Somebody must see him ! Where is he now ? "

" According to the papers, he and the Countess have left London for his castle in Cumberland."

" I say, sir, shall I go ? " cried the Secretary. " I'll telegraph first, of course. He loves wires. Do let me go, please ? "

They did. He went—explained, and returned with the great sportsman's cordial agreement.

The M.U. subscription was a guinea a year while A.A. members paid two. To reduce the latter was

agreed to be unsound, " And yet," said the M.U.
plenipotentiaries, " our people will have just cause to
complain if they are made to pay double."

There was a way round. Careful management of
M.U. funds by the Chairman of its Finance Committee
and the Hon. Treasurer and other clever men had
succeeded in building up a reserve fund of £8,000.

On the strength of this admirable nest-egg, it was
decided to allow every existing M.U. member a run of
three years with the amalgamated body at his former
subscription rate—a guinea a year.

" By that time, gentlemen," said the Finance Chairman, who had conceived the idea, " we hope to prove
our worth so convincingly that everybody will come into
line, and hardly anyone will drop out."

Three months' devotion to problems which were in
turn solved by the melting rays of goodwill brought
the big task to a close.

The Agreement was concluded, signed and confirmed
by the respective general Committees. To the M.U.
membership figure of eight thousand, five hundred and
twenty-seven was added that of nineteen thousand,
five hundred and thirteen A.A., making (the then quite
formidable) total of twenty-eight thousand and forty,
which was something to talk about.

The last Press announcement of the great amalgamation
had been sent off. The last inquiry had been answered.
The telephone operators had gone home. A few seniors
at Fanum House filled the Secretary's office with smoke
from pipes of peace.

" And to think," said he, " that just over five years
ago we had only ninety members, hardly anything in
the bank, and the hand of almost everyone against us.
We ought to be very grateful ; we've been lucky, eh ? "

" Rather ! " said the next senior. " It was an awful
worry, but what a splendid finish ! "

" FINISH ? " laughed the Secretary. " It isn't a
finish—it's a *beginning* ! "

CHAPTER XIV

STILL EXTENDING

ELIJAH, erstwhile Secretary to the M.U., was settling down to his job as Secretary of the Road Board, and Elisha, newly appointed secretary to the amalgamated body, went to see him. Many matters remained to be settled. They were more or less of a domestic nature in that they concerned the staff of the recently united organizations.

"I'm taking the senior book-keeper of the old M.U. with me," said Elijah; "but the second one is almost as good, and you will like him. Then there is a young legal chap, very bright—he learnt Parliamentary work at my knee, so to speak; and there is a qualified engineer, who ran our Technical Department and Aeroplane Section, and one or two others. Several good women, too! I hope you can blend them all in with your people!"

"Rather!" said Elisha. "In a year or less you won't tell t'other from which."

"That's very good," said Elijah. "And now! There is one I am rather concerned about, and I want you to help me. In a way he is on my conscience."

"How?"

"Well! When our people were fighting your people, I got a grant from the M.U. Finance Committee to institute a new venture—a Travelling Organizer. So we advertised for a man and got lots and lots of replies."

"But what was he going to do?" asked Elisha. "What was his job?"

" His job was to—well—it was to—travel—and—organize ! You see my point, I hope ! "

" I suppose I do ! "

" Very well ! " he went on. " As I said, we had lots and lots of replies, and one chap stood out from the rest so clearly that I simply had to get him, so we raised the salary we had offered in the advertisement in order to make it worth his while to leave his job and come to us."

" But he shouldn't have left a certainty for an uncertainty ! " said Elisha.

" Perhaps not, but he *did*. He was an architect, but his hobby is motoring. He loves the road and exults in road problems, and propaganda. He ran a County Motor Club in the Midlands. It was affiliated to us, and well I knew it. They gave me no peace. That's why I snapped him up." Elijah wiped his brow.

" A good man ! " admitted his friend and successor. " But, I ask you, what do we want—what *can* we want with a Travelling Organizer now ? "

" That's my greatest concern," said Elijah. " Here am I, leaving the M.U. for higher things. I entice this chap to leave his profession—he does good work for about six months, and then—there's a chance he may be left in the lurch. That must not be. Promise me that you will look at him and look after him ! "

" Certainly ! Don't worry any more," said Elisha. " Amalgamations are like omelettes. You can't make one without hurting people or the other without breaking eggs. But we won't hurt more people nor break more eggs than we can possibly avoid. We'll put him in somewhere."

Elijah said, " Thank you ! "

Here was the first occasion in the short life of Motoring's Youngest Organization where a job had got to be found for a man, as distinct from finding the man for a job ; but it had to be done. Elijah's warm heart had to be relieved of unrest, and Elisha, incorrigibly superstitious, wondered if the finger of Fate would waggle, as it so often had done, when the Good Fairy of the A.A. wished to give a sign.

So a telegram was sent—" Come to Fanum, London, please. Wire time arrival." And the reply came—" Thanks. Arrive eleven-thirty to-morrow morning."

He arrived, and was found to be likeable on sight.

" A Midlander, eh ? "

" Yes. I was Hon. Sec. of a Club affiliated to the old Motor Union. I've been in all the rows."

" Oh, you like fighting ? "

" Very much."

" You're joining the right regiment for it," said his future chief. " I can't yet see where we can fit you in. Finding a job for a man is something new to us. However, let us try."

They considered possible openings. The road staff ? There was no vacancy for a senior official. Headquarters ? No ; at any rate, not yet. A Branch Office ? The very thing, but it would have to be a new one. This nominee of Elijah must stand on his own feet.

The map of the then United Kingdom was laid out on the table. It showed that in addition to Fanum, London, and Caxton House, Westminster, the A.A. and M.U. flag flew over Manchester, Leeds, Glasgow, Edinburgh, Dublin, Belfast and Norwich—yes, and Paris. Not so bad for five years' work ! These pocket Fanums were managed respectively by Lancashire men, Yorkshire men, Scots and Irishmen, each in his native element. That policy had been learnt from Scotland, and it paid.

The map showed middle England somewhat vacant, and Nature abhors a vacuum. The New Chap was a Midlander. His motoring experience, knowledge of the country, and organizing attributes generally, marked him as one who could give effect to the slogan " Service on the Road."

" I have it," cried the Secretary. " I'll ask the Committee's sanction for a Fanum at Birmingham, and you shall run it. You may as well go back and hunt for offices in Birmingham, as central as you can get them, with room to expand. That's about all for to-day."

" I will, and I'm very grateful for the chance," said the New Chap as he rose to go. " And if I may say so," he added, with becoming diffidence, " I hope and think that we shall—shall get on well together ? "

" I'm sure of it," said the Secretary. " And mind, you needn't expect to stay in the Midlands all your life. One of these days we may want you at Headquarters. There is plenty of room at the top. Good-bye and good luck ! "

While during the following few years Fanums were established and developed at Exeter for Devon and Cornwall, and at Cardiff for South Wales, Fanum, Birmingham, fully justified expectations. It proved a remarkably fine pivotal point in a district which combined glorious motoring country, calling for enjoyment, with factories producing the vehicles for that purpose.

The Midland Branch, A.A. and M.U., expanded in membership to the proud position of third on the list of Fanums—close upon the heels of its elder brother Manchester.

Elijah's planting had borne good fruit.

. . . . . .

On a certain very wet Sunday afternoon in December, 1913, a touring car pulled up and decanted its passengers, father and son, at an inviting hotel in Birmingham.

" We've had enough of this rain ! " said the parent to the driver. " It's useless going on. Make yourself comfortable and be here sharp at 8.30 a.m., for Fanum, London, in time for lunch to-morrow, please ! "

Later the telephone-bell rang in the home of the A.A. Midland Manager.

" How are you ? Sorry to spoil your day of rest, but I've broken a most uncomfortable journey from

Liverpool to spend an evening in the dry. Could you come along for a bite of food ? "

" Certainly ! Delighted ! "

" Thanks ! And, oh ! Will your wife join us—it isn't fair to leave her out, eh ? "

" Very good of you to think of her. She'll love to come along."

" Right. I've got Junior with me. He's rather too young for late dinners, so I'll fix him up with a meal in our rooms, and we'll have a nice talk."

So *that* was settled.

During dinner came a message.

" No. 242. That's you, sir, wanted on the 'phone."

" Bother ! It can't be for me," said the parent to his colleague. " You go, please ! It must be Junior up to his tricks."

It was. The young monkey had seen, standing by his bed, a telephone asking, mutely, to be played with ! Right—ring up the Governor and hope he's enjoying his grub !

That explains the interruption—and it didn't much matter. What *did* matter was that while the Midland Manager's wife and his Chief were marking time, the latter suddenly broke in upon light conversation with—

" I'm glad to tell you that your husband is doing very well. I say, have you ever contemplated the possibility of his being transferred to London ? How would you regard *that ?* A bit of an upheaval for you and the children, eh ? You might think it over. There's no hurry."

" It doesn't need thinking over," said his guest. " We will go anywhere, suffer any inconvenience, when it means getting on."

" Good ! That's the spirit ! It's impossible to say when, but your man shall be next wicket for Headquarters ! "

Fate took a hand.

On the following Sunday morning, at half-past three,

the telephone-bell rang insistently in a certain house in London. Not a boyish prank this time, but tragedy. The very bright young Assistant Secretary, A.A., was lying in the Middlesex Hospital in a grave condition.

" Collision, street-refuge, greasy road, car dashed out from turning, nothing to save a skid, injured terribly—come at once."

Within a clock-round the poor boy was dead.

The following few days were a maze of grief, dismay, and inquest, which meant inquisition—and then came the last sad honours to a fine young worker who had promised to go so far in This Motoring.

" What a waste ! " said a Committee member—one of the boy's many admirers—a kindly Scots lawyer—and wept. The kindly one was fated to meet with sudden death too, in a railway accident, soon after the Armistice.

.   .   .   .   .   .

But the A.A. had to " carry on," and within a fort-night of that snatched conversation on a certain wet Sunday evening in Birmingham, when Junior had been monkeying with the telephone, the Midland Manager was transferred to London, in due time to become Deputy Secretary.

CHAPTER XV

FIRST-AID

THEY say that the road to Hell is paved with good intentions ; so was the A.A. and M.U. road to fame paved with good ideas, many of them supplied by members.

As a shining example : the head of a famous medical requisites firm telephoned one day to fix a time for discussion, and arrived to the tick.

" I'm a founder-member, as you may know," said he. " Our patrols are splendid, but they can be made even more valuable. I bring you an idea."

" Oh, thank you ! But I would gladly have come to you—it doesn't seem fair."

" Never mind that. My idea is this : Train our men to render first-aid on the road."

" In accidents ? "

" Yes, you know, St. John Ambulance Brigade. Splints for a broken limb, and binding up wounds, and so on."

" I say ! That's a wonderful idea ! It flames," said the grateful Secretary. " Do you think the St. John people would be good enough to help—to lead us up the strait and narrow path, so to speak."

" Of course they will. I'm on the Council, and can put you in touch with the people who count."

" It's jolly good of you. Our fellows must attend classes in the evening, and sweat up for examination to get their—what do you call it ? "

F . 141

" First-aid Certificate."

" Thanks, that's it. But just one difficulty—they're spread about the country, and they can't go far from their beats."

" That's all right. St. John have branches and centres and what not, and it should not be too difficult. I'm glad you have jumped at the idea. I thought perhaps it wouldn't appeal."

" Of course it appeals. It's splendid. Our men will need equipment, though. That means money. We're young yet, and not well off."

This founder-member had a heart as large as his big business.

" I've thought of that," said he, " and I'm coming to it. Our fellows must be properly equipped. It's no use being stingy. Do it well or not at all. My idea is a smart web cross-belt, carrying an oblong pouch made in the best patent leather—none of your shoddy stuff—in A.A. colours, dark blue and yellow, and fixed with the best possible gadgets. Here is the list :

2 bandages $2\frac{1}{2}$ in. × 3 yds.
1 bandage 1 in. × 3 yds.
1 triangular arm sling.
1 tourniquet.
4 packets absorbent cotton.
1 packet absorbent gauze.
1 tin aromatic ammonia.
1 tube court plaster.
1 tin adhesive plaster.
1 tube pins.
1 tube camel-hair brushes.
1 packet jaconet.
1 small bottle castor oil.
1 pair scissors.
1 bottle ionized iodine (1 oz.).
1 book instructions.

" How does that appeal to you ? " he concluded.

" It frightens me, but we'll jolly well try to afford it. The Committee are always game to——"

" *Do* let me finish ! I'm as keen as can be on this— it's my baby. To make everything sure, my firm shall give you as many complete equipments as are needed by our patrols for, let us say, the next two years. And after that——"

" After that we can buy ! Oh, easily ! We are ever so grateful to you. The Committee will jump at your generous offer."

" That's all right ! " said he. " And they needn't go making me an Honorary Member or anything. I'm content to pay for service ! " So saying he departed, amid a shower of blessings.

The Committee *did* jump at it, and to it.

" What a fine chap, and what a FIRM ! " said the Chairman, in the course of proposing a hearty vote of thanks.

" Yes, indeed ! " said the seconder. " We must go one better than merely expressing appreciation. This is a big thing—it will be something more for our members, and the public. This idea must not be allowed to drift, if you know what I mean. It must go with a bang."

" Well, why shouldn't it ? " asked another. " We've got the men, and we've got the equipments—promised— and——"

" I know what my colleague is driving at," said a quiet one. " He's wondering what will happen if our fellows don't want to work for their First-aid Certificates. You can lead a horse to the water——"

" Exactly ! That is what I did mean. We must give the men encouragement. I have it ! Extra pay—even if it's only a shilling a week."

" The very idea," said the Chairman. " Good conduct or efficiency pay, like they give in the Army."

He put it to the meeting—" When each man qualifies for his First-aid Certificate he shall wear a special badge—they like decorations—and have an extra shilling a week."

Carried with acclamation, and left to the Secretary to get on with it.

. . . .

The Assistant Road Manager was presiding at a meeting which comprised a Superintendent or two, a few Inspectors, more Sergeants, and still more patrols, who had been brought in to a schoolroom kindly lent for the purpose. Under the regulations licensed premises were out of bounds for A.A. men in uniform, and this particular regulation has always been strictly enforced.

" I've been instructed," said he, " to come down here to attend this meeting, as well as other meetings all over the country, to tell you about a new idea which a gentleman, who is a member, has put up. Our Committee have agreed to it, and the Secretary has told me to get on with it. So here I am in the Chair at this meeting, and—gentlemen, you may smoke."

He paused for breath, amid a chorus of " Hear ! Hear ! " " Pass the matches," and " Lend me a fag, Bill ! "

" When I say I'm in the Chair," he continued, " it isn't exactly a Committee meeting, like those up in London. You can't vote or anything like that. You can only listen when I read the instructions about this new idea of A.A. first-aid on the road, and then ask questions, if you like—but not too many—like we did when I was in the Navy."

The instructions were duly read.

" Any questions ? "

" It looks like going back to night-school again," ventured one.

" That's not a question, but a statement," said the Assistant R.M., late R.N., feeling like a real Chairman. " I rule it out of order. Besides, a bit more of study will do you good—keep you out of mischief. It's better

than wasting your time playing darts at the Crown and
Anchor."

(Murmurs of " Hear ! Hear ! "—some rather faint.)

" Please tell us again what we're going to get, sir,"
said another.

" That's a question, and quite in order ! You're
going to get an extra shilling a week when you have
qualified."

" Equalling six pints of beer," said an ex-Army man.
" Not so bad. Sir ! you can put me down as a starter
for the Poultice-Walloping Stakes."

" The *what ?* "

" Just what I said, sir ! " replied the expert mental
arithmetician. " In my unit we always called the
Ambulance Section, Poultice-Wallopers, because they—
well ! they mix up a poultice and sort of wallop it on.
See ? " He looked round for approval, and not getting
any, closed down and extended his calculations to gallons
per mensem and barrels *per annum*.

Whether the extra pay meant beer or ginger ale, or
in fact without either attraction, the good A.A. fellows
applied themselves diligently to the innovation. Winter
was coming, with its long nights, and there were no
cinemas then to distract their attention from what, after
all, was a rather fascinating study. Thanks to the
splendid St. John Ambulance Association, the classes
were arranged to fit in with hours of road duty and
length of beats.

The Exams were a source of mingled amusement and
concern.

" We must pass the first time, you know, for the credit
of the service."

" I wish I wasn't so weak in poisons," said one to
his neighbour.

" Or me in stopping bleeding," was the reply.
" Somehow I can't find the blessed artery with my
thumbs. I've practised on my landlady's eldest boy
until his thighs are black and blue. It cost me half a

crown to keep him from telling his mother, and she's
sure to find it out on bath night ! "

" Never mind ! Make up on fractures what you lose
on arteries, and you'll pull through somehow."

They did. Hardly any of them failed to qualify,
and those few exceptions got through the second exam.

.   .   .   .   .   .

Oh, very smart, those first-aid pouches, and justly proud
the wearers when they sported them on the first day.

" Hello ! Our A.A. man looks extra nice. He has
something new on," said the wife of a doctor member.
" Do let us pull up and ask him about it ! "

" Good morning ! " said the husband to the patrol,
when they had stopped. " You're looking very smart
with your nice cross-belt."

" Yes, sir ! It makes me feel as if I was back in the
Regiment, doing Orderly Corporal."

" And what's the idea ? "

" First-aid, sir ! First-aid to the injured."

" Oh ! Have you qualified ? "

" Yes, sir—look at my badge ! "

" Um—that's official enough. Congratulations. Very
enterprising. Your people seem to be for ever breaking
out in a fresh place. You're going to take some of the
bread out of our mouths. I'm a doctor, you know ! "

" Beg pardon, sir, but we shan't do that. We shall
do our best to patch the people up and keep 'em going
until you come along."

" A good answer," said the lady, pulling her husband's
arm. " Now come along, and leave him in peace."

" Just a minute," said the doctor, who obviously
wasn't very busy. " It's a fine morning, let's have a
little fun. Now, patrol, I'm allowed to give you a tip—
a present—because I'm a member ? That's so, eh ? "

" Yes, sir, thank you ! "

" Right ! I will ask you three simple first-aid

questions, and if you answer them properly there is half a crown for you."

" Thank you, sir ! "

" First question. What would you do for a chap with a broken thigh ? "

" I would tie his body, hips, thigh and leg to a broom-stick and lift him carefully into a cart for the nearest doctor."

" Right ! " " Second question. If you found a fellow, with no bones broken, but all shaken up after a smash, and inclined to faint, what would you do ? "

" I'd give him some brandy, sir ! "

" And if you hadn't any brandy, what would you do ? "

" Is that the third question, sir ? "

" Yes ! "

" I'd—I'd—promise him some, sir ! "

" Ha ! Ha ! That's not what I expected, but it's good. Here's your half-crown."

" Make it five shillings, George," said the lady.

" All right, dear, it's worth it ! Cheero, patrol," and off they went.

How many thousands of times, during the years ensuing, that brain-wave of a generous member reacted beneficially upon This Motoring need not here be flaunted. It was available to all who used the King's Highway. Many a cyclist, having ridden not wisely but too well, had cause to bless A.A. first-aid for expert bandaging, or a timely whiff of smelling salts.

Even dogs ! Oh, yes, please ! Only a simple story, one of many, and it won't take long.

An A.A. man was out for a Sunday morning walk, with his daughter and one of their dogs, properly led, as dogs on a main road should be. They came upon a little man obviously in great trouble, and simply had to stop. A terrier of uncertain ancestry was limping pitifully, dropping blood from a paw which had been cut by broken glass while roaming in the hedgerow. His eyes spoke his distress.

"Poor darling! How did he do it, and what can we do for you?" said the daughter, getting out an absurdly small handkerchief to use as a bandage.

"That's not much use," said her father. "Try mine"—and produced the usual large one.

The little man, poor, and so tidy, choked his thanks.

"It's very good of you—I'm worried. This is the first time I've let him off the lead, and—I don't know what the wife will say when I get home—if I get him home—and that's two miles down the road, and I've got my new overcoat on, and—they'll never let me get on the bus with him bleeding and bleeding. I don't know what I shall do"—he choked again. A pathetic little man.

"Now, cheer up," said his new friends. "We won't leave you until it's all right!" They tried again to stop the bleeding, but the wound defied even a man's handkerchief.

"How silly of us!" cried the daughter. "One of our A.A. patrols went by, a minute ago, on his bicycle. Can't we catch him or something?"

"Of course." A passing car was held up—the situation explained.

"And you'll stop him, won't you, please, and tell him to come back as fast as he can?"

"Certainly," said the car-owner. "We've dogs of our own. Consider it done." And dashed away.

In a few minutes, the patrol rode up and dismounted.

The little man, in his new overcoat, stood rather dazed watching the efficient application of first-aid to his terrier, by a big fellow dressed in khaki uniform, who took it as part of his morning's work.

The terrier, although of uncertain ancestry, was a perfect little gentleman, and didn't snap at all. He seemed to know.

Antiseptics were duly applied, lint, a quite professional bandage, and there he was, all nice and safe.

" Now they'll let you take him on the bus, and you won't spoil your new overcoat."

The little man's eyes were wet. He fumbled in his pocket. " What do I have to pay, please, although I can never repay the good deed ? "

" The pleasure is entirely ours," said the A.A. man.

" Especially mine," said the daughter.

That was true, and so is this little story.

CHAPTER XVI

THAT objectionable person, the Road-Hog, thoroughly deserved his name. It was largely a question of manners. His was the type of inhumanity which would barge through a hotel swing-door, or jostle inoffensive people in a queue—just to save an unimportant moment, to gain a personal advantage at another's expense.

The thruster is nuisance enough on foot. On a horse he can be dealt with. On wheels he became a menace. Fortunately he was rare. The question was how to diminish the species.

Picture, for a moment, any road—plenty of traffic, but room for all decent folk. Cars, cycles, carriages, coming and going on their lawful occasions.

One of his type, still chasing that unimportant moment, pulls out and tries to pass. In doing so he takes someone else's part of the road. He has done it many times before and it has come off—this time it won't.

That Someone, pursuing the even tenor of his way and, like every good Briton, resentful of aggression, says under his breath : " No, you don't ! you bad-mannered something. You jolly well get back to your proper side. This side of the road is mine ! " Very often, before their respective telepathies can connect and before Bad Manners can pull in again—CRASH.

One more Road-Hog has learned his lesson—thrusting in haste to repent at leisure—and to pay in full.

This sort of trouble naturally attracted the attention of the defenders of This Motoring, whose good name was at stake. The Committee pondered the human problem with grave concern.

" Can't we do something to weed our own garden ? " asked a member. " I mean, something in the nature of putting men on observation duty—noting cases of bad driving, and, if regrettably necessary, prosecuting the offender ourselves ? "

" Prosecute one of our own members ? "

" Well, it might come to that, you know ! " observed an otherwise quiet colleague.

" Never ! Never ! " cried another. " Don't let us get hysterical, or lose our sense of proportion. Our Association came into being to fight for freedom, not to play the schoolmaster. We exist to serve our members—not to censure them."

" I know what you mean, good friend," soothingly interposed the Chairman, " and I agree. If we were to do anything of the kind, heaps of our most decent members would resent it."

" Quite so, sir," said another. " Walter is right. Our members do not pay their subs. to be treated like schoolboys. Now, there must be a way round or a half-way house, or something. Here is an idea, for one."

(Chorus of " Thank you ! Good ! Let's have it ! ")

" I suggest we form a Complaints Committee, or a Department, if you like, and let it leak out discreetly through the Press—that's the Secretary's job—how much we deprecate these road incidents (don't call 'em accidents) caused by bad behaviour ; and if any aggrieved motorist will send in his complaint, with full particulars, including the registered nnmber and description of the offending car, the A.A. and M.U. will take the matter up with the owner—and—and——"

(Chorus of " And what ? ")

" Well ! Ask him what he has to say, and—oh, I don't know how to put it—try to make peace somehow, and hope he won't offend again."

" And if he does ? "

" I have it, Mr. Chairman," said the Never ! Never ! Objector. " Our colleague is helping enormously, and I think we can finish for him. Prosecute our own crowd —Never ! Never ! as I said at the start ; but I haven't the least objection to our dealing with every really bad case under one of our Rules."

" And which one is that ? " asked the Chairman.

" The one giving us power at a meeting specially convened for the purpose, with at least two-thirds of the Committee present, and voting, to—to——"

" Well ! "

" To turn the offender out—that is, to request his resignation."

This excellent idea was acclaimed and adopted.

The news leaked out according to plan, and to good effect. Complaints were sent in and handled with care and discretion. Many a delinquent was checked and his road-manners improved by carefully-worded representations. Many an irate complainant was soothed by a frank apology, gently instigated, and many a Police Court action thereby avoided.

Rule 33—the " turn 'em out " one—was invoked only in extreme cases, and those cases were not made public. Here was good and lasting work, and a better job than washing the motorist's linen before a critical public, and to the glee of the " Anti-motorists."

It was extended—always with the velvet glove—to public services—meaning motor buses, lorries, and the like. For example :

See an indignant A.A. member, calling on the hop— that is, without an appointment.

" Woof ! " he blurted, breathlessly. " Good of you to see me, and all that. I'm boiling, and——"

" That's all right ! Do sit down, please. Cigarette ? Better still, keep your pipe going. Good stuff, a pipe —now, you were saying—— ? "

" Thank you " (puff)—" glad you don't mind a pipe. I didn't like to come puffing away in another chap's room, so I kept it warm in my glove. As I was saying, I'm boiling, with rage—not so much as I was when I came in—nice room this, eh ? "

" So glad—but you were saying ? "

" Oh, yes, thank you—well, your Complaints Department—jolly good idea that—I have a complaint, a very grave one, and I want you to prosecute the confounded fellow—nothing less. Prosecute him—get him fined and his licence endorsed " (puff).

" Who is he ? "

" He's a driver of one of those confounded motor buses, which take up all the road " (puff) " and push us into the ditch without so much as a ' by your leave, please.' "

" Oh, yes ? "

" Yesterday morning, at exactly 11.35—I've got it all down in my notebook ; just a minute while I get it out " (puff—puff). " Oh, bother, my pipe's gone out. Never mind—As I was saying, at 11.35 I was driving to Brighton—just past Purley Corner, and rounding a bend near the Red Lion Inn. I kept quite properly to my near-side and saw another car approaching well on its proper side, and this motor bus close behind ! What does this confounded bus driver do but barge towards me, shave the other fellow by a wing's-breadth and cut in between him and me, the scoundrel ! I jammed my brakes on—so did the oncoming car. I finished up with my near-side wheels well in the ditch and my missus in a faint. But I got the confounded fellow's number, and the rest is up to you ! "

" A deplorable error of judgment, and a bit of disgraceful driving."

" Yes, indeed ! and I want the scoundrel punished

—it will serve him right if he loses his job. My wife fainted, I tell you."

" Quite so," came soothingly from his listener. " Now, fill your pipe, please, and let us look at the matter from both sides."

" Certainly ! " said the injured one—and puffed away.

" From your side there is no doubt that the bus driver behaved abominably."

" Yes."

" From his side, it *may*—mind, I only say it may— have been the only time he has behaved so badly."

" Um ! Don't think so, but go on ! "

" Thank you. He might, for an unhappy moment, have had his mind off his job. Your wife fainted ! True. After he had scrambled through the—the— crisis—and realized that it was his fault entirely—oh, yes, he probably did realize it—I expect he jolly nearly fainted, too ! "

" Well " (puff), " what are you driving at ? "

" Just this. We want to improve road manners and road behaviour, but it's no use dog eating dog. Let us try gentle measures first. Don't urge a prosecu- tion. Think what a conviction may mean to this bus driver."

" He ll get the sack ! And serve him jolly well right."

" Just a minute, please. And his wife and children. What about them ? "

" What about them ? What have they got to do with it ? My wife fainted, I tell you."

" Yes, but she's recovered. Now ! Do you really want his wife and children to go hungry ? Could you really enjoy your dinner ? Oh, come now ! Give us a chance to get you satisfaction, without smashing up a home."

" How ? "

" We will write one of our nice velvety letters to the man's employers, setting out your complaint, and emphasizing the enormity of the offence."

" Um ! "

" Then we'll point out that our member, rightfully indignant, but generous, would—that's conditional, not a future tense—would, or rather might, refrain from prosecuting if—if——"

" If what ? "

" If they will have their man on the carpet and put the fear of Section One of the Motor Car Act into him and tell him that but for the good nature of the gentleman whose safety he endangered, and whose wife fainted, he would be discharged forthwith. His employers have everything to lose by bad driving, and may be relied upon to watch his step in future. How's that ? May we try, please ? "

The injured one said, " Yes."

And the man's employers said, " Thank you. We accept and will act upon your friendly suggestion in the spirit in which it is offered."

And the man said to his wife, " Lummy, old girl. They didn't half tick me off, but I deserved it, and the chap what drove that blinking car is a gentleman—that's what he is—a gentleman."

And the wife said—but never mind what she said.

.   .   .   .   .   .

So much for road manners. There still remained the hidden dangers of the Way.

In the matter of warning signs, Authority had certainly done something—overdone it, in fact. There had been evolved a simple triangle in the hope that it would be recognized and respected as notifying DANGER.

Unhappily, these triangles were erected so indiscriminately that their value as a warning waned to the point of being negligible. The country was ablaze with them—signs without significance.

" Easy, John ! " would say John's wife ; " here's another of those triangles, cross-roads, perhaps," but when for the nth time the triangle was found to protect nothing more dangerous than a carriage drive, John and his fellows not unreasonably said, " Bother the things, they mean nothing, and we'll just ignore them."

Regrettable, but there it was ; so the motoring organizations came to the rescue, and put up signs which indicated in a word or two the kind of danger to be expected —thus :

DANGEROUS CORNER. CROSS ROADS. CONCEALED TURNING.

" Let ours be true warnings," said the Committee ; " none to be erected without previous inspection. We'll satisfy ourselves that the danger is real. Therefore our signs will be respected, while the plain iron triangles are not. Continue on those lines and hope for the best. Let A.A. and M.U. be the hall-mark. This will set a new standard."

It did.

All A.A. and M.U. signs were finished in enamel, a blessing by no means unmixed. Could they brave the weather ? Oh, yes. Also they responded to cold water applied with a wash leather by the patrols during the off season.

" Keep 'em clean, my boy ! A dirty sign is a bad advertisement ! Take my tip. Keep 'em clean." Thus had said the Honorary Treasurer, of lamented memory, in the course of a run back from Manchester Office to H.Q.

Like the Finance Chairman, he was of the old M.U.—prince of industry, and faithful lover of This Motoring.

" Look ! " said he, as the car passed an A.A. sign, all spick and span in the sunlight ; " that's what we might call our high-water mark, but it must equally be our Plimsoll line. Keep 'em clean, my boy ; there's a lot of sense in the housewife's motto : A shining door knob is as good as a smiling face."

That good advice was followed. Thereafter the presence of a dirty A.A. sign in a district was regarded as a personal reflection upon the official in command, and dealt with accordingly.

So far so good, but stone-throwing became a perfect curse. Whether inspired by England's national game of cricket, or prompted by original sin, the lads of the village joyfully hailed each newly-erected sign as a target for their prowess.

"Charlie!" yelled one of them, "here's another of those Aunt Sallies. I'll bet you that I'll chip the D out of Danger in ten shots," and the little demon proceeded to win his bet. He changed the word DANGER into ANGER and went home to tea in triumph, having spoilt a perfectly good warning-sign that had cost the best part of one member's annual subscription.

Multiplied by hundreds, the young barbarians at play might cheer the hearts of sign manufacturers, but they worried those who had to foot the bill.

"This is sheer waste of money," complained the Chairman of Finance at a Committee meeting, "and it must be stopped. I hate waste. Can't somebody suggest anything?"

A hand went up, and its owner said: "I have one idea, but it won't entirely solve the difficulty."

"And that is?"

"When and wherever possible let our signs be put up on a friendly cottage or other building, close to a window."

"Whatever for?"

"The young beggars will be afraid to throw at our signs for fear of breaking the windows. How's that for logical deduction?"

Applause greeted this wise Committee member, and his bright idea was put into practice—with such success that A.A. signs, so astutely placed, stood fast for twenty years, and still stand.

But that didn't settle the trouble. Thousands of

signs simply had to be on posts in open country, otherwise
they were of no value. What about them ?

Another hand went up at the meeting. This time
from the paid official.

" If you please, Mr. Chairman——"

" Go on ! "

" Stone-throwing is damage to property. Our signs
are our property, therefore we can prosecute stone-
throwers for wilful damage."

" But how can we catch the young barbarians at
play ? "

" Offer a reward, sir."

" A reward ? How much ? "

" Forty shillings, for information which shall lead
to the conviction of the offender. The big idea, if
you will excuse me, is that we fix a small plate, enamelled
like our signs, just below them, stating that a reward of
forty shillings will be paid for information leading to
the conviction of any person or persons damaging these
signs."

" What do you think of that, gentlemen ? " asked
the Chairman. " I think it is good."

" Agreed ! "

" And," he continued, " when we catch the young
barbarians we must prosecute them, eh ? "

" Agreed ! "

" Even if we pay their fines," put in the Reverend
Member—affectionately called the Chaplain. " We
mustn't be too hard on them, you know. They've
probably got good mothers."

" All quite good," said the Medical Member ; " but
good mothers ought to spank their bad boys. Spare the
rod and spoil the—sign."

So, there were prosecutions—a few, and somewhat
desultory.

The A.A. solicitors didn't press the charges. One
of them would say : " May it please the Bench, my
clients, the Automobile Association, don't want to be

vindictive ; they just bring the charge as a warning that
property is sacred—must be respected, and all that.
A nominal fine, or even a caution, or, if it would please
your Worships, to admonish, or—or—better still—bind
the young defendant over on an undertaking by his
father to administer corporal punishment—give him a
good hiding, to put it colloquially, your Worships."

The outcome of all this was distinctly Gilbertian.
The young barbarians quite sensibly connected a good
hiding with the small reward plates and focused attention
on them—to such an extent that the ten times larger
and more expensive warning signs were left unscathed.

.   .   .   .   .   .

The youngsters — bless them — produced another
problem. Schools situated on main roads called for
protection. It was not the fault of This Motoring that
Those-In-Authority had made a point of placing the
schools in dangerous localities, upon which a flood of
little ones would pour joyously out from the class-rooms,
and race across the road for home and dinner or tea.
In big towns their dispersals were effected under the
safeguard of teachers, male or female, and by the extended
arm of a gentleman in blue.

That was all very right and proper, but in villages
the protection of young Britain by a gentleman in blue,
at certain specified times, was not feasible. He had a
long beat to patrol, miles and miles, and, as he explained,
" If I'm there when the kiddies come out of school I'm
only too glad to give the teacher a hand in seeing 'em
across the road, but I can't be in two places at once
—not even me ! and after all, nobody would have
thought of holding up the traffic in a village for the
kids to go home, before these motors began to come
through."

" Oh, very well ! " was the answer, " we will do
something." So they surprised and pleased the countryside by putting up neat signs which read : " Caution,

159

School," and which were interpreted by every reasonable motorist to mean :

" If you drive past this sign somewhere about 9 a.m., or noon, or 4 p.m., remember that plenty of children may be crossing the road. Think of your own children and take especial care."

School signs needed no pushing. Directly the idea became known applications poured in from all parts of the country and the finances of the amalgamated A.A. and M.U. were strained to comply with the requests.

" Now," said they to the school authorities ; " it's your turn to do something for the kiddies."

" Anything in reason," they replied.

" Will you teach Safety to the children, if we help by providing you with a large show-card setting out in simple language what the scholars should do and should avoid doing in the interests of their personal safety ? "

" Certainly ! " was the answer. " Send along your show-cards and we will give the children brief lectures on Road Sense." That was done, and much good accrued.

.   .   .   .   .   .

All of this went a long way to establish the fact that motorists were good citizens. For years they had chafed under the stigma of being treated as criminals, hence organized scouting to keep them out of police traps, and organized legal defence to fight in the Police Courts for those who got caught.

They had asked, with reason, " Why won't you other road-users realize that we are as well behaved as you who walk or cycle ? This Motoring has come to go as well as to stay, so join with us to make the going safe. As cyclists—only a generation back—you were named ' road hogs,' and you have outlived the stigma. Now you are among the critics of the new traffic—which is illogical. You don't like to go into the ditch to avoid being run into when we cannot see you on a dark night, and of course you are right. You don't like us to dazzle you with headlights—and you are right again. But to be consistent—why don't you carry *something* to make you visible ? The more visible you are the less we shall have to dazzle you. We motorists carry a rear light. Why not a reflex light on the cycle ? "

Earnest talk in this strain was being carried on at an A.A. and M.U. Committee meeting one afternoon when the Honorary Treasurer thumped on the table, and got a hearing.

" Here's an idea," he said. " Let us offer reflex lights, free, to our brothers and sisters of the bicycle. A thousand—five thousand—ten thousand—we can afford it, or if we can't I will gladly help. Think it over, gentlemen. It would be a fine gesture."

" There's no need to think very long. The idea is good, eh, gentlemen ? " said the Chairman. Proposed, seconded, and carried with acclamation.

" Shall we put advertisements in the dailies ? " asked a member.

" I don't think so," replied the Honorary Treasurer. " A simple Press paragraph should suffice."

It did.

" On receipt of a postcard—name and address in block letters, please—A REFLEX LIGHT FREE." Within two months ten thousand were issued. A friendly gesture was accepted in the spirit in which it had been made, save only by the Cycling journals, whose contributors rather ungenerously flogged the argument that it was the motorist's responsibility *not* to run down the cyclist, and—by inference—it was not up to the cyclist to protect himself against such a contingency. They derided the gift as a selfish move designed by This Motoring eventually to enforce rear-lights on bicycles.

Nothing could be further from the truth.

CHAPTER XVII

ONE STAR DIFFERETH FROM ANOTHER STAR IN GLORY

MUCH unkind criticism has been levelled at the British innkeeper, but there are two sides to every question. Tragic must have been his lot and difficult his problem when, about seventy years before motoring appeared, stage-coach and post-chaise traffic was ruined by the coming of the railways.

Consequent upon that, the bed-and-board part of innkeeping went to sleep for half a century.

Think what this meant! All the happy clatter of arrival and departure gone. The stables empty. Drivers and guards and ostlers and waiters and serving maids on the unemployed list, with no dole. The hay-and-corn-chandler bankrupt. The butcher and baker and candlestick-maker going much the same way. The turnspit silent. Beds and blankets and glassware and cutlery no longer needed—often sold off at beggarly prices to help pay the rent and keep things going. All that cheery noise and bustle portrayed so delightfully by Dickens fading into oblivion.

Thereafter the roadside inn had perforce to shrink within itself, dependent for its owners' meagre existence upon the villagers' capacity for liquor and the chance custom of a commercial traveller, known then as a bagman.

Here, surely, was a sickness approaching unto death, from which it seemed hardly possible for an industry to recover.

Many a genial spirit must have been crushed by the iron wheel, stern and cruel.

Think what it meant!

Let us imagine the scene, somewhere on the Great North Road, one evening in autumn. A sad little group is gathered round the porch of the Duke's Arms, waiting for the stage-coach, due almost any minute now, to pull up, change horses, and pass on her final stage—for the last time. For years this beautiful, lovable, living thing, with horses, coach, coachman and guard complete, one and indivisible, has swung round the bend and pulled up, all standing, to the tick. "Set your watch by the Duchess? You can, sir—ay—danged if you can't!"

For years the simple village mind has revelled in a rather equivocal way-bill which tells the world that the Duchess leaves the Duke's Arms punctually every day at a quarter past six. And now!

The horn which heralds her arrival sounds a bit cracked. The guard may have a lump in his throat. He isn't the only one.

"Whoa, my beauties!" Ostlers run to their heads, reins are handed down over the whip, off the box steps Sam the coachman, into the cosy bar for his usual rum and water with the landlord—for the last time.

"And to think that this is the end!" says Sam. "When we get to Nottingham to-night, and stable the team, it'll be for the last time—and to-morrow! nothing, nothing but selling off the horses and coach and gear. Thirty years on this road, man and boy, and now! What's to become of us?"

"Poor Sam!" sighs the landlord. "Never mind—you're not the only one. What's to become of *us?* How long the poor old Duke's Arms is going to last when you've gone I don't know. Bad luck to that Scotchman who thought of steam engines."

"Time, gentlemen! Passengers aboard, please.

Shake hands, Sam ; come and see us soon. Always a welcome for you. Good-bye—good-bye ! "

The beautiful, lovable, living thing, nearly empty, is all ready for her last stage. It is a solemn moment. The horses stand quite still. They seem to know.

Everyone is silent. Something is passing from the gentle life of this little English village, never to return. The church clock chimes the quarter. That breaks the spell. Sam the coachman pulls himself together and barks to the guard : " Sound ! Joe, dang you, man—sound ! "

Joe does his poor best. A few try to cheer and give it up. The women cry quietly. Sam twirls his whip, game to the end, and clucks a command. The team obey as one horse, and the Duchess, queen of the stage-coach realm, rumbles away down, down, down the road into the limbo of things forgotten.

Think what that meant !

.   .   .   .   .   .

It softens the lump in one's throat to reflect that new life was brought back to the innkeeping industry by This Motoring.

Here was something really good which came out of the internal-combustion engine.

That last, lost chord of Joe the guard, which had trembled away into silence, was to speak again in the honk-honk of a motor car, pulling up at the old Duke's Arms for refreshment of man and engine.

The pneumatic tyre was restoring what the iron wheel had killed.

" Mary ! " cried the third generation of the Duke's Arms to his wife ; " it's wonderful ! Here's life and hope coming back to the old house—in motor cars. Just think of it, five of 'em stopped here to-day and we've served fourteen meals. Never mind if they *do* smell different from horses. Here they are, I tell you, waking up the road, waking us all up. New life, business

—coming back. It's good enough to make Grandfather turn in his grave. Bustle, Mary! We must show 'em that we know our business. Fancy! the old times coming back! coming——"

" Yes, John ! and now stop talking and start working," replied his very much better half. " You must do something more than hang about in the bar parlour. These new folk will expect clean tablecloths and new cutlery, and napkins to wipe their fingers on. And good beds and blankets and sheets—sheets, mind you, changed for every customer. That and about fifty other things will be my department. The Lord send we can borrow the money to buy them. And Emma must leave school and help with the books. Your job is to talk straight to the butcher and get more credit —make him understand what all this may mean to him as well as us. Then to the baker, and greengrocer. Make them understand too ! Then go along to the brewers—they ought to give us an extra loan, enough to buy all the things we want for the house. It means quite as much to them as it does to us. And another thing : these people will want motor spirit, petrol—or something like that—instead of hay and corn. The stables aren't much use, but the coach houses can be turned into a —what's that French word, John ? There seems to be a lot of French in this new business."

" It's ' garage,' Mary. I saw in one of those new motor papers——"

" Yes ! that's it—and—there . we go again, what do they call the men who drive ? "

" Chaffours, or something like that ! "

" Yes ! Well, we've got to feed them, and they can't take their meals with the gentry, you know. So we must have a special room for them, like Grandfather had for the post-boys and grooms ; that's very much what they are, really, in spite of their outlandish name. We shall soon be having to get some more maids, not too good-looking either, with those ' chaffours ' about !

And who knows, we may be able to afford a real waiter again ? Oh ! there's a lot to be done."

Something like this dialogue was being spoken in a thousand or more British inns. Whether as Rip van Winkle, or Sleeping Beauty, according to their structure, the old places were waking up in earnest, and a new life was extended before them, thanks to This Motoring.

As the novelty of pulling up for meals during a day on the road wore off, the refreshment of man and engine increased in interest and importance. Comparisons were frequent and invidious.

" We won't stop there again, George," would be the decision of Mrs. George ; " only to get foreign meat and custard powder when we pay half a crown for a lunch. It isn't good enough." Or, to quote the same lady at her own tea table : " My dear ! we found a perfect *duck* of a place, the Swan's Nest, on the so-and-so road, about thirty miles out. You simply *must* try it. Everyone there is *so* polite. It's as *clean* as a new pin. Upstairs too—you know what I mean—and everything served up *hot*, although we didn't get there until half-past one. *English* meat, my dear, and *fresh* cream," and so on for five well-filled minutes.

Talks of this nature meant much to the inn and hotel industry. They marked an interest which was not likely to wane in a hurry.

Cleanliness, comfort, and courtesy were looked for and acclaimed wherever they were found. Food, a topic ever dear to the English heart, headed the list of things which simply *had* to be good, and wine found a place in the cellars after half a century's absence. Beer and spirits had, of course, always been wanted—and taken.

. . . .

It would be unfair not to record with gratitude the fine spade-work by that excellent body, the Cyclists' Touring Club. Its familiar sign displayed over the porch was the first of the kind to link up innkeeping with organized touring, a decade or two before an automobile appeared on any highway.

Congratulations, then, to the C.T.C. for this and other evidence of imagination and enterprise. Not any of those qualities lose in value by the fact that still more was needed by motoring.

To that end, therefore, the Committee of a certain Association — getting much more respectable and respected now, thank you, with a membership running well into five figures and several newly-formed branch offices—sat round the table for their monthly, self-imposed—and unpaid—job of moulding the destiny of This Motoring.

The Minutes were read, confirmed, signed. The little things disposed of. The Chairman spoke : " I will now call upon our Secretary to bring up an important matter—not on the agenda. Now, Mr. Secretary ! "

" The hotel problem is very much in evidence," said the Secretary. " Here are three letters on the subject. Two complaining about the attention our members did not get, and one praising a certain hotel up to the skies. The last one asks why we don't do something."

" What does he mean by ' do something ' ? " asked a leading member.

" Just a minute, Walter ! " said the Chairman. " We're coming to that. Carry on, please ! "

" Right, sir ! Here is our problem. We are hard at work appointing hotels and decent inns and allowing them to display our sign. In this we are following the excellent lead of the C.T.C. It is about the only idea we ever borrowed from any organization. Now our people are asking us to go one better. Several have called here to talk about it. They say, in short, that it's all very good to see our sign, and better still to turn up a page in the Handbook when they seek a place to lunch at or dine and sleep ; but their needs vary so, and there isn't anything to guide them. Nothing to show what kind of accommodation they may expect, and this is particularly important when they are going to stop overnight. It's quite a problem."

" In support of that, Mr. Chairman," broke in a member, " let me tell the Committee my, or rather our, experience last week-end. I say ' our ' because the women in our family party were most concerned. We pulled up at a dainty little place, about seven o'clock, after a long day, with three punctures—hungry and really tired. The dinner was plain but good, and after that we didn't feel like moving on, so—although the place was small—we decided to risk it and stay the night. There was nowhere to sit except in the bar parlour, or a rather chilly drawing-room, poorly lit by gas, with uncomfortable chairs and ornaments everywhere. So that meant that our wives must go to bed while we two had a smoke and drinks in the bar parlour. The bedrooms — well — they weren't bedrooms as we know them."

" Clean ? "

" Oh, quite, but so poky. You know the kind, where you have to open the window in order to change your shirt. Neither gas nor oil lamps, just candles. The tiniest cupboard—useless as a wardrobe—and only wire nails on the door. And as for other conveniences— ugh ! the less said the better. Our wives were wretched, and my friend Bill and I got the reaction."

" But didn't you complain ? " asked someone.

" Funnily enough, we didn't ! You see the landlord and his people were so perfectly willing and anxious to oblige. It wasn't their fault, poor things. They haven't the money for improvements. You see, if Bill and I had been by ourselves, with our bicycles, and nothing but a razor and a change of socks, it would have been a peach of a place. However, the next morning, only ten miles on our way, we saw a much bigger place, with the A.A. sign ; and early as it was, we got out to look and found it to be everything we could have wished. Now, Mr. Chairman, if only we had known. If we could have had guidance from the Handbook—I don't quite know how—we could have plugged along these extra ten miles and the ladies would have been comfortable instead of wretched, and our week-end a success instead of a failure. That's the lesson my friend and I learned, and I put it up for discussion."

"Gentlemen," said the Chairman, "Charles Two, our colleague, is quite right. There is more in this problem than meets the eye. Again we must lead. Has anybody anything to suggest?"

"If you please, Mr. Chairman!"

"Certainly! Quiet, please, gentlemen—carry on."

"It's nobody's idea in particular, but that doesn't matter much. It's just this. We all know how brandy is labelled——"

"Brandy? What on earth has brandy to do with hotels, except in the bar?"

"Bear with me one minute, please. We are able to select average drinkable brandy according to the number of stars on the label. Very well, then. Let us star our appointed hotels."

"Well, I'm—but go on."

"You see what I mean, don't you? Three-star brandy is calculated to please the majority—it's not too poor for the average taste, and not too dear for the average pocket. So let it be for hotels.

"We can take a really decent average middle-class hotel, like, say, the Lion at Guildford, with good food, English meat, beds, and other comforts, which no reasonable motorist can cavil at, and make that our standard three-star. Those below that standard of construction and management can be starred down to two and one. Those exceeding its standard in size and luxury can be starred up to four and five. It's not so complicated after all."

"Yes, thank you! That's well worth thinking over," said the Chairman, "and, in tackling this problem thoroughly, we shall render real service to our members, and that's reward enough. Agreed, gentlemen?"

"Agreed."

So far as the Committee were concerned discussion ended and staff-work began.

. . . . . .

After decision, action. This new work called for the powers of selection, inspection, discrimination, discretion. The staff must be chosen and trained. Chosen for their qualities of integrity, patience, and politeness, trained in the rest.

Hotel-keepers, and such as they, were acutely sensitive of their dignity. They knew their business and were not at all inclined to be lectured by any young man, however bright, who might arrive in a two-seater, present his card of authority, and proceed to throw his weight about.

A few thus chosen from the road staff sat, as it might be in a class, to learn.

"To begin," said the teacher, "we must tread lightly, and mind each step. Above all, remember who you are, and what you serve. Some hotel-keepers—not many, thank goodness, but some—will try to buy you. Whenever you go inspecting with a view to recommending appointment, make this a golden rule, that they shall not know who you are until you have lunched or dined and slept at whatever place is on your list for that day. NEVER, *never* accept a receipted bill except in return for your money, which is our money. You know what I mean by that. The only possible penalty for such behaviour would be dismissal from the service.

"You must guard against all sorts of little tricks. For instance, when you look into a bed, after peeping under it for possible dust, and find sheets with two obvious sets of creases, they are not clean sheets—they have been used before and pressed in order to look clean.

"You must not miss a thing. Bathrooms and

avatories claim especial attention. A dirty hair-brush— horrible thing—a roller-towel, cloudy from excessive use — scrappy, messy bits of soap — tablecloths with smudges—serviettes with finger-prints not traceable to you—knives and forks with cleaning-powder carelessly left on—plates with spots of obstinate mustard. Look out for all this and other evidence of slovenly attention, to be used, when found, in evidence against. Is that quite clear—yes ? Good ! A score of other points will occur to us—every one important."

" May I speak, please ? Just an idea."

" Certainly ! "

" I suggest we all ask our wives, if we are married, and our mothers or married sisters, if they can give us any other points for observation ! "

" Excellent idea. Agreed, gentlemen. Please note."

The lesson went on.

" So much for inspection and discrimination, with discretion. Now for classification. The management of an hotel or inn is one of our considerations, and its size, quality of building, and furniture another. Don't mix up the two. Classification must be according to the house as it is built and furnished—or laid out. That, and only that. No house, however large and well decorated, may hope for the A.A. appointment, or prevent its being withdrawn, if it is badly directed. No landlord or manager of an hotel which is not large enough to merit more than two stars, can expect to be graded higher on the score of good management or the charm of the landlady's smile.

" It doesn't need much vision to see how this work, if properly done, will influence the innkeeping mind. We can imagine the landlord's lady of the Crown and Anchor looking down on Mrs. Blue Boar, because the former boasts a two-star grade while the latter has only one. There will be no rest until that second star has been earned. That kind of rivalry is what we want and will make for everybody's good.

"Again, we are not charging for our appointments, but what is given can always be taken away. It may not be realized yet, but one day, not so very far distant, the value of that gift will rank high in an hotel's list of assets, and the loss of it will be regarded as a dreadful stigma.

"Can't you hear them in a small town ? I can ! Something like this : ' Have you heard about the trouble up at the Crown and Anchor ? ' ' No ! what's up ? ' ' Why ! ' in a whisper, ' they've had their A.A. sign taken away.' ' Ooh ! and serve 'em right seeing how '— et cetera. You can fill in the rest for yourselves. Enough then, for the time being, of theory. How shall we start putting all we are considering into practice ? "

" I have an idea, please, sir ! "

" Good chap ! Let us hear from you."

" It's like this. Couldn't you take a few of us on the road, during a week-end, to lunch and dine and sleep at one or two of our appointed hotels, and study the classification problem, so to speak, on the spot ? "

" Thank you ! The very idea. We'll borrow an extra car or two from our good friends in the Trade, and make up a small expedition. Now let me think ! Yes ! Another idea. We'll all go down to the good old Lion at Guildford. No need there to look under the beds for dust—you could sleep under them at a pinch. And the food—well—just wait and see !

" That is a typical three-star A.A. hotel, with its typical manageress, buxom, smiling and efficient, and dear old Robert, the head-waiter, with twenty-odd years' service, known and respected throughout Surrey, or for that matter, Britain, as the best man in his profession. If we take the Lion as our three-star standard, we can grade others from it. Next week-end then, gentlemen ! Good night."

The class broke up.

It followed that on a Friday evening in the late summer of never mind which year, a happy hopeful party arrived in four motor cars at the Lion's hospitable porch, carefully, and one at a time, because the High Street is so hilly.

" Very glad to see you. Go where you like and see what you want to see, gentlemen ! Don't mind us," said the incomparable hostess and the inimitable Robert, to both of whom the great idea had been unfolded.

So, after dinner a tour of instructional exploration was made of the famous old house, under their friendly and ample wings. This took a solid two hours, and when the class had compared impressions, asked all sorts of questions, and made copious notes, the exploring party went contentedly to rest, feeling that the foundation-stone of hotel classification had been well and truly laid.

What happened during the following two days need not be unduly laboured. Between London and Brighton there were found inns and hotels, each of which was characteristic of what a one, two, four or five star should mean to the motorist, who thenceforth would, when touring, enhance the comfort of his womenfolk and menfolk by—consulting the A.A. Handbook first !

And that is how it was done.

CHAPTER XVIII

INSURANCE

ONE morning the Bright Young Insurance Manager called at Fanum by appointment, complete with cigarette and happy smile.

" Now we are sailing comfortably along under one flag, or rather one Badge," said he, " the next thing is to increase the benefits to members. Am I right, Mr. Secretary ? "

" Entirely ! All ideas gratefully received and considered," was the reply.

" Good ! My Company, as you know, are building up a reputation for settling claims more promptly and more generously than our rivals."

" Very sound business, too ! "

" Quite so," said the B.Y.I.M., and continued : " While the good work of getting together has been going on, I have been earnestly considering the problem of disputes—you know what I mean : where the car owner isn't satisfied with the way he is treated in the settlement of a claim or repairs to his car after an accident. At present he is entirely at the mercy of the company, or the broker, to take what they give him or do for him ; otherwise he must spend his own money on a solicitor and possibly risk an action at law."

" That's true. He is very much in the position that our members were with the Motor Car Law until we introduced Free Legal Defence."

" Exactly ! Now, my idea is that under the A.A. and M.U. policy issued by my Company exclusively to your members, all disputes shall in future be referred to your Committee, whose decision shall be final." B.Y.I.M. paused for breath.

" That sounds rather like a lease, but it attracts. Do you really mean it ? "

" I mean it in its fullest and widest sense. There shall be no appeal by my Company from your Committee's decision. There shall be no limit to the amount of your Committee's award in any and every case. How does the idea strike you ? "

" Good from the word ' Go.' But just a moment. This new work will take up a lot of time, and our Committee work purely for love, you know. They don't draw directors' fees—not even expenses."

" The work must not take up much of your people's time, and it shan't. We will see to that."

" How ? "

" Well, it will be my Company's job to regard disputes as the plague, and every man on our staff will do all he can to avoid them. The mere fact that every member of the A.A. insured with us can appeal to you when he has a grievance, or thinks he has, will act as a red light to all our claims assessors and engineers. It will make them keen to satisfy even the unreasonable. See ? "

" I see ! And admire ! You had better put it all in writing for our next Committee meeting, and there can't be much doubt about the reply."

" Good ! " said B.Y.I.M. " But I haven't finished. Here's another valuable concession, also quite new, and entirely for the benefit of your members."

" Oh, philanthropist ! Go on."

He went on. " Insurance policies are tricky in their wording. They have to be, for quite good reasons. Many a time a fellow may have trouble against which he thinks he is protected when he isn't, and then he grumbles."

" But he could appeal to our Committee, couldn't he ? "

" He could," said B.Y.I.M., " and even then he might

not get anything, because his particular accident was not provided for in the policy—and your Committee are to be judges ! That is to say, they can award but they can't give. Let us take, for example," he continued, " the case of a driver who skilfully avoids running down a foolhardy person who has blundered into the road in front of his car, and in doing so rips his gears, burns his brakes, and ruins his perfectly good tyres. Technically he would have no claim. Any company could turn him down, because he had not actually collided with anything. Yet, he deserves consideration. It would be hard luck for him not to get it, wouldn't it ? "

" Yes, indeed ! And that is only one instance among thousands."

" Well ! We propose to give your Committee power to make what we call *ex gratia* payments from a special fund which my Company will place to the Association's credit in your own bank. Again ' no limit,' as the bookmakers say. Think what a protection both of these benefits will afford your members. Now ! " he wound up with his usual smile, " how do you feel about the whole thing ? "

" Since you put it so clearly," was the reply, " I feel as if you were selling me a purse with a sovereign inside it, all complete for eighteenpence. I only hope the sovereign is a good one. Meanwhile you deserve lunch, and I will pay."

The sovereign *was* a good one. The Bright Young Insurance Manager's optimism was justified, and His Company, as he loved to call it, thereafter never looked back. The day was to come when it proudly carried the largest motor-premium income in the world of insurance—over a million sterling ; and when, too, the Great Powers who had given it a year at the most, saying to each other, " It can't live ! you know," would invite his Company to sit with them in the seats of the mighty.

Well played all !

CHAPTER XIX

L.I.A.T.

" ONE of the best things we have brought into the
great amalgamation is membership of the International Touring Alliance, known as the L.I.A.T."
Elijah said this to his successor, as they chatted over
the fire.

" Oh, yes ! " he went on, " we heard all about your
negotiations with the Touring Club of France in 1908,
and how the A.A. engineered its triptyques and customs
facilities. Bright, very bright ; but, my boy, the M.U.
was fixed up all over the Continent long before your
people began to think about such things. You see,"
Elijah continued, " I was on the Council of that excellent
national institution, the Cyclists' Touring Club. We
obtained free passage across frontiers for our members
with their bicycles, in conjunction with the Touring
Clubs of France, Belgium, Holland, Germany and others.
I believe the Belgian Club holds the proud distinction of
having initiated that valuable document, the triptyque,
for motor cars and motor cycles, which metaphorically
wiped out frontiers and started a veritable boom in
International Touring."

" That was fine," conceded Elisha, " but where does
all this lead ? "

" Patience ! Help yourself and listen. These Clubs
had founded the L.I.A.T. In turn, the others obtained
authority from their Governments to issue triptyques,
and the path of the touring motorist was made longer

and easier. We did not at that time need a triptyque, because foreign motor cars were admitted into Great Britain free of duty. We had already been elected by the L.I.A.T. with open arms to full membership, and have been good friends ever since."

"That, too, is splendid!" said Elisha. "What about the Royal Clubs?"

"Oh, yes! We must be fair. They certainly got together to foster the sport, and in due course they obtained similar authority. Anyway, the point is that since the old Motor Union set out a few years ago to plough a lonely furrow, eventually to link up with its affinity, the A.A., we have been able to supply every reasonable foreign touring need, and that valuable benefit of membership is now handed over to you. Make the most of it."

"We will, indeed, and thank you very much! Good luck to the L.I.A.T.," said Elisha feelingly.

"I haven't finished yet," said his host. "The Royal group have an office in Paris, and all meetings are held there. Our group meets every year in a different country; each organization in turn extends hospitality to the visitors—Belgium, Switzerland, Austria, Holland. England too. Oh, yes! we went shares with the Cyclists' Touring Club and gave our friends a good time. They turned up from all corners of Europe, with wives and daughters complete, and loved it. And by the way," wound up Elijah, "the next L.I.A.T. meeting is at Geneva. Of course you will go. You must. You've been there before?"

"N-no!" said his rather overwhelmed guest.

"Lucky man! You'll have a wonderful time, and you'll do the cause good," Elijah generously added. "Nice people intuitively link up with their kindred spirits—even as you and I did—and they are a good lot, hard-working, simple, and honest. Speak French? Like an Englishman? I thought so. You had better rub it up before you go. Your German too, if you know any. If not, learn some phrases, however few. It's a compliment to them, and they will appreciate it. We British are too insular. Our European brothers don't like our reserve. It's your job, as it once was mine, to break down that reserve—to wash out barriers. This Motoring is international—mark that—and keep to it."

"It is all splendid," said Elisha; "but I shall feel rather lonely with these good people."

"Possibly you will, but here is an idea. On the old M.U. Committee I had a friend, a soldier, retired and very keen on international touring. His father was English, but French is his mother-tongue. He was simply invaluable as one of our delegates at the meetings in Munich, London, and Brussels. He acted as interpreter, and spared us much embarrassment. I'll bring you together—get him to go with you to Geneva. He will probably take his wife—a nice woman, and daughter—very nice too."

Elijah was as good as his word, and the Anglo-French ex-Regular officer, complete with wife and daughter, fulfilled all expectations. Portly and genial, he presented an unmistakable portrait of a British gentleman, which, combined with a perfect French accent, surprised and charmed his colleagues from Amsterdam to Athens, and from Stockholm to Stamboul.

He knew them all, and they loved him. " A Johnny Bull who speaks French in a fashion all that is of the most perfect," they shouted, and thumped his broad back. His lady, too, and his little Miss. " Hear her pronounce what you call in Ingleesh ' counterpane.' Now, Miss, please," and Miss would purse her lips and say " kueue—vair tueuurrre " in accordance with the best traditions of her grandmother's race.

Splendid—all of it—making, as it did, so effectively for better understanding—breaking down racial prejudice ; establishing the truth that the Colonel's lady and Judy O'Grady were sisters under the skin.

Elisha was thrilled with the thought that the mantle of Elijah had so many pockets, and that this one, containing international touring brotherhood and sisterhood, was easily one of the richest.

In the following year the L.I.A.T. meeting was held in Vienna. In the year after that, Amsterdam—then came Britain's turn.

By this time Elijah's genial ex-Regular officer nominee had so cemented friendships and affection that the prospect of entertaining a modern Tower of Babel for four or five hectic days no longer was fraught with terror.

" Our bank balance is healthy ; let's give 'em a real good time. Let us all chime in with hospitality," said more than one Committee member.

" Very well, don't all speak at once, gentlemen, please," admonished the Chairman.

" Quite right," said the Reverend Member. " Speaking as a motor cyclist—I can't afford a car—don't let us forget our friends and allies, the Cyclists' Touring Club. But for them, you know, we might never have been in this wonderful International Touring Alliance."

" I support the Chaplain," cried another Old Timer, as they called themselves. " I'm a life member of the jolly old C.T.C.—money well spent, too ! Ask 'em— they'll jump at the idea."

Accordingly the C.T.C. was asked, and *did* jump.

As became a diplomat and, in the years that were to follow, a statesman, the Chairman curbed his Committee's enthusiasm with a gentle warning.

" You are all unselfishly and generously eager to help, gentlemen," said he ; " but please don't misunderstand my suggesting that we mustn't overdo things."

" In what way, sir ? "

" Well, don't let us—how shall I put it—oh, yes, don't let us commit the mistake of trying to wipe the eye of our European colleagues. They might resent it."

This sound advice was followed by the mixed Committee of C.T.C. and A.A. Simple entertainment should be the keynote, and the visitors should have one or two free afternoons and evenings.

"That will set the L.I.A.T. a good example," said one experienced in these matters. "We were almost choked by the hospitality of never-mind-which Club. Our hosts, bless 'em, hardly allowed us an hour to ourselves, even for shopping."

Simple entertainment. "We must take them down the Brighton road where we started our fight against police traps," said an A.A. man. "We'll borrow an idea from the Guards to Hastings day, and get our members to provide the cars."

"Agreed! And what about showing them Father Thames?" asked a C.T.C. colleague.

"Good idea! Let's hire a launch and share the expenses. And then there is lunch!"

"I'll give everybody lunch in my orchard," said the Vice-Chairman, an M.U. enthusiast. "I live quite near the River, and after that they can enjoy a motor run through nice country."

"Members' cars again—to my place," said the Chairman of Finance, also an M.U. stalwart, "and I'll give them all tea. Let them wander round my old-world garden, and play tennis too, if they feel like it."

.   .   .   .   .   .

Thus these very good-natured gentlemen set the seal of success upon the L.I.A.T.'s second visit to England. Tickets for the opera, or a play, or a musical show, were offered and taken. All went well until the last official day, when they who rather prided themselves upon "good staff work," tripped up badly.

At that time Earl's Court Exhibition was a popular resort. The band of His Majesty's Guards discoursed sweet music, while London's work-people perambulated slowly in keeping with the "Blue Danube," or quickly for "The Man Who Broke the Bank at Monte Carlo."

The Big Wheel turned ponderously on its axle, and

was subject to attacks of engine failure, when unlucky
occupants of the dozen or more suspended carriages
which remained in the air beyond reach of the highest
ladder would be stranded for hours—sometimes for
a whole night. For compensation the Directorate paid
each sufferer a guinea. This was attractive. Passengers
were rarely alone. Solitude in two was sought, for
reasons into which it would not become a history so
sedate as this to probe too deeply. The Big Wheel
thereby became a vogue—whatever that may mean—
and the shareholders profited accordingly.

There were also side-shows, stalls, scenic railways,
and other attractions, and—the Welcome Club, which
merits a paragraph to itself.

Exhibitions might come and Exhibitions might go, but
like a river the Welcome Club flowed on for—nearly—
ever. It was an oasis in a desert of gravel. Reception-
rooms, cloak-rooms, bars, and other amenities of
civilization converged upon a restaurant wherein man's
and woman's appetites were first excited and then
assuaged by clever catering. At this delectable spot a
well-meaning Entertainment Sub-Committee of the
C.T.C. and A.A. & M.U. unanimously decided to hold
the final function.

" It shall be our swan-song," said the Chairman.
" The last evening of the L.I.A.T. congress shall be a
star turn. Dinner at the Welcome Club, speeches
short and—we hope—sweet, and after that—Fun, with
a big F."

But nobody thought of the weather, and when evening
came it rained—oh ! how it rained.

The last Meeting of the World's most influential
Touring Organizations convened and held for the
second time in delightful England was drawing to a
close. The Secretary of the Alliance, a right trusty
and well beloved Dutch gentleman, who combined a
capacity to speak in several languages with the discretion
to keep silent in many others, had expressed on behalf

of his colleagues, the visitors, their heartfelt thanks, in commendably few and well-chosen sentences.

The right trusty and well beloved Chairman of the A.A. and M.U. had replied in suitable terms, and the equally trusty and beloved Chairman of the C.T.C. had identified his Committee and himself with the sentiments so ably, and if he might add, so exquisitely expressed by his colleague and friend in the Chair.

Loud and prolonged applause.

Then from the Chair came an announcement, eminently befitting the imagination of a future statesman. It anticipated by much more than a decade the British Broadcasting Corporation.

"We are now closing down for two hours, and then we shall switch over to the Welcome Club, Earl's Court Exhibition, for dinner, light music, and pleasant intercourse."

So far, that was all excellent, but within half an hour the rain started. Real London June rain—steady, persistent, pitiless.

The chief paid official was nearly at breaking-point. "This is the Blue Alsation limit!" he wailed. "Just think of it! We award each other medals for organization, and imagine we deserve 'em, and here we are, with nice men and charming women, gaily dressing up in their best to go to our final function, and—just listen to the rain! Why on earth didn't one of you fellows—oh, that's not fair—why didn't it occur to *me* that Earl's Court would be a wash-out if it rained? *Damn!* DAMN!! DAMN!!!"

Devoted colleagues shared his distress, and sought to soothe him.

"Don't give way, sir," said one. "We've been in tight places before and have come out smiling. Let's order a couple of motor buses to take the guests along."

"Thank you! That's not at all a bad idea. But the buses must stop at the turnstiles and then everybody will have to slop along for a quarter of a mile or so in the rain on soddened gravel, in thin shoes, and with influenza as an extra dish in an otherwise attractive menu. Where we were wrong," he continued, " was in omitting to back our fancy each way ! "

" Each way ! How ? "

" We should have emulated Harris in ' Three Men in a Boat ' and asked—like he did—' What about when it rains ? ' "

" And then ? " asked one.

" Don't be silly ! We could have fixed up to cancel the Welcome Club, and held our winding-up dinner here, dry and warm in this hotel ! But it's too late now."

Thus did the best-laid schemes of mice and motoring gang agley. Yet not entirely.

The motor buses rolled up to time, and This Motoring's descendants of the Tower of Babel entered and seated themselves with hopeful confidence.

" After all," they thought, " this is England. Anything can happen in England—therefore, why worry ? "

The Good Fairy of the old A.A. happened to be on duty that evening. Imprecations uttered by the one who should have known better but didn't, had broken in upon her particular and personal wave-length. She construed them into a prayer, and took action.

" What luck ! " cried the worried one. " Here we are at Earl's Court, and it has stopped raining. All we have to do now is to carry the ladies to the Welcome Club." That was done in great style, with the exception of a few generously-proportioned ladies, who thought it safer to walk and dodge the puddles as best they could.

Vast mats at the Club entrance displayed WELCOME in wet letters. Food and drink and good service made everybody try to forget damp feet, and treat a fiasco as a joke.

Nevertheless, the dinner as a function was not a success.

" This is awful," whispered the Chairman. " It's

going flat, and the confounded rain has started again. What shall we do ? "

" More speeches, sir. Make one of your topping speeches about brotherhood and all that. Great nations gathered together to make the path of tourists easy. Frontiers vanishing with a wave of the magic wand of our Alliance. Then get our friends on their feet to reply, one after the other. That will keep us going until we can get the motor buses along. We told the drivers not to leave the Exhibition, and arranged supper for them."

" All right ! Keep the wine waiters busy," said the Chairman, and proceeded to bridge an awkward gap in his best parliamentary style.

The Congress was held in one of London's largest hotels, and most of the visitors stayed there. This afforded one last despairing chance of ending the imperfect last evening of a perfect week on a less depressing note.

A self-appointed Sub-Committee of three crept out for a consultation.

" Here's an idea," said the paid member. " Let me telephone the hotel manager and tell him our trouble. Perhaps he can fix up something."

" Certainly ! But what ? "

" Well, if we could get them all back into one of those gorgeous rooms or lounges, with thick carpets and settees and curtains, and plenty of light, and coffee and sandwiches and drinks, it would help them to forget the rain. See ? " He paused for breath.

" Yes, of course. Do it, and persuade him to let us stop up as long as we like. We can square the waiters."

That was agreed, and done.

The Hotel Manager chuckled through the telephone : " Right, sir, leave it to me."

So the Sub-Committee crept back to the dining-room. More whispering to the Chairman. He smiled appreciatively, finished his ginger ale, tapped on the table, rose, and—

"Ladies and gentlemen! Friends one and all! (*Très bien! Ganz gut! Molto bene!* Hear, hear! from around the table.) "Thank you! We have tried, and you, our esteemed guests, have most generously helped us, to combat the misfortune which our infernal— I mean, our uncertain English weather has so inopportunely intruded upon our last evening. I am sure our joint hosts, the Cyclists' Touring Club, will support my earnest plea that we shall not say good-bye to each other yet! You, our friends, must not depart to your several homes in Europe with this infernal rain—I mean, our uncertain weather, pattering wetly on your memory of a successful week."

(*Molto bene. Ganz gut. Très bien.*)

"Thank you, ladies and gentlemen. The motor buses now await your pleasure. I beg to suggest that we go back to the hotel to finish the evening."

A babel of approval brought sighs of relief from the hosts.

Oh, yes! The English always muddle through. Curtains, carpets, settees, lights, sandwiches, drinks, smiles, and friendly talk, combined to save the situation. Earlier discomforts were forgotten under the spell of warmth and conviviality.

"Smoke your pipe if you prefer it. No more ceremony—we are at home! What about another whisky and soda? or a brandy—what you call a ' push coffee '? When you come to think of it, a liqueur does push the coffee, eh? "

(*Très, très bien!* Ha! Ha!)

The Hotel Manager beamed upon the results of his staff work, carried out at notice so short. He was spotted by the self-appointed emergency Sub-Committee and pulled into a merry group.

"Here is the sportsman who helped us out," said he who had cause to be especially grateful. "Come along everybody and shake hands with him. Now, Mr. Manager, let us present you to our esteemed Secretary-General of the L.I.A.T., of Baarn, Holland. Also to Herr Blank of Hamburg, Signor Blank of Milan, Madame and Monsieur Blank of Brussels. By the way, what particular nation has the privilege to claim you ? "

The beaming Manager bowed and replied, " I am Sweess."

.   .   .   .   .

A week later. The not-too-unhappy guests had departed, the accounts had been checked, agreed with the C.T.C., and settled, and the relieved Committee met in a small room in the British Empire's leading hotel just prior to the Annual General Meeting.

" We have much upon which to congratulate ourselves, gentlemen," said the Chairman. " Our finances are sound, the membership is growing by leaps and bounds. Three thousand, two hundred and seventy-nine new members have just been elected, bringing the total to eighty-nine thousand, one hundred and eighty-nine. Within less than four months we shall be occupying our usual Stand at the Olympia Motor Show, thanks to our friends, the Society of Motor Traders, and our Secretary wishes me to tell you—but let him tell you himself. Go on, Mr. Secretary."

" Thank you, sir. I have every reason to hope that by Olympia Show time we shall be *one hundred thousand strong*. Surely a World Record."

" Bravo ! We must give a dinner to celebrate that," said Charles One.

" Yes—a big one, and invite all the Press ! "

" Rather ! And friends of other motoring bodies— especially the trade, who have helped us so much," cried another.

Carried with acclamation.

The Committee then followed the Chairman into a

larger room for the Annual General Meeting, at which everything passed off in accordance with happy tradition.

" Good-bye ! Mr. Chairman.   Good holidays to you." His hand was wrung by many admirers.

" Thank you—the same to you, gentlemen, and to you, Mr. Secretary.   When we meet again after the holidays our scoring board will mark *the first hundred thousand*, eh ? "

" Yes ! thank you, sir.   I hope so, and think so ! "

.   .   .   .   .   .

But the Secretary was wrong. The Good Fairy of the A.A. must have gone on holiday, too ; for the scoring board had to be turned to the wall.   The big dinner to celebrate achievement of the First Hundred Thousand was indefinitely postponed. Holidays were cancelled. The Olympia Motor Show was not held.

Why ?

The answer is easy, now !

This happened in July, 1914, and within three weeks Europe was at WAR.

CHAPTER XX

FOR KING AND COUNTRY

THE Reservists were called up. The A.A. patrol staff was automatically depleted by one third.

The Territorials were mobilized, which meant depletion of indoor staff. Kitchener called to male Britain. More depletion.

The Committee was in meeting—Secretary speaking :

" And, Mr. Chairman, the Staff wish me to convey to the Committee, through you, sir, our unanimous agreement to a reduction forthwith in our pay, of twenty-five per cent., because nobody knows where this awful upheaval may lead, nor when it will end. Nor, too, in what way the Association may be affected. We feel that we must sacrifice something."

This gesture was accepted in the spirit in which it was made, with one reservation by the Chairman of Finance—who was always thinking of those not so prosperous as himself—that when things settled down, if they ever did, and the atmosphere cleared—he hoped so—full pay should be resumed and sacrificed pay returned.

Meanwhile, there should be separation allowances for all who joined up, and everyone's job should be kept open.

" And may those of us who wish to, join up, please ? " asked the Secretary.

" Why certainly ! " replied the Chairman. " I'd go myself if only I were twenty years younger."

Depletion of staff was thereby accelerated.

What to do next ? An idea ! Form a Volunteer Motor Corps for Home Service, and offer it to the Government.

With the help of military experts the scheme was completed to the last button on the tyre covers, printed in a style most attractive, and presented to the War Office " for approval and necessary action, please."

But approval was not forthcoming. Instead, there was received a rather stilted request that " The Chairman and Secretary be good enough to attend at Room Number So-and-So, War Office, on Sunday, the 16th instant (August), at 4 p.m."

It read like a Jury Summons ! Never mind. Our country before our pride. The summons was obeyed. A Great One addressed the jurymen.

" We have considered your proposal, but, thanks, it isn't needed. All we require is a matter of a hundred and forty of your fellers to stand by with their cars, at a given centre, for eight days, or it may be ten, until Territorial mobilization has linked up with our Defence Scheme. The show will be over in three months. Good afternoon."

Did he add " Mind the step ? " It seemed so.

In that curt way a fortnight's soulful work was squashed by one who sat in a high place, and thought he knew !

" Never mind ! " said the Committee, " we won't let all this fine work be entirely wasted. Idea ! We'll turn the Motor Corps scheme into a Voluntary Service Corps ; then the lady members can join."

It was done. Within a few weeks the A.A.V.S.C. numbered nearly twenty thousand of all ranks and both sexes, doing all kinds of duty anywhere, and at any time, such as transport of the wounded from railway station to hospital ; taking the convalescents for a breath of country air ; acting as taxi-men and -women —without the clock—at the call of Military Authorities.

Regimental, Divisional, and Command Headquarters had good cause to appreciate this A.A. activity.

There were regrettable incidents, inevitably, but only a few.

As an example, one afternoon an honest Yorkshire tradesmen burst into the A.A. Office in Leeds.

" Look here," he said, " I've got two sons doing their bit in France. I filled up one of your forms, and was doing my job thoroughly, but I'm finished with Voluntary Service. I'll do no more ! It's like this. I turned up yesterday afternoon at one of the Headquarters, and a gawky chap with tabs and brass hat and spurs, and all, clanked out and stepped into my car as though it were his own. Not so much as a ' thank you,' but I didn't much mind. Serving my country, says I, and left it at that for the moment. But mark you, I was wild. I drove this officer-chap up hill and down dale for over three hours, with him lolling in the back of the car, and me at the wheel like my poor chauffeur who went down in the *Cressy*."

He wiped his brow.

" And then ! We were half way between Selby and York, about three miles from a village either way, when something happened to the engine and the car stopped."

He wiped his brow again, and went on.

" I got down and began tinkering with the works, found out what was wrong, and was just putting it right, when this officer-chap, getting impatient I suppose, barked at me—that's the only way to put it—and said : ' Look here, my man, I can't be kept here all the blessed afternoon—I'm in a hurry ! ' Imagine that ! ' My man ! ' *His* man ! And I could buy him up—ten of him. And my two boys at the front ! I *was* wild. Just then the engine gave me the O.K. and I knew she'd start. I kept that to myself and I said to his Lordship, ' I'm doing my best—but—just get out for a moment ; I want some tools from under the back seat.' So like a great gawk he stepped to the side of the road, and said, 'All right, but hurry up, I can't wait all the——'

" And before he could finish I hopped back into the driving seat, and said, ' In a hurry, are you ? Your man, am I ? Well, see here ! I've had enough of you, with your spurs and your tabs and your swank. You can something-well walk home.' And I let in the clutch and left him—gaping !

" But ! " concluded the honest tradesman, " now I've got it off my chest, I'm just wondering if—you see we're at war, and we've all sorts of laws in war—D.O.R.A. and suchlike. Can they do anything to me up at Head-quarters, do you think ? "

The A.A. sympathizer—a Yorkshireman, too—smiled and replied, " You did quite right ! and I'll tell you another thing "—wagging his finger—" that officer-chap won't say a word. He feels too much of a fool. And don't stop doing Voluntary Service, please. They are not all like him."

"'Oh, very well," said the injured one. " I'll carry on."

· · · · · ·

Next ! A circular letter was issued to what remained of the potential fighting force of the A.A. staff. The wording was purposely unofficial. " Your King and Country need you, and the A.A. doesn't. Every one of us who can get past the doctor is joining up. What are *you* going to do ? "

The answers to that appeal came promptly. The depletion of Staff was accelerated. Early in September a hundred and fifty patrols made a brave show as, com-plete with bicycles, they marched from Fanum House, Coventry Street, along the Embankment, up Queen Victoria Street, past the Old Lady of Threadneedle Street, along Old Broad Street, to entrain for Colchester, there to form the first two Companies of the 2/8th Cyclists' Battalion, Essex Regiment.

What next ? Ambulances ! Oh, yes ! A special fund

was opened, and over ten thousand pounds was quickly subscribed. Members gave their cars for conversion into ambulances. Many themselves defrayed the cost thereof in their eagerness to give and keep giving. His Majesty King George reviewed the first fifty in the garden of Buckingham Palace. Those went to France, others to Belgium, others were allocated to the War Office, the St. John Ambulance Corps, and kindred organizations.

．　　　．　　　．　　　．　　　．　　　．

One morning, those at Fanum, Birmingham, who were trying to keep the home fires burning, received a call from a bluff Midlander who, past military age, devoted all the time he could spare to making jig-saw puzzles for convalescent soldiers and attending the hospital-trains, which were arriving with dreadful frequency from the coast.

He went straight to the point.

" Four- and five-seater cars carry the minor injuries quite efficiently, but those who have two-seaters can only take one. These motorists are working themselves to death on munitions, but they are quite willing to come along to the station, even though it means waiting two and three hours before the train actually arrives. At the same time, they don't feel they are doing much good in carrying one man. Further, there is a shortage of ambulances for the stretcher cases. Now," continued he, " I have invented a trailer-ambulance. It is a light car on two pneumatic wheels, with a canvas awning, which will take two stretchers. Towed behind a two-seater it increases the capacity 200 per cent. and gives the motorist a real job. It is cheap—£50 or £60 against the £500 and £600 of the ordinary ambulance."

" Bravo ! " said Fanum, Birmingham.

" Thank you ! I took it to the War Office. It's unpractical, they said, and turned me down—flatly. I reminded them that gun-limbers were trailers and were not exactly unpractical, but the Brass Hat had spoken, and that appeared to settle it. Do come down and see it."

" Certainly ! "

Fanum, Birmingham, knew a good thing when he saw it. He whipped up the willing members, with the result that quite soon afterwards a column of trailers was working day and night in the Midlands—and the idea was copied throughout the country.

" Unpractical ! " had said the Brass Hat.

. . . . . .

While good work of this kind was going on, the A.A. had broken out in a fresh place. There were about four hundred miles of overhead and underground cables to the Continent which needed guarding by day and by night, because—well, because you never know, you know ! The police were busy enough, and their forces, too, were being depleted by the demand overseas. So the A.A. did it until the police could take over and carry on.

. . . . . .

The papers were preaching " Business as Usual." That slogan looked well enough in print, but—" Business as Usual ? " said the eager and devoted. " Don't be silly ! There's a War on ! " So the slogan died.

Depletion was not confined to the staff. Members were flocking to the colours by the thousand upon thousand. The membership figures were dropping persistently, pitilessly, like the rain on that last evening at Earl's Court. Never mind—what next ?

Another brain-wave.

" Let us help recruiting ! What we may term the cream, is getting thin. Conscription is not yet contemplated. The eager ones have gone already. There remain umpteen thousands of worthy men not perhaps so impulsive, but not any the less willing. They need to be talked to. It's like an ordinary peace-time business.

After the first rush for a new article—those who want to keep the sales up must get out and—and—scratch for customers. That's what the dear old Recruiting Officers have got to do, in order to keep up the supply. Let us help them to get out and scratch."

" Certainly ! But how ? " seemed a fair question.

" Let us provide them with cars—free. Remember the Guards to Hastings scoop, and how A.A. members rushed to help ! In the present crisis they will do it again, anywhere and everywhere."

It was true. Those who couldn't join up, and those whose dearest *had* joined up, were aching to do something—waiting only for a lead.

It followed, therefore, on a certain morning in October that the " War House " received a visitor from This Motoring. He went straight to the point.

" Would it be of value if your Recruiting Officers throughout the country were afforded motor-car transport *free*, with the result that they could tour their districts—you know, like a Candidate for Parliament has to tour his constituency canvassing for votes ? Motoring is expensive."

" Indeed it is," said the Staff Officer, " and don't I know it ? I'm a member of the A.A. I drive a ' twenty.' It costs me eightpence a mile."

" Very well, sir. If we could give you a million miles of *free* driving, would that help ? "

" Splendid feller ! It would be wonderful."

This Officer was one of Britain's brightest and best. Tall, lean, fit, with legs which simply were made for a top-boot—that is, no calves ; a rather formidable nose, twinkling grey eyes, and—yes—even dimples. He smiled away most of the gloom with which earlier the well-intentioned ambassadors of This Motoring had been smothered. (" No, thank you ; it will be over in three months. Good afternoon—mind the step.")

" You like the idea," said his visitor.

" Like it ? I love it. Now let us get down to details."

They were soon settled. A well-conceived appeal to A.A. members, to be signed by the Chairman, with a postscript endorsing the appeal, to be signed by—whom ?

" Do you think you could get the Greatest One to sign it ? " asked the visitor.

" 'Fraid not." The twinkles faded out for a moment. " He's too busy, we can't get near him, but I'll get the next biggest to sign it. Rely on me. Good-bye for the present—splendid feller ! "

The " million-mile scheme " was a triumph. A.A. members, and members' wives, and members' daughters, and sisters, and sweethearts, jumped at it.

It was all done by kindness, and post cards. Kindness proposed—post cards disposed—in this way. Every Recruiting Office in the Service in due course was gladdened by a batch of yellow post cards showing who would drive, in what kind of cars, with how many seats, and when ! Telephone numbers added for mutual convenience.

" Bless these people," said the overworked R.O.'s ; " now we can get on." And they proceeded to do so.

The umpteen thousands of worthy ones—perhaps not so impulsive as their brothers who formed the First Hundred Thousand of immortal fame, but not any the less patriotic—were reached and talked to and, perhaps for the first time, who knows ? were offered a ride in a fine car, driven by a bright girl—who would say, " My brothers are out there. I say, now, hop in behind— there's room for three of you and we'll run you along to the Recruiting Office, only ten miles, and—What ? Oh, yes ! I'll drive you back here again—after you've been sworn in."

The Greatest One, of lamented memory, acclaimed this particular A.A. activity in a speech at the Guildhall, London.

.   .   .   .   .   .

What next ?

The air raids. Another good idea. Special Con-
stabulary. A special A.A. Motor Section was formed,
composed of members unfit for active service, but keen
to do their bit. Their bit consisted of turning out at
any hour of the night, in all weathers, to drive through
the streets, without lights, sweeping the unthoughtful
into safety, crying " Take cover ! Take cover ! " while
taking not any themselves. Their orders were to carry
on until the all-clear signal was given. That job didn't
seem much, but it called for courage, and got it.

A year passed. The female staff were dribbling away
to join the W.A.A.C.'s, and the W.R.E.N.'s, and later
the W.R.A.F.'s.

Another year. The membership figures were down
to sixty-seven thousand, but the spirit of the members
who remained was inspiring. " We're getting practically
nothing in return for our subscription," they wrote,
" but never mind ! we will keep on paying. It's the
least we can do."

Even more inspiring was the fact that at every Committee Meeting there were always some—not many—
applicants for election. And at one Meeting in the
dark days of 1917, Britain and Mrs. Britain gave evidence
of their unquenchable optimism in that one hundred and
eighty-one of them took up Life Membership at a fee,
then, of fifteen guineas.

Three years of war. Membership down to forty-
eight thousand. The staff on Service by now was
decimated. Killed in action. Died of wounds.
Torpedoed. Those who were invalided out were coming
back to resume duty. One brave soul appeared
pathetically with an inferior and unworkable false
leg—the best that a hard-driven Medical Staff could
furnish. To wear it involved such discomfort that he
preferred to take it off and stand it in the corner, like an
umbrella.

" We can't allow this," said the Committee. " Let's
get the poor chap a really fine one—aluminium, springs

and all that—the nearest approach to the one he left in France."

" How much will it cost ? "

" Sixty pounds ! "

" Never mind ! "

.   .   .   .   .

Four years (within a month or so) of War. At the Annual General Meeting the membership figures stood at thirty-six thousand, six hundred and sixty-three. "What price our hundred thousand now ? " was a pathetic and pardonable question.

" Never mind ! The War can't last much longer. Carry on ! "

.   .   .   .   .   :

Then, at eleven o'clock one Monday morning, after a week-end of hopes and fears, the explosions of maroons heralded ALL CLEAR ! That magic lead off was followed by motor horns, bells, cheers, tears, hand-shakes, embraces, thumping on the back, kissing, and other excusable evidences of mild hysteria.

The War was over !

CHAPTER XXI

WITH a calm characteristically British, the Committee met as usual on the morrow of Armistice Day.

Outside Fanum House mild hysteria still prevailed. Piccadilly was the centre of revelry, emulating Hampstead Heath on a fine Bank Holiday—but the Committee met as usual.

"And now, gentlemen," said the Chairman, "we must get back to work. For goodness' sake let us close the windows—that row in the street is most unseemly. Where was I? Oh, as I said, we must get back to work. How do we stand exactly? And what shall we do?"

"Our position is somewhat ironical," said the Finance Chairman. "We've dropped in membership from ninety thousand to thirty-something; but, thanks to our sportsmen and sportswomen who have paid their subs. while getting nothing much in return, we've heaps of money in reserve."

"Good!" said Charles One. "Let us spend some of it?"

"Why?"

"Why not? Hang it all, it belongs to our members, doesn't it? They didn't subscribe it for it to be tucked away in a stocking. Remember the parable of the talents."

Somebody gasped, but Charles Two seized the point.

" He's right. Let's go all out after that First Hundred Thousand. Flood the roads with A.A. patrols. More telephone boxes—Publicity—Get a move on—Wake things up ! Why not ? "

He puffed at his cigar, and gazed rather truculently —for him—at all and sundry.

The Committee, responsive as ever to enthusiasm, " signified the same " in the usual manner.

" Bravo ! Quite right ! Let's get that six-figure membership, and hang the expense ! "

" Agreed, gentlemen ? " asked the Chairman.

" Ay, ay, sir ! "

Left to Finance Committee and Secretary to devise ways and means.

.   .   .   .   .   .

Ways and means ? Here, indeed, was a problem calling for bold decision. No one could forecast with any degree of certainty whether This Motoring would boom or slump.

" Never mind ! Take a chance in the hope that it will boom. Wake things up and that will *make* it boom."

The war spirit seemed reluctant to die out at the behest of a few maroon signals. This was all to the good. Enthusiasm is ever a healthy germ. The staff were dribbling back, some rather diffidently, though they had no grounds for fear. They were greeted by " Splendid ! So glad to see you ! There's plenty of work ! Hang up your hats and let's get on with it. Things are in rather a mess. We'll clean it up together ! "

" We'll clean it up together, but mind," said the Senior, " it means work with a capital W. There must be no passengers on the A.A. boat. In the words of our faithful major domo, we haven't room for the type with one eye on the clock and your hand out on a Friday."

" Rather a mess " was a mild way to describe conditions of This Motoring.

The roads of Britain were in an appalling state. No longer could they be proudly acclaimed " smooth as a billiard table from here to so-and-so. Finest in the world, you know ! "

Heavy motor lorries, bearing munitions of war, had rumbled " good-bye to all that." Britain's star road-engineers had been busy making roads behind the Front, and had perforce taken steam-rolling plant and labourers with them. Hardly a highway retained a decent surface. " Business as usual " had been side-tracked. As and when the surface crumbled under heavy traffic, it was just shovelled to the side. That which didn't crumble, but, like the immortal British front line, could be bent but not broken, was very sadly bent.

The motor industry was in a state of chaos. Every factory had been put to munitions. Cars were scarce and prices prohibitive. Until the boys could come home repairs were being held up to such an extent that anything which would stand up and look like a motor car found a ready and quite irrational market.

" This is fine," chuckled a few lucky garage pro-prietors, who had kept going somehow. " Hope it will last."

It *did* last for a few months ; then the situation was eased by the release of cars and lorries sent home from the War area. But prices remained high, profiteeringly so, as witness :

Early in 1915 one of the innumerable patriotic A.A. members, ordered to India, offered his brand new 12 h.p. touring car, of classic make, and beautiful, as a gift outright. Fanum replied, " Very sporting of you, and keenly appreciated, but, don't ! *please*, give it—just lend it to us for War Service, and nothing *but* War Service. Then, at the end, we will return what is left. Who knows ? It may be worth a tenner or two."

" All right, thanks ! " said the member, and promptly forgot all about the matter. Being, as it was, British throughout, the car was quite fit and well after three and a half years' careful usage.

Its original price was four hundred pounds. Its owner was still in India—a Civil Servant. The process of cleaning up in due time brought the matter of LB. 4—— forward for consideration and settlement.

He who had driven it during intervals of home duty was quite sentimental. " I've grown to love that bus," he said. " She steers like a yacht and has never let me down, I wish I could keep her, but that's out of the question. What shall we do ? "

" There's only one thing to do," said the Particular Personal Secretary—of the weaker but so often wiser sex. " Stifle your feelings, give her a thorough paint and varnish, sell her for the best price we can get, and give our member his money back."

" All right, Miss K.—we'll do it ! "

LB. 4—— was reconditioned at a cost of thirty pounds. " We'll throw that in, eh ? She saved us ten times that amount."

Looking as good as new, she fetched seven hundred and seventy-five pounds. The full amount was transferred by cable to the Chartered Bank of India in the name of Mr. Blank. That gentleman cabled surprised and pleased thanks in a few well-chosen sentences.

The cable was filed for reference and the A.A. turned its thoughts back to the problem of the first hundred thousand.

. . . .

Hotels ! A rather pretty mess here ! A rare state of things. Five-star and four-star had managed to keep their end up, but from those bearing one-, two-, or even three-star A.A. classification the tail had dropped clean out.

Poor things ! It couldn't be otherwise. With ration cards, synthetic foodstuffs, unsympathetic mortgages, brewers' and distillers' loans, to worry them, and practically all that fairly profitable custom hitherto derived from This Motoring gone, hotel and innkeepers were in a bad way. Furniture worn to threads. Bed-linen frayed. Table-linen stained. Male staff away fighting, female of the species doing their men's work, pinched and drawn the while, living on war rations and an all too infrequent visitor's tip.

The clock had been put back. Dark rings of anxiety had thickened round the eyes of Boniface and Mrs. Boniface. In cottage windows were displayed, proudly at first, cards notifying that :

> " A man from this house is fighting for his Country."

Pathetically, then, a tiny black ribbon would intimate that " is " had been changed by grim strokes of the great Reaper into " was."

The clock had been put back, almost to the time when the Duchess left the Duke's Arms for the last stage of her last journey.

Think what that meant.

Recovery came, slowly but surely, to these brave and patient people.

The brewer's collector sensed an improvement in the atmosphere of This Motoring, and acted in accordance with the best traditions of *his* office, which were to encourage trade. Called with British reticence a mere " Collector," he was, in fact, a General Staff Officer, first grade, to his Army Headquarters, the Brewery.

He administered an area of inns and hotels either owned by his brewery and rented to Boniface, with the stipulation that only the brewery's beer could be sold there, or on which large loans had been made on First Mortgage, also with the stipulation that only the brewery's beer could be sold.

That is how the breweries quite rightly did most

of their business, and that is what was meant by the term—being in the hands of the brewers, or tied.

It is easy, therefore, to see that a Collector held a position of responsibility and power far exceeding the modesty of his official title.

A Distiller's Collector, at any rate in England, was not so great in importance because beer was the first item on the agenda of an English hostelry. Spirits and wines came second and third.

The shine had dropped out of A.A. stars. The work had to be done all over again as part of the 100,000 membership campaign.

Recovery in this connexion meant a thorough re-combing and re-inspection, in order that the A.A. Handbook should, within a year or two, again be worthy of trust.

Boniface had cause to bless A.A. inspection. He welcomed the bright young Area Road Manager, back from War Service. " Just called in, you know, for a chat and a look round. Yes, thanks, I'm staying the night. How are things ? You must have had a rough time, even as we did. But never mind. Thank Heaven it's over. Did your son George come out all right ? "

" Yes, bless you ! " said Boniface. " He's one arm short, but he's back at work, and we're pulling the business round by degrees. But, listen ! The missis and I could do so much more if we could only coax a bit more money out of our brewers. The place fair makes us weep. We took such pride in everything being spick and span, and—look at it—ceilings cracked and wallpaper mouldy ; the very chair you're sitting in has a leg loose—be careful. A few hundred pounds would help us to get back to our pre-war smartness. It fair makes us weep."

" What about your Collector ? "

" He's a good chap, but I suppose even a brewery has its troubles, what with D.O.R.A. and restrictions on production, and so on. If we could kind of squeeze

him a bit—you know what I mean—bring some pressure
to bear——"

"Pressure!" said the A.A. man. "You want
pressure? Why shouldn't!—I say! take me over
your place, now, before we settle down for the evening.
I've got an idea—*and* a notebook."

. . . . . .

The A.A. Area Road Manager had paid his bill in
full, in accordance with the strictest traditions of *his*
office, and was saying good-bye. "Now! don't get
the wind up when our official letter arrives. It will be
a stinger!" He winked as he let in the clutch. "Don't
get the wind up, and mind you let me know. Mark
your letter ' Personal.' Good-bye, Boss; good-bye,
George! No more Mespot, eh?"

. . . . . .

The Collector was taking tea. He looked worried.
"Let me read the A.A. letter again!"

"' Reluctantly compelled to withdraw the official
appointment. Take down the A.A. sign.' Take it
down!—but that's dreadful! Think what that means
to our prestige. How the Rose and Crown will jeer.
How the townspeople will talk!"

"But, sir," said Boniface, remembering the wink,
"you see what the A.A. letter goes on to say, and it's
signed by the Secretary—not a rubber stamp, or *per pro.*,
or anything. It says *unless* I can have the place put in
proper repair, and new furniture and beds and bed-
linen, and tablecloths, and so on, and two extra lavatories
—well! it's not so hopeless! I've worked it all out,
and got an estimate. Five hundred will do it. At
five per cent. that's only ten bob a week. We can get
that back ten times over in trade. Couldn't the brewery
help? Now—come!"

"You're right," said the Collector. "The brewery
must help. I can't promise, of course—but I'll certainly

recommend it! The A.A. sign to come down? Oh, no!"

The Collector got into his car, said good-bye, drove away, and Boniface, beaming, cried: "Here! Mother —George! Collector's gone, and we've 'clicked.' We're through! We'll get the extra loan. The A.A.'s done it!"

.   .   .   .   .   .

The garage man—the roadside repairer—had had a thin time, too! How he even kept a roof overhead is a wonder and a lasting credit. He suffered, but, in accordance with the best traditions of *his* race, managed to keep a firm chin above rough water. Thereby he was a potent factor in the recovery of This Motoring.

No brewers' loans for him—oh, no! The long, long trail a-winding to munition factories afar had pulled away his workmen. The stream of motoring traffic, from which he had extracted a modest living, died down and down to a mere trickle. With Dick and Walter away, of course, Mary and Ethel had put on overalls and were carrying on bravely, but despite their efforts trade had gone from bad to worse, even as with Boniface. True, petrol reached as high as four shillings a gallon, but there hadn't been enough buyers to pay the rent.

Comparatively few people troubled to realize the immense needfulness of the local repairer, and what an important factor he and his were—and still are— in the peace and comfort of This Motoring.

The A.A. had always been his champion. When cleverly conceived enterprises for Co-operative Trading in motor accessories were launched, the A.A. stood aloof. "This Motoring needs the local repairer. He must live, and prosper, and be afforded his moderate profit to that end." Thus said the Executive Committee.

The Motor Trade Association had received this statement of A.A. policy, at an Annual Dinner, with outward applause and inward reciprocal sympathy.

The A.A. spokesman, standing on a chair, with one foot on the tablecloth, had said : " We are not in favour of Co-operative Trading, which aims to kill the small trader. Our members need repair service, supplies, and so on, just as close as can be to the spot where those needs occur." He went on : " If one of ours is hung up near Pitlochry in Scotland, or Pwllheli in Wales, with his last tyre-cover burst to bits, or his big-end seized, what's the use of Co-operative Trading to him ? ' No ! ' he says, ' damn Co-operative Trading. Give me the A.A. Handbook '—and he's right."

That statement cemented an understanding which meant much for motoring and the industry that thrives upon it.

.   .   .   .

" Here's an idea ! That hundred thousand ! Let's put it up to the Committee," said the Secretary to his colleagues. " We've got to inspect all our agents and repairers over again. Why not employ the system on which our hotels are appointed, and——"

" And what, please ? "

" Star 'em."

" Well, that's an idea, certainly ! What does our Engineering Department think about it ? "

The head of that Department had recently taken over. He had been chosen not merely for having rows of letters after his name, but mainly for hard and possibly bitter experience as an owner of a repair business.

" Splendid ! " said he, " and it's easy to work, with care and discretion, of course. We mustn't hurt anyone's feelings, and they've had an awful time. Don't I know it ? "

It was a good idea. The Committee approved, and it did work. One and two stars for modest supplies, and expert motor-cycle repairs done by men who could take one to pieces, put it together again, and have nothing left over. Three and four stars for garages suitably equipped and staffed to undertake repairs and adjustment, as well as carrying a good range of supplies, and having adequate garage accommodation. And that was another step towards Recovery.

.   .   .   .   .   .

Recovery of A.A. service could not keep pace with the immediate post-war needs of This Motoring. War had popularized mechanical transport to such effect that the average young warrior, drawing his gratuity, proceeded to " bust " most of it in a motor cycle, or a second-hand crock of a car. Sister W.A.A.C. and Sister W.R.E.N. did a little in the same line, too. And of course those who had stayed at home, to make money, stood, metaphorically, in a queue, cheque-book in hand, waiting for delivery of the best stuff. All these had to be looked after.

A.A. membership was booming. The far-seeing Committee had ordained enthusiastic progress ! Wake things up ! and keep them moving ! So when, at a meeting early in April, 1919, the Secretary diffidently asked for " fifteen thousand pounds, please," the Chairman didn't faint, but just asked for further particulars.

" That's for a start, sir, thank you, and it's like this ! Our men are resuming duty in batches, and scores of ex-service men are being taken on and trained. The roads are really looking more like pre-war, and members are flocking in. Two thousand and sixty-nine for election to-day, making a total of forty-one thousand, one hundred and seventy-nine. We're climbing steadily back to pre-war strength, but our men, as you know, are on ordinary bicycles, and they can't work a beat longer than eight or ten miles. We have a scheme to accelerate our progress as well as that of the patrols."

" All right," said the Chairman, genially, " you will have your atmosphere, eh ?   Now what is it ? "

" It's to establish a fleet of Road Service Outfits—motor-cycles with sidecars, specially built, and painted in A.A. colours. Mechanical first-aid. Miniature repair shops, in fact. We've worked it all out in conjunction with our Engineering Department, and of course the Road Department. There is plenty of personnel available—trained men back from the War—Army Service Corps mechanics, you know. This service will go far to fill the gap in what may be called ' running repairs ' until our A.A. Agents get back to pre-war efficiency. I hope that's clear."

" Not quite," said a quiet member. " We mustn't get mixed up in trade, after keeping ourselves unspotted and respected by the Industry."

That gentleman spoke with feeling and authority. He held the twenty-four hour record for Brooklands Race Track, together with another record ungrudgingly accorded to him as the " best seller " of his time.

" No, sir ! " was the reply, " our copybook will remain unsullied. Nothing shall be sold, even to a sparking plug, except at full retail price, and supplied or replenished as may be necessary by the A.A. Agent on the beat."

" Good ! Now what about cost ? "

" Well, sir, we estimate that each outfit will cost one hundred pounds to buy and seventy-five pounds per annum to keep going, but, naturally, the ' beats ' will be extended materially. In fact, two men on motor-cycle outfits should, we think, out-class in utility and equal in advertisement five men on pedal-bicycles. Here is a drawing of the proposed side-carrier. We hope the Committee will like it ! "

" H'm," said the Medical Member. " It looks like a coffin ! "

" Surely the colours yellow and bronze-blue will avoid that ? "

" Perhaps ! I hope so, but it looks like coffin, all the same."

" The Doctor ought to know," said Mr. Solicitor. That got a laugh, and diverted attention.

" Anyhow, Mr. Chairman, this is going to wake things up," said Charles Two. " Let 'em get on with it. I propose therefore," etc., etc., and—bless them, it was carried unanimously.

But the Finance Chairman looked thoughtful.

CHAPTER XXII

THE FIRST PETROL PUMPS

THE War had shown how entirely dependent Britain was on sources overseas for supplies of motor fuel.

Petrol was sold on the basis that it was worth all it would fetch. Prior to 1914 the three leading motoring organizations had combined in an earnest effort to encourage home production of motor fuel, principally benzole, which could be extracted from coal and was then much cheaper than petrol.

But much of this was so inferior in quality that it became suspect and unpopular.

Recovery brought about two reassuring developments. First, a standard specification of benzole to which all the leading by-product manufacturers readily undertook to conform. Second, the historic A.A. ten-thousand-mile test on a famous British car, and a five-thousand-mile test on an equally famous British motor-cycle. The mileage per gallon in both tests was most satisfactory, and the engines, taken down and examined on completion of the runs, showed perfect condition.

So benzole was restored to public confidence and the National Benzole Association, formed by the leading producers, started out upon its successful career, aided and encouraged in every possible way by motor users and traders alike.

The A.A. Honorary Treasurer was a great traveller. It was his habit to spend the winter abroad, now in his Villa on the Riviera, then in California—motoring always.

Returning from California he button-holed the Secretary. " We can all learn something, can't we ? " said he.

" Yes, Mr. Treasurer, that means you have an idea ! "

" I have. The first thing to irritate me on arriving home is the bother of messing about with two-gallon tins of motor-spirit. It's silly. Just fancy. There isn't a single roadside fuel-supply station in Britain, in this year of (dis)grace, 1919. Whereas, over there I got all I needed from pumps, and never saw a tin."

" Oh ! that looks promising. Couldn't the A.A. start the ball rolling ? "

" Exactly ! my boy," he said gleefully. " Let's show 'em the way. We want to wake things up. I've made inquiries. We could put up a complete outfit, including pump, tank, and what they call ' free air ' installation, for five or six hundred pounds ! "

" Have you any pictures ? "

" No, but I can cable for some, and have them over in time for our next meeting ! "

" Splendid, sir ! "

And off the cable went.

. . . . . .

" We hope the Committee won't mind our putting forward another scheme, please, Mr. Chairman."

" How much do you want to spend now, pray ? "

" Well, sir, the Honorary Treasurer has given us the idea, and it isn't worked out thoroughly yet. A matter of six thousand or so, to start with—but it's a perfectly topping scheme."

" Let's hear it first ! " said the Finance Chairman, looking thoughtful.

" We want to put up ten fully-equipped Roadside

Filling Stations for motor fuel at different points in England, manned by our own men in uniform, painted in our colours, yellow and bronze-blue—a gorgeous advertisement. They would be available only to A.A. members, on pain of dismissal to any patrol disregarding that rule. Fancy! Mr. Chairman and gentlemen! We, the A.A., will be the very first to introduce Roadside Filling Stations to the British motoring public. Think what *that* means!"

Some members of Committee caught their breath for a moment; but then came applause, loud and prolonged.

The quiet watchful Motoring Industry Leader said: " But surely this means the A.A. going into trade, and I thought it was agreed that——"

" Not at all," broke in the Honorary Treasurer, " if my friend will pardon me interrupting. I've been warned of that already by our Secretary, and—but let him explain."

" Well, sir," and the Secretary took up the tale, " we propose to supply the outfits and man them, but instead of going into the motor-spirit business we will let the local A.A. Agents take it in turn to supply the spirit at the proper retail price. That will cement still further the good understanding between the retail trade and ourselves."

" Good! I'm satisfied, and the idea to provide ' free air ' for members' tyres is excellent," was the frank reply from the Motoring Industry Leader.

" And the publicity!" said another.

" Yes! with illustrations."

" And have a ceremonial opening—with sandwiches and drinks! Fine!"

Enthusiasm prevailed.

" Just one more point, please!" came from the lower end of the Committee table.

" Well, Mr. Secretary?"

" The price of petrol is what it will fetch!"

" Yes ? "

" The National Benzole people are working hard to get a market, and we want motor-spirit of different kinds. Competition is good for the user ; therefore, let the A.A. Filling Stations begin by supplying National Benzole only, please ! "

That, too, was agreed.

The Chairman of Finance looked thoughtful, but smiled cordial approval.

He signified that approval in a practical manner by journeying long distances, in his own car, and on his own benzole, to perform the ceremony of declaring each A.A. Filling Station open, making it clear in his speeches that the A.A. was not concerned in trading in motor-spirit, or any other commodity, but was content to act as pioneer of a very desirable development, and to allow the local A.A. Agent and retailer to use the installation for selling motor-spirit in the most up-to-date and practical manner.

. . . . . .

A leading light in the petrol world, highly respected and very likeable, met an A.A. man at lunch, and, over coffee, went straight to the point :

" What exactly is the idea of this Automobile Association Americanization of motor-spirit distribution, if I may so express it ? "

The A.A. man smiled and replied : " If I may venture to emulate your brevity of expression, we are indulging in what might be termed an orgy of utilitarian publicity. That is to say, we do good not in any way by stealth and delight to find it fame——"

" Well hit ! " said the Likeable One, smiling too. " But you'll be imitated, surely, and what then ? "

" The A.A. won't care very much. So long as we lead, others can follow. In the matter of Filling Stations our commitments are limited to ten. No more. We wish merely to demonstrate that roadside petrol pumps

n Britain are as feasible and desirable as in the U.S.A. ;
and then, when the Petrol Interests—you, for example—
see fit to take over and carry on, the A.A. will say,
'Good night, everybody. A.A. Filling Stations now
closing down ! ' That's fair, eh ? "

" But, my dear chap, you don't seriously expect our
people to sell through pumps. Why, our brand would
go to perdition ! We *must* keep to tins. We *must* ! "

" Are you sure ? "

He was not sure, and very honestly said so.

Within five or a few more years, roadside petrol pumps
were even as the lilies of the field, albeit not quite so
pretty, and the Likeable One's company was one of the
first to put them up.

By that time National Benzole had become National
Benzole Mixture. Never mind how or why ! And
presently the great petrol combines had followed the
drum so fairly that they, too, were rightfully accorded
their measure of A.A. recognition ; which meant that one,
two, three, or four of the leading brands took turn and
turn about in the tanks of the A.A. Filling Stations.
And the Honorary Treasurer, driving down the Great
North Road, chuckled.

" Look at 'em ! Twenty-five pumps between Newark
and Stamford. I've counted them, and the A.A. did it ! "

" No, sir ! *You* did it."

" No, my boy ! *We* did it—all of us—the family,
you know ! "

Which, after all, was true !

. . . . . .

Just a postscript. Brands of motor-spirit might take
turn and turn about in A.A. Filling Station tanks, but
the rule to serve A.A. members only was rigidly enforced,
on pain of " dismissal without the option." And quite
right, too !

One afternoon a car was held up for a minute or so
on the Brighton road at Bolney Cross Roads (A.A.

Filling Station). One of the occupants, a girl—a mere child—cried out, " I say ! Look ! There's a car being filled up at Our Filling Station by Our man, and it has the Other badge on—not Ours ! Surely that can't be right."

" Take the number of the car, darling ! " said he who obviously was connected with the girl by marriage " and I'll write to the A.A. about it. Well done ! Chocolates for you when we get to a shop ! "

And he did write, and the matter was investigated. It was found that there were other sins of omission or commission to the debit of the A.A. man i/c Filling Station, and he was discharged, in order, as Candide would put it, " to encourage the others."

. . . . . .

The esteemed and lamented Honorary Treasurer, who had come over with the old Motor Union, and inspired Roadside Filling Stations, conceived also the idea of keeping Fanum, London, open for the round of the clock, throughout the year. The Secretary was politely dubious.

" It looks all right, as a gesture, as window-dressing, but, frankly, I can't see reason in keeping a staff on duty all night and every night merely on the chance that somebody may happen to want something at a time when all good motorists should be in bed ! As a gesture, yes, but——"

" My boy ! " said the slightly older but far more successful man, " Filling Stations were a gesture, but they justified themselves. Let's try a twenty-four hour service—as a gesture, if you like. We can cut it out if it doesn't prove to be worth while. Let's try it."

" When you talk like that, Mr. Treasurer," said the Secretary, " I'm almost persuaded. We'll get our teeth into your idea, if only from affection for you."

" How much will it cost ? " asked the Finance Chairman at the next Meeting.

" To do the job properly, a couple of thousand a year—not more, sir."

" Very well ! It's a fair risk, gentlemen, eh ? Agreed ? "

Agreed, and left to the Secretary to complete.

" Now," said that partly-converted sceptic to his colleagues, " we have got to make this new idea flame, for the dear old Treasurer's sake. We need eight bright young men, for a start, allowing for week-end and holiday reliefs, and for the present unmarried."

So departments were combed, and the potentials duly reported for instruction.

" First," they were told, " those who are selected for this new job will get extra pay and allowances. Second, the work calls for special tact and imagination, and anyone who fails will revert to his Unit."

" What exactly shall we have to do, please ? "

" It's difficult to say. Nobody knows what kind of inquiries the new service will attract, nor what may prompt a member to telephone at any hour of the night. Except for warmth and light you will be on a kind of outpost duty, to be shot at from all quarters, with problems instead of bullets."

" Couldn't there be a reserve line, please ? " asked one of the potentials.

" What exactly do you mean by that ? "

" Well, sir ; personally, I'd like to feel that I could telephone a senior officer for guidance when necessary."

That good idea cemented the scheme. A reserve line was formed by the heads of departments, who could be rung up at their homes.

The A.A. night emergency service was a success from the word " Go." It engendered a comforting sense of security. Somebody to hold one's hand.

Even as a wave-length would convey the sympathetic voice of a B.B.C. announcer, saying, " Before we give to-night's weather forecast, here is an ' S O S.' Will Mr. So-and-So, who is," etc., etc.—so did the private branch exchange at Fanum House transmit far more than fifty-seven varieties of trouble, some small, some serious, with which the omniscient and omnipresent A.A. was called upon to deal.

. . . .

Three o'clock on a horribly cold and very frosty Christmas morning.

Ting-a-ling-ling-ling !

" Is that the A.A. ? "

" Yes, sir—A.A. Emergency Service—what can I do for you ? "

" I'm broken down on the Great North Road and am speaking from the A.A. box at Girtford Bridge. Can't get a kick out of the confounded engine. Stuck here for the last hour, and I must—simply must—get on to Slocum-in-the-Wilds for our Christmas party. The magneto isn't sparking. Can you get help to me ? And how soon ? "

" That's bad luck, sir. Let's see. What have you tried doing ? "

" I've done this, and that, and that."

" Oh ! but you haven't detached the earth-wire from the mag., have you ? "

" No ! "

" Well, try it."

Five minutes later :

" I say—is that the A.A. ? Yes ? You've done the trick, and the old motor is going fine. Thank goodness for——"

" That's all right, sir. Don't forget to put your money for the trunk call in our box."

Mutual " Happy Christmases." And so—not to bed, until the world began looking in its Christmas stockings, and the A.A. Day Shift came to relieve the Night Watch.

. . . .

" My husband is motoring somewhere in France. He's expected at Lyons to-morrow. His mother is very ill. We want him to return. What can you do ? "

" We're very sorry for that, madam. Which hotel will he stop at ? "

" I don't know ! "

" Well ! it's fairly certain it will be an A.A. hotel. There are three in Lyons. We'll telegraph to each of them. Leave it to us, please."

" Oh ! THANK YOU ! "

.   .   .   .   .   .

These were but two of many hundreds of serious troubles. There were others in lighter vein, as witness.

Night Emergency Service calling again on the reserves.

" Is that double-one-two-one Westcliff ? Yes ! Oh, is it you, sir. Very sorry to wake you up, at one-fifteen ack emma. Mr. So-and-So, of somewhere quite North, is holding on another line. He was motoring to Folkestone for the morning cross-Channel boat and broke down at Ashford. What ? Oh, he's all right. He's snug and warm at the Bakers' Arms."

" Well, what is he worrying about ? "

" He wants to cancel the shipping reservation to-morrow, but must be assured that the freight charges he paid will be refunded, otherwise he will have to get a tow to Folkestone to ship. What shall I tell him ? "

" Tell him to go to—that is, tell him we'll arrange that he'll get his money back."

This at one-fifteen ack emma !! Ooh !

.   .   .   .   .   .

Troublesome ? Yes, but well worth while. Warming, too, to be able to help the member anyhow, anywhere—anywhen ; to be able to answer the bell—be it 'phone or door.

Or door . . .

Ting. Ting. Ting. Zero hour.

" Sorry to knock you up so late, but I'm a member and saw a light."

" You're quite welcome, sir."

" Thanks. The fact is, I've just had a cable and must leave in a few hours for East Africa. I want the car taken care of until I return. Overhauled, etc. I wondered if the A.A. could look after all this."

And, of course, the A.A. did.

" Leave it at the door, please, and let me have the key. I'll turn your instructions over to the Engineering Department when it opens."

" Thanks tremendously. I must apologize for troubling you when you are closed."

" That's all right, sir ; *we are never closed.*"

CHAPTER XXIII

MAINLY FINANCIAL

THE agreed principle of going all out for a six-figure membership—waking things up, and be hanged to the expense—was being carried out joyously. Secretary and staff revelled in the work, and were unafraid.

Village and Direction Signs were put up by the thousand. Patrols—ex-Service men, of course—were taken on by hundreds. A.A. Branch Offices were reconstituted as Areas, with a Secretary in command, and complete with Road Manager, Touring Department, Legal, and in many cases Engineering Departments. " Pocket Fanums," they came to be called.

The budget for Road Service alone was in the region of a hundred and twenty thousand pounds for the year. The campaign for home-produced fuel was costing a cool thousand a month. Political work almost as much. A monster A.A. petition against the prohibitive price of petrol had been presented to the Prime Minister. It took months to prepare and was signed by one million two hundred thousand people.

Home routes could now be reconstructed. At one time every route card had been written out by hand from a map or an experienced mind. After a while they were typed, but only one at a time. Yet this was absurd ; so those who were responsible considered the possibility of mass production.

Some said, " It can't be done ! "

" Nonsense ! It must be done ! " decided the Secretary.

" But you'll spoil the individuality of the route, the personal touch, and we're so proud of that. Must it go ? "

" Sorry—but there's no alternative. Your idea of tea made fresh for each customer is all very pretty, but it simply won't work when we have armies of members to supply."

A bright mind called attention to the fact that A.A. routes were still typed on cards. " Why not on sheets," he asked, " with a strong cover to keep them flat ? "

" And why not print them ? " asked another.

" Of course ! That's the very idea of mass production. Let's get on with it."

It took months, and cost thousands—but it worked ! The time soon came when A.A. routes could be boomed throughout the membership, whereas before it was hardly safe to attract requests for fear that they couldn't all be supplied in time. Mass production became a mild fever.

" This is splendid ! " said the joyous ones. " Home routes are going to be a star turn—an attraction to be shown prominently in A.A. windows. We must have filing cabinets and the latest ideas in card index. Let's get an expert in. Printing estimates. Wake things up —that's the stuff."

The timid ones were proved to be wrong. The routes were even better than those prepared like tea—fresh for each customer. Later there was equipped a fleet of cars, driven by bright young men with road sense highly developed, and aided by the last word in gradient meters and other products of science. Their job was to log every mile an A.A. member would one day traverse. Thirty thousand miles marked the first season's work— and it was good.

The next development was with Foreign routes. How far afield this work progressed was evidenced one summer morning when Royalty from Southern Europe honoured Fanum with a personal visit. He evinced keen interest in the Routes Department. So something was taken out of the A.A. " window "—that is, a map of Europe was laid out on the table.

" If your Majesty would kindly ask for a route from anywhere to somewhere, please."

" Certainly." A Royal finger indicated from " here to there "—a thousand kilometres from home.

" And note the time, please ! "

It was a teaser, and no doubt meant to be, with hardly a main road. But like magic it was built up with sheets drawn from mysterious pigeon-holes, and it was presented within five minutes.

" Good ! " said Majesty, and the chief of A.A. Routes Service whispered to himself ; " Good be blowed, it's *right !* "

Oh, yes ! Routes by the million cost a fortune, but the money came back tenfold in new memberships.

.   .   .   .   .   .

The cost of practically everything was up by thirty or forty per cent. Small wonder that the Finance Chairman began to look thoughtful, as he sanctioned commitment after commitment.

In October, 1919, the Auditor called by appointment. He, too, looked thoughtful, and said :

" On the figures for the first four months of this financial year, May to August inclusive, we show a most disquieting deficit. In fact, if you don't pull up soon, the A.A. will go bankrupt ! "

" Ooh ! " said the Secretary. " Is it as bad as that ? "

" It certainly looks like it."

" But we're doing it with our eyes open. We have the reserve funds ; it's all part of an agreed policy for Recovery ; and look at our membership returns ! They're wonderful. We added two thousand, six hundred and sixty-six in one week !—that's nearly one new member a working minute. Our total to date is eighty-five thousand

and sixty-five. That's splendid," went on the Secretary,
" and at that rate we ought to reach six figures by next
Spring. Why should we get the wind up, Mr. Auditor?
Even if we do finish this year with a big deficit, it will all
level up next year!"

" That may be," said the Auditor; " but my duty is
to the general body of members; and I tell you straight
that you can't go on spending thirty shillings for every
pound you receive, without eventually going bankrupt.
You had better put the brake on before it's too late."

He gathered up his papers and left, and a very thoughtful quartette applied themselves to the problem his
plain remarks had engendered.

" Hang the chap," said one of the four. " He may
mean well, but he gets on my nerves. We're going
ahead like one o'clock, reconstructing and raking in new
members—waking things up—and then he dashes a
bucket of cold figures over us and leaves us gasping."

" Don't shoot the Auditor; he's doing his best—he
only wants to help!" said another.

" After all, figures don't lie! We are most grateful
for the warning," said the Secretary.

" Mind you! I'm not afraid," he continued, " but I
feel rather like a little boy caught in the act, and I'm
wondering what our respected Finance Chairman will
say when he sees the accounts. We may still be on the
right side. I think we are, but never mind that. Sup-
posing we are *wrong*. Let's apply ourselves to that
possibility. What can we do to cut down expenditure—
if we find that we must?"

" We can't sack anybody!" said one.

" No! That would be suicide, not economy."

" We mustn't close down any departments or Area
Offices."

" Agreed."

" We can stop recruiting for the road staff."

" Certainly."

" And ease up the fuel campaign."

" Yes ! "

" And charge a small fee for routes ? "

" Worth trying—if it comes to a pinch."

" And only issue the Handbook on demand, instead of generally. That would save a few thousands."

" Yes ! "

These and other potential savings were agreed for submission by the Secretary at the next Committee Meeting, with a faint hope that they might not be deemed necessary. There was no waste. That always had been anathema. To use a sheet of new notepaper for an unimportant note or message was regarded as a sin. Inter-departmental memoranda must be written on second-hand sheets, and transmitted in envelopes used time after time, with the aid of gummed labels stuck across the flap. These were but two of a hundred similar economies.

. . . . . .

The fateful day arrived. He put on his hat to go to the office. He felt rather sick. She noticed it.

" What's the matter ? "

" I don't feel at all well, dear. I wish I hadn't to go. It will be a most trying Meeting. I ought to be in the pink of condition—on my toes, if you understand me— full of go and grit, and all that, and instead, I feel anyhow. I don't know how they'll take the figures.'

" Nonsense ! " said She. " Pull yourself together— there's nothing the matter with you. Now run along and don't be so nervy ! It will come out all right ! "

He went.

. . . . . .

The Minutes were read and approved and signed. Correspondence was dealt with. New members were elected, and then—the Finance Chairman presented the accounts.

" At first sight the situation is disturbing," said he. " Our first four months show a deficit of forty thousand

pounds. If we go on at the same rate we may—I don't
say we shall, but we may—be a hundred and twenty
thousand overspent at the end of this financial year.
That's what we have to visualize ! "

" But look at the members we've just elected ! Look
at the progress we're making ! " cried he who was
affectionately termed Charles Two.

" Quite so, and very good," was the reply. " But
according to the figures we may find ourselves in a bad
way at the end of April, 1920—if we don't pull up ! "

Deep depression. Further outlook unsettled.

" What are our reserves ? " asked the Chaplain.

" About one hundred and fifty thousand ! "

" Thank you for that timely question, Chaplain,"
broke in Charles One. " The situation isn't so bad as
it looks. What, after all, have we to worry about ?
We pledged ourselves to a policy of Recovery, and we're
carrying that policy through amazingly well. A hundred
and fifty thousand ! Gracious ! I remember the time
when we hadn't three hundred. After all, we may be
spending money, but we're not wasting it and the
reserve was built up for just the present contingency.
We want members, more members, and still more
members ! We must keep going, and keep serving
them ! "

The Doctor caught his enthusiasm, and cried : " I
support that ! Let us stick to the policy we agreed.
Let's sail close to the wind."

" And what shall we say at the Annual General
Meeting ? " asked the Finance Chairman. " Of course
I'm with you. We'll face the criticism, even with a
hundred thousand pounds deficit—if that's the view of
you gentlemen."

" Well spoken, sir," cried the Doctor. ' Face the
music—that's the stuff. Why should we apologize
for having done what we knew was for the best. After
all, as the Jingoes used to sing, ' We've got the ships,
We've got the men—We've got the money, too ! ' ' "

The Secretary listened with relief, and caught the Chairman's eye.

"I can assure you and the Committee that your Staff realize the seriousness of the present situation, and have it in mind. We want that six-figure membership. We were getting quite near to it when War broke out and stopped us. With ordinary luck we shall reach the hundred thousand mark by next March. That will be a triumph. Meanwhile, the brake shall be pressed well down upon expenditure, with the earnest hope that you, sir, and gentlemen, can enjoy the Annual General Meeting with a six-figure membership but not a six-figure deficit."

The Finance Chairman smiled approval. "I am content," he said. "The Secretary has put up to me —unofficially—seventeen separate and distinct ways of curtailing expenditure. Some of them are good, some may be bad in that they will irritate the members— and we mustn't do that. We must be like the cup that cheers but does not inebriate. I agree with our colleagues who have spoken. We won't apologize for the deficit. We'll take pride in it."

The Finance Chairman was right. In February 1920, the long coveted hundred-thousand mark was reached, and acclaimed with musical honours at a small dinner.

．　　　．　　　．　　　．　　　．　　　．

He tidied up and went home. "Well, how did it go?" She asked.

"Oh, splendid! Such a relief. They are good chaps! So full of understanding! And pluck? Oh, rather! They don't care a—I mean that they know we are doing the right thing for our members, and as one of 'em put it—'The only time a decent chap need worry is when he's wrong!' Oh, yes! It's a great relief. I don't feel sick any longer."

"Oh! you don't! That's good!"

"What do you mean by 'that's good!?'"

" Well ! you looked positively awful this morning when I packed you off to Fanum, but it wouldn't have done any good to tell you so ! Men are such babies when they're ill ! "

. . . . . .

At the Annual General Meeting in July, 1920, all went merrily as a marriage bell.

" Our accounts show a big deficit," said the Chairman, " and I'll leave the details to be explained by our friend the Chancellor of the A.A. Exchequer. But, gentlemen, just think of it. In the short space of twenty months— that is from November, 1918, to this morning, our membership has grown from thirty thousand to one hundred and forty thousand ! We are now, and I hope forever shall be, the world's largest motoring organization." (Loud applause.)

And the Finance Chairman said, among other things :

" For the first time in our history I present you with a deficit. And as a good Irishman says—(I'm Scotch myself)—' I'm proud of it ! ' The deficit amounts to seventy-one thousand pounds. But for foresight and devoted management by our staff—never mind about me—it might have been double that huge figure. That by the way. It was *your* money, gentlemen. We are the trustees of *your* money. We pay it out to the best advantage of you all. You have enjoyed the benefits which this big deficit occasioned. It may not be untimely or unreasonable for me to remind this meeting that we, your Committee, serve this great organization with affection and without gain. Whenever a function or a journey is involved, we pay our own expenses. Please remember that."

" Just one more point," he continued. " We have ample reserves to meet the deficit to which I have re- ferred with pride, as distinct from diffidence. We are solvent. You may also be assured that when, as I hope, we all meet again next year, the accounts will show a surplus—not too great—but, still, a surplus. I now formally move the adoption of the Accounts."

That was seconded and carried with acclamation. Votes of thanks, pats on the back, and the meeting broke up in perfect harmony.

.   .   .   .   .   .

The next year's accounts disclosed a surplus of income over expenditure amounting to twelve thousand pounds, which, replacing a previous deficit of seventy thousand, looked healthy.

Membership was wonderful. During ten weeks the net increase totalled twenty thousand, and the two hundred thousand mark loomed in sight.

"We must rebuild Fanum, gentlemen," said the Chairman, "and start without further delay. The situation is pleasant but embarrassing."

"Indeed it is, sir," added the Secretary. "The staff are working overtime and holiday time, and in turns over the week-ends, because there's no room for additional clerks, unless——" He paused.

"Unless what?"

"Well, one of our senior men told me that if we go on like this much longer, we shall have typewriters ranged along the window-sills and clerks billeted in the corridors—and that wouldn't be efficient."

So plans for the great rebuilding were agreed.

Much quiet staff-work had already been done. An estate agent, keen and discreet, had acquired the necessary freeholds and leaseholds, without disclosing names or details which might have opened the mouths of the respective vendors. The young and hardly-known architect impelled admiration by the beauty of his "elevation," and his offer to build one-half at a time. thereby lessening materially the strain on the staff. The building corporation undertook to complete the whole job in so many months, later to assume virtue for being only a year over their contract time. Troubles innumerable and discomfort immeasurable were borne cheerfully by a loyal and sorely tried staff, with the reflection always that it was all in the day's work, and that one day it would be lovely ! Enthusiastic minds vied with each other in suggesting improvements, labour-saving devices, and time-economizers.

" I think we ought to have a kitchen and a luncheon club on the top floor," said one. " Let's put it up to the Chairman."

" I most decidedly think not," said that experienced and calculating gentleman. " We're building a work-shop, not a restaurant, and judging from past experience we shan't have enough room for our ever-expanding staff, even before these high-speed contractors have taken down the scaffolding."

A sympathetic Buildings Committee of the L.C.C. had approved the maximum height permissible, and Fanum House, London, W.1, showed a fine elevation of ten spacious floors, brightened by acres of handsome windows. " Plenty of daylight," it had been urged. " Let's give our people light—it helps to keep them cheerful—and glass doors from end to end to render supervision real instead of merely academical."

Three years saw the task finished. There was no formal reopening, nor even a house-warming. It happened just after the general strike, and everyone was too busy recovering, but the membership figures marked the great event by turning the three hundred thousand mark.

The Chairman's foresight was borne out. Fanum House, the beautiful, the spacious, which had earlier been regarded as meeting the last word in A.A. requirements, could accommodate four hundred workers, and no more. A few succeeding years of progress and prosperity enlarged the staff to five hundred and fifty.

" Who said kitchen and luncheon club " asked he who had turned the idea down—and laughed.

" All right, sir. Your trick ; but it goes to show what

a wonder the A.A. really is. Our wildest dreams are exceeded before we have, so to speak, got out of bed. What next, I wonder ? " said the happy Secretary.

County offices were established to relieve the pressure at Fanum, London. The very bright Area Secretary, who had built up both Eastern and Western districts, was called back to Headquarters, where he rightly belonged, to bring up the young county secretaries in the way they should go.

The Department tucked away behind Piccadilly Circus, known as the Workshop, was kept going—soon to be adapted for a double shift similar to munition works during the War—with a private telephone line.

In Camden Town, a few miles away, a three-storey building was erected, primarily as a repair department for the fleet of Road Service Outfits, motor cycles, and staff cars—later to accommodate clerks, addressographs, gammeters, and " stop press " printing machines—also with a private telephone line, of course.

" We must have the latest and quickest and best of everything, eh, gentlemen ? "

" Yes, indeed ! " said Charles Two. " Our motto must be penny foolish and pound wise ! We want the last word in internal telephones—a branch exchange—with the cleverest and most amiable girl operators obtainable. Good shop-window dressing that."

.   .   .   .   .   .

To put a crown on all this inter-communication, came yet another brain-wave.

" May we spend a little money on a new idea, please, Mr. Chairman ? Only a very few hundreds."

" What, again ! and why, pray ? "

" Well," said the Secretary, rather diffidently, " it's like this "—(it always was " like this ")—" I feel that we're in danger of losing that very valuable personal touch with the staff. It has always been one of our strongest points—our long suit, in fact—and now, with

our people spread about in three separate buildings
it's hardly possible to maintain contact. We propose
to cross that particular bridge by something quite new
—and rather attractive. Broadcasting ! "

" But you don't expect to get a special A.A. wave-
length out of the G.P.O., do you ? "

" Oh, no ! We don't need a wave-length. We
propose to install a microphone, with loud speakers
distributed over Fanum and Windmill Street, and
Camden Town, connected up by wires, or as they call
them, land lines, and then with the aid of our existing
private 'phone lines, we can broadcast to the whole
staff, whenever we like. A.A. news—copyright reserved
and all that. We've tried out the idea with a borrowed
microphone, and a hundred feet of wire—and it worked
and a big firm assure me they can fit us up. We'll get
all the money back in resiliency and increased efficiency
within a year. We shall, really ! "

" By Jove, I support that—it's a great idea," said the
Engineering Member.

" I, too, Mr. Chairman," said he who still held the
Brooklands twenty-four hours' record, as well as that
of ' Best Seller.' " The idea alone is worth the money
—in publicity."

So that was unanimously agreed and acclaimed. The
work was done efficiently, as befitted a famous firm, and
discreetly, in that nothing was allowed to leak out. The
great day came and, for the very first time in the history
of modern business, a regiment of A.A. workmen and
work-women gleefully stopped dictating, typing, drawing
writing, " for just ten minutes, please," the while to
hear a senior official, whom they might or might not
have met in the lift, on the stairs, or at a staff cricket
match, or dance, say : " Good afternoon, everybody
This is rather wonderful, don't you think ? " and pro
ceed to tell them all about everything.

.   .   .   .   .   .

Christian names of simple form abounded in the A.A. Committee.

Charles Two had materially strengthened a strong team by inspiring the co-option of a Charles—his co-director and close friend, a city magnate and world traveller—and the Chairman, himself a Charles, introduced the second medical member, also a Charles.

Yet another Charles had come over with the conquering Motor Union to be one of the two Vice-Chairmen. A Walter, a John or two, an Alfred, a Frederick, a Francis a Richard, and a Philip, combined to maintain this eminently Anglo-Saxon flavour.

Charles Two further introduced another stalwart, a leader in the motoring community, known more familiarly as George.

Then to the lasting grief of all who knew and loved him, Charles Two died suddenly and tragically, whereupon the Committee, in a body, begged his brother to join them.

" Never mind how you feel about it—we know, but please fill his place. After all these wonderful years we can't imagine an A.A. Committee without the honoured name of your family."

The dear man blushed. " Oh, very well, Yes ! "

His two most importunate friends said, " Thank you, Joe ! " and he was welcomed with open arms.

All too soon after this most desirable acquisition, came a second tragic loss, that of the Treasurer, who had given the A.A. the brain-wave to be the pioneer of Roadside Filling Stations in Britain, and many other valuable ideas. His Christian name was William. Charles Two's brother generously took over the duties of Treasurer, by unanimous request.

Good or bad events, certainly bad ones, seem to run in threes, for within a year or so the second medical member, who may be called Charles Six, passed away. His place on the Finance Committee was taken by the gentleman known as George.

One day a Big Man—capital B and capital M, please —said to another : " This A.A. is really wonderful ! What's the secret of its success, do you think ? "

The other replied, " TEAM WORK, my boy ! Have you ever studied the list of Committee names ? No ? Well, look at your A.A. Handbook. Workers all ! And Unpaid. There isn't one showman. I know a few of them," he continued. " They know each other and pull together for the Association's good, and never for their own. That's the secret."

CHAPTER XXIV

POLITICS

ELIJAH started it. He had retired from the Government Department which War had rendered rather too somnolent for one of his energy and ideas. Elijah liked starting things. Quite a few healthy National Institutions owed their existence to his initiative.

"Let's get together for political work," said he. "Form a Committee, put up some money—plenty—find a good man or two, pay them well—and there we are."

It was a good idea. Post-war motoring was becoming the object of legislation—local and general—and seemed easy prey. D.O.R.A.'s body lay a-mould'ring, but her spirit marched on, intoxicating those in brief authority —all in a plausible endeavour to make of Britain a land fit for Heroes.

Easy prey? Oh, rather—with motoring so much divided in the face of what once was its natural enemy, namely, any Government for the time being.

One organization thought "this," and said so. Another thought "that," and said so. And Government said: "You fellows evidently don't know your own minds. So we will do as we think fit."

The A.A. Committee and staff liked Elijah's scheme and promptly agreed to be one of the political group.

The great Manufacturers' Society liked it also, and agreed to join in.

There was much to be done.

The Transport Bill was before the House of Commons. Motoring was in danger of being legislated and regulated out of existence. In Parliament, Reconstruction was becoming a disease ; everybody seemed anxious to reconstruct everybody else—forgetting that the War was over, and the Sergeant-Major " de-mobbed." Nobody, apparently, was quite sane—yet.

During the War, when a bunch of great ones found themselves at a loose end, they would form a new Ministry of something or other, commandeer an expensive building, fill it with an expensive staff of officials, harass a despairing G.P.O. for innumerable telephone extensions, and call for Returns.

" We couldn't stop that, with a War on," said the Motor Trade to Fanum ; " but we had better stand together and fight this new Transport Bill tooth and nail, or else we'll find motoring tied up in knots."

" Right ! We're with you. We must ask the Other Powers to come in too, eh ? "

" Of course, but if they won't—yet ? "

" If they won't—yet," said the A.A. spokesman, " we'll go on by our two selves. How much ought we to guarantee, do you think ? "

" Up to a limit of ten thousand pounds ! "

" Very well, we'll go halves with you."

" Splendid ! " said the Trade, and that was settled.

Nothing could have been more opportune than this friendly agreement.

In accordance with British tradition, a Committee was formed then and there. Advertisements for a Secretary were inserted, shoals of applications were received and considered by a Sub-Committee. Oh, yes ! Almost the first duty of a British Committee, after selecting a Chairman, is to appoint a Sub-Committee— never mind what for, it must be done. In short, a Sub-Committee proposes in order that the Main Committee may dispose.

The shoals of applications were thus boiled down to three, and the Main Committee met, like a Grand Jury, to choose a Secretary.

One candidate turned up in full War kit, except, of course, for his tin hat. He had a merry blue eye, ingratiating smile, good teeth, hardly any hair, and a row of real War decorations.

The second was a big, upstanding, steady-looking chap from North of the Border, whose age obviously explained his civil attire. He produced convincing testimonials to his capacity as a political organizer, having worked for one of the greatest.

The third was very good, too.

He who had taken the Chair, almost as a matter of course—none could be fitter—put the candidates through their paces, asked them to retire, and having expressed his opinion, waited for that of his colleagues.

" I like the Scotsman," said Elijah.

" I favour the Warrior with the merry blue eye," said his friend Elisha.

A bright business mind, representing the Trade, solved the problem.

" Let's have both of them. We've plenty of funds. We've heaps to do. This is not the time to split hairs, or strain at gnats, or anything. Let's have both ! "

And that, too, was settled.

Elijah, who was ever a good judge of workmen and workwomen, added to these two entirely opposite mentalities a third—feminine—learned, almost a bluestocking, sound and reliable in every way. A couple of rooms and a typewriter, notepaper, a telegraphic address, telephone number, a typist, and an office boy, completed the establishment of The Motor Legislation Committee, of which the unpaid chief of the A.A. Committee, naturally, was Chairman. Elijah was appointed Deputy Chairman, and the blue-eyed Warrior and the Scotsman of over military age were respectively

General and Parliamentary Secretaries. Four or five
others, without portfolio, made up a team of first-class
fighting men.

"And now we want a press man—a publicist!"
said the Chairman. "Our first big job is to fight the
Transport Bill—not to kill it, you know—it may prove
to be for our common good—but to see that our interests
are thoroughly safeguarded. We must have a publicist.
Who can suggest one, please?"

And Elijah said, "I know the very man for the job
—if he'll come. He's been in the Press gallery of the
London County Council, editor of a municipal paper,
and is keenly interested in public affairs. He's on the
Committee of that big political Club which was bundled
out of its marble halls to make room for some Ministry
during the War—he's the very man, if he'll come."

He was. He did—to the lasting benefit of this new
political machine.

The Warrior fought the motoring cause as well from
an office chair as he had fought his country's cause in
the trenches on the Western Front. The big, calm
Scotsman sapped and mined in the lobby of the House
of Commons. The new man, also over military age,
and weight, worked his machine-gun, spraying para-
graphs with diligence and precision, to such effect that
the at-one-time detested and feared Transport Bill
became smaller by degrees and infinitely less in its
potentiality for evil to the interests of the reasonable
Motor User and Trader.

"Hang these people," said Authority, legislative and
administrative. "They are like the inhabitant of the
Zoo—dangerous. When they're attacked they defend
themselves. We'd better do something to placate them.
We'll offer to put a clause in our Bill—the Transport
Bill—giving the Minister powers to set up Advisory
Committees, and we'll ask the motoring crowd to
nominate members. There's a brain-wave for you,
eh? *That'll* keep 'em quiet."

It was a brain-wave, but it did not act quite up to expectations. It *didn't* keep them quiet.

The clause was adopted, the invitation was extended, and the nominees duly paraded for necessary action.

Elijah was one, Elisha was another, and the Warrior a very good third. Fighters all ! Several other faithful representatives of motoring in its various phases made up the team.

The greatest Road Engineer since the time of McAdam presided over what was officially termed the Departmental Committee on Taxation and Regulation of Road Vehicles in Great Britain and Ireland.

.   .   .   .   .   .

The Committee was quite a success. At a long, narrow table Motor User and Trader faced Bureaucracy, and each found the others to be quite nice people, personally.

Above the quite nice people, personally, and beyond the reach of criticism or anathema were, however, the Big Ones—Ministers of this and that.

So, when on the vital subject of a Taxation formula for motor cars, the Departmental Committee unanimously recommended a flat-rate of duty on petrol, with continuance of the existing rates on motor vehicles—in short, " pay as you run "—the big people said, " Thank you very much, but we don't agree. The petrol duty has got to go, and that's all about it. Now get to work again upon a formula based on Horsepower."

The A.A. said " No ! "

Weeks of discussion ensued. That beloved offspring, a Sub-Committee, toiled at the job of fixing the amount per horse-power which would provide the several millions sterling needed to put Britain's highways in repair. Statistics were misleading. The War had destroyed their efficacy. The Sub-Committee did its best, and recommended that the tax on motor cars should

THIS MOTORING

be at the rate of one pound per horse-power ; motor-cycles, thirty shillings and three pounds, according to weight, with an extra pound for a sidecar. This system was approved by the Main Committee.

The A.A. said " No ! " and in so saying stood alone !

" What's the good of sticking out against the H.P. tax ? " asked several people. " You've heard what the Big Ones say—the petrol tax has got to go ! "

" That doesn't turn black into white," came the reply. " The system is wrong. Even if special taxation of motor owners, for road costs, were right—and it isn't—the system is still wrong. We're to be taxed according to the cars we own, and not, as it should be, according to the use we make of our cars. It's inequitable, and unjust. Take whisky. Eight shillings and sixpence duty is payable on a single bottle—for revenue purposes. We may like whisky—you may not. What would you say if you had to pay fifteen pounds a year for duty on whisky whether you consume five bottles or fifty ? "

There was no effective answer to that reasoning—at any rate, so far as the privately-owned motor car or cycle was concerned.

The First Interim Report of the Departmental Committee was duly completed, submitted and published. It was signed by twelve members, and it recommended the Horse-Power Tax.

There was a Minority Report signed by one—the A.A.

The A.A. was convinced that it was right—and this conviction was given full endorsement one memorable night when the People's Representatives of all Parties tucked their knees under a great dinner-table at the House of Commons, and—later—avowed with one voice that " Taxation according to Use " was the only logical basis for motoring to make roads fit for itself.

The Debate in the Commons was long. For hours the seemingly irresistible arguments were marshalled by eloquent speakers who—thanks to good staff-work —knew their brief.

But in the face of the divided counsels, the single-handed fight was lost !

.   .   .   .   .

It was rather an unpropitious start for the Motor Legislation Committee to have a measure of disunion in the first big fight, but Britain has a curious way of beginning badly and ending well.

Thereafter, in practically every case, accord reigned and discord was avoided. The M.L.C. did splendid work, and it still does. The number of contributing organizations expanded from two to ten, making an imposing show on the official notepaper. The atmosphere was healthy and invigorating : a Committee composed of workers, ready to combat anything and any Corporation, Municipality, Urban or Rural Council in the House of Lords, or House of Commons, or in the Press. Ready to beard the Chancellor of the Exchequer in his den. Ready, in fact, to do any old thing for the good of the cause.

The Agenda read like a Menu.

Soup. Minutes read and confirmed.

Fish. Apologies for absence—not many, and correspondence—not much.

Joint. " Here's something into which we can get our teeth," said the Chairman. " The Blankester Corporation is promoting a Bill for greater powers. Among other things it aims to provide that motor cars shall stop every time a tram stops to pick up passengers. We can't allow *that*, can we ? "

Chorus of " Fight it ! "

" Good, gentlemen ! The Bill will come before a Select Committee of the House of Lords. That entails briefing Counsel to oppose it. It will cost—how much do you think, Mr. Secretary ? ''

"Oh ! Anything up to five hundred pounds, sir ! But we'll get in touch first with the promoters and see if we can induce them to withdraw the clause. Otherwise ! Fight 'em ! ''

" Here's another ! The Blank District County Council want to increase the charge for water used in washing motor cars from twenty shillings to twenty-five shillings per annum.

" Here's another ! A Borough Council has promoted a Bill which, among other things, aims to prohibit pillion-riding. That's interfering with the liberty of the subject. They might as well try to stop the working man from giving his tired mate a lift on the step of his bicycle.

" Well, gentlemen, our policy is clear, eh ? We'll speak them fairly, but, if that doesn't suffice, oppose them strongly."

" Agreed ! ''

Sweets ! Letter from the Ministry of Transport. " It is proposed to issue new Regulations concerning the size and shape of number plates," or something equally innocuous. A perfectly phrased letter meaning in effect : " Have you anything to say about it, please ? '

" Rather ! And a pat on the back for the Ministry Nice people ! And commendably human. They don't put on side."

" We can safely leave this to our Secretary, eh, gentlemen ? He'll telephone for an appointment to talk the matter over, and, what he may agree, we confirm.'

. . . . . .

Time sped, and in due course the Chairman of this very practical community of workers for the Cause had to resign. He had been promoted to a place in His Majesty's Government. That was the first step to one of the highest offices in the State, later to a seat in the House of Lords. His necessary resignation was accepted with regret blended with pride in the reflected glory, and signified by a delightfully conceived testimonial, which no doubt would be made an heirloom of his family.

Who was to succeed him?

The Manufacturers' Society, which had gone halves with the A.A. in this great and eminently successful adventure, said, generously, " Our exalted friend was an A.A. man. He was fine. Let's have another A.A. man."

So they chose the A.A. Finance Chairman—never to regret it.

More changes. The Warrior, he of the merry blue eye, was wanted and taken to be chief paid official of the great Manufacturers' Society. And the Committee appointed in the Warrior's stead the capable publicist of machine-gun press-notice fame, also never to regret it.

CHAPTER XXV

MAINLY LEGAL

HE who a decade or so earlier was recommended
by Elijah as a bright young mind, with legal
attributes, had gone from good to better in A.A. service.
He added Parliamentary erudition to that of Law, acted
as Junior Counsel at Motor Legislation Committee
meetings, making sure that no point should be missed by
the A.A. spokesman, kept track of the proceedings of
the Departmental Committee, and read Hansard with
his morning cup of tea.

Under such nursing the legal and political work at
Fanum, London, and the Fanums everywhere else
flourished apace.

" What more can we do for our members ? " was an
ever-recurring question.

" Well," said Legal ; " we defend them free—that's
pretty good—but sometimes the case goes against us
and sometimes it's unfair. Suppose a member wants
to appeal, to save an unjust endorsement on his licence
for example, it may not be a point of what we call public
interest, which would of course justify our fighting his
case right through the Appeal Court, and paying all the
costs, but it may be very vital to him or her, personally—
prestige—what the neighbours say—you know ! "

" Quite good," said his colleagues. " What if the
A.A. were to go halves in the expense of an appeal—
up to a limit of, say, twenty-five pounds—granted always
that we are convinced there has been a grave miscarriage

of justice, and that there is a fair sporting chance to win ? "

" Good ! We'll put it to the Committee," said the Secretary.

And the Committee answered, " Yes ! "

Another idea ; civil cases—comparatively unimportant but irritating. For example, a member would have a dispute with a local repairer—not an A.A. Agent, of course. The bill might be excessive. He had the unpleasant feeling of being " done," and yet it was only a matter of a couple of pounds. He was a busy man. " Silly," he would mutter, " to have gone to anybody who didn't hold the official A.A. appointment. Better pay up and be done with it. But, half a minute, before doing so, why not let the A.A. know and see what they think about it ? It might be worth while."

" Leave it to us ! " he was told. " We'll take it up with the repairer, quite nicely ! He may see reason."

" And if he doesn't ? "

" Then he can issue a County Court Summons, and we will fight the case for you."

" Thank you," said the member, and went away content.

The need for taking so firm an attitude gradually disappeared as post-War conditions got smoother and tempers calmer. Many a misunderstanding was cleared up by a tactful letter or two, and in most cases the local repairer concerned in due time earned inclusion in the A.A. Handbook.

" We must be resilient and sympathetic," said a prominent Committee member in Meeting. " Times are difficult for everybody. Don't let us stick too closely to our Rules and By-Laws, but stretch them. Temper the wind to the shorn lamb—that's the way to maintain confidence."

" Good ! Agreed ! "

On the strength of this admirable decision, an ex-officer received a pleasant surprise when he called at

Fanum to tell his woes. " I've been in a dreadful mess," he said. " Just avoided a conviction for Manslaughter at Blankshire Assizes. I had to get a big man from London to defend me, and I'm nearly ruined by the expense."

" But why didn't you come to us before ? "

" I know ! I know ! But let me tell you ! One unforgettable night on the so-and-so road, I was nearly home, driving quite alone. It was pouring with rain and pitch dark. I hit something—the wheel was nearly jerked out of my hand. I pulled up, got down, and searched anxiously with my electric torch for about a quarter of an hour. I was soaked. I found nothing, and concluded I must have brushed the branch of a tree, so I went home, to bed."

" That's a pity ! You should have called in at the nearest Police Station to report the incident, just in case."

" I know ! " said the poor chap, " but I didn't think of it. The next day the Police came to my house, and asked to look at my car. It had a bent nearside wing."

" ' Were you out last night ? ' I was asked, and I replied :

" ' Yes, on the so-and-so road about four miles north of here '—and I explained to the officer what had happened."

" Well ? "

" It wasn't at all well ! I had hit the handle-bar of a cycle in such a curious way that machine and rider were hurled down a bank, and—you can judge what happened. I was horrified. My wife and I did everything possible for the poor man's widow, but local feeling was strong. I was regarded as one of those callous people who had become used to slaughter—having got the D.S.O.—and nothing could prevent my standing in a dreadful dock at the Assizes, looking like a criminal and feeling almost like one.

" Now I'm exonerated, but broke ! It cost me nearly four hundred pounds to get off."

" Never mind," he was comforted. " Your case
shall be put up to the Committee for sympathetic consideration. Our Meeting is next Tuesday—you may
expect to hear from us by Thursday at the latest."
He received a letter on the Wednesday morning
containing a contribution towards his law costs—" as an
act of grace."

.   .   .   .   .   .

There were bigger things than deeds of chivalry to
the individual member in distress.

" We must be ready for the new Motor Traffic
Bill," said Legal. " It occupies a pigeon-hole in White-
hall and is taken out and dusted every time a fresh
Government comes into power. One of these days the
Cabinet-for-the-time-being will call for the Bill and throw
it at an unsuspecting House of Commons."

" Yes—and it is our job to see that the Commons is
not caught unawares. What can we do about it ? "

" Well, the question of the twenty-mile-an-hour
speed limit is the biggest risk. Much publicity has
been given to the idea of raising the limit, but retaining
the principle. The A.A. has always fought for abolition.
We have opposed speed limits as being arbitrary, and
proved them so. The point now is how many of our
members are ' Pro ' and how many ' Con ' ? "

" That is only one way of settling that," said Legal ;
" and that is to take a vote on this point—and also on
those others which affect the motorist vitally."

Out went the questionnaires, and back they poured,
to a total of one hundred thousand.

Pros and Cons—Ayes and Noes—were collated by
an expert staff of tellers—and the vote was :

92% for the abolition of the 20 m.p.h. speed limit.
81% for the abolition of the 10 m.p.h. speed limit.
98% for legislation to penalize joy riders, and
97% in favour of a tax on motor-spirit to replace the
Horse-power tax.

With this Vote of Confidence from its constituents
the A.A. stood its ground. And it came to pass, in the
very fullness of time, that the Traffic Bill *was* rudely
jerked from its pigeon-hole—to receive the shock of its
sequestered life. It was passed—and, with it, passed
the speed limit—into oblivion, to join the Shades of
P.C.'s X and Y, who ran that " Trap No. 1 " on the
Brighton road a quarter-century back—but for which
there would have been no A.A.

Speed Limits had served at least one good purpose.
Out of Evil, etc.

CHAPTER XXVI

OVERSEAS

CANADA was calling. A project to send somebody on a visit to the Western Hemisphere for propaganda and peaceful penetration had had to be shelved '14 for " the duration."

It was revived and submitted to the Committee.

" I support that strongly," said the Vice-Chairman. We must build up our Overseas connexions, not only cross the Atlantic, but throughout the Empire in time. suggest that our Secretary goes, and treats the trip his annual leave. We'll pay all his expenses, of urse."

" I support Charles One," said his neighbour ; " with slight amendment. Let's send two. Then we can ll it a Mission."

" Very well ! " agreed the Chairman. " One of our ommittee, eh ? Hands up, please, anyone who would ke to go ! "

" Just a moment, please," said the Finance Chairman. This matter of a Mission raises an important point policy. While I am entirely in favour of the idea, on't let us forget what I said when presenting the ccounts at the last Annual General Meeting but one— We serve our great organization with affection and ithout gain.' Therefore, unless any other member is een to represent us, I will go, on one condition—that pay my own expenses."

" Splendid of you. And while you are about it, you

can look in at the United States, too ; don't you thin
so ? "

" All right ! "

The matter was settled—the Mission duly appointed
Plymouth, New York, Washington, Pittsburg, Cleve
land, Chicago, Detroit, Buffalo, Toronto, Ottawa
Montreal, Boston, New York, and Plymouth, made up
rather hurricane itinerary, lasting only seven weeks
The Missionaries were dubbed " The Hustlers from
Britain "—a title quite well earned.

It was heartening to note the genuine pleasure with
which the A.A. Hustlers were welcomed in every city
" You've taken the trouble to come to see us," said, in
effect, each Reception Committee. " We're friend
now. We can write to each other without formality
We will surely return your call one day—not in singl
spies but in battalions."

Those promises were fulfilled. The tendency o
motoring visitors to Europe, complete with famil
and car, had been to land at a French or Italian Port
Thereafter they were inspired to have a look at Britai
first.

The General Manager of the Back of Beyond Moto
Club saw to that.

" Land in England, Fred ! " he advised. "We'll fi
it all up for you with the British A.A.—membership
badge, papers, and everything, before you start. You'
be received with a salute at Southampton, ushered ashor
like a Prince, and saluted like a General all along th
roads by the A.A. men. Your people will be tickled t
death. And then, go to London. I'll give you a lette
to my opposite number, and he'll greet you—with
siphon in one hand and——"

And Fred would say, " That sounds pretty good
Gil ! Call it a deal ! "

Thus, it may be claimed without immodesty, wa
really started the " Come to Britain " movement—
decade later to become National and official, and backe

by a Government grant—all too insufficient, but, still,
a gesture of encouragement.

The A.A. did it !

.   .   .   .   .   .

" Blood is thicker than water, my boy, and, to quote
a war-time chorus, ' We don't want to lose you, but we
think you ought to go.' And what is more, we'll keep
your job open, just in case you are able to come back."

The man to whom this was said, choked a little, and
tried to smile his appreciation. He was the Irish-born,
New Zealand-bred, Olympia Motor Show journalist at
a loose end, who had been taken on the strength to build
up A.A. Ireland, and having done so with commendable
efficiency, had been moved to A.A. Midland Area to
take over from Elijah's original nominee, hurriedly
transferred to Head Office to fill the gap so tragically
created by a skid on a wet Saturday night in December,
'13.

" I hate to have to leave this wonderful show, but
what can I do ? " he had said. " We're New Zealand
people—my wife's mother is calling her. I promised
that she should go back if ever she was wanted, and I
can't break a promise, can I ? "

" Of course, you can't. Blood's thicker than—but
I said that before. Now, let's think for a minute. How
much good can we extract from this very regrettable
situation. Everything is said to happen for the best,
although it isn't easy to believe that—at the time."

" Couldn't I do something for the A.A. on the way
out ? "

" Of course you can ! " said his Chief. " Our successful mission to Canada and the U.S.A. provides the very
idea. Send your wife and little one out direct. She
won't mind that purely temporary separation. Clean
up and hand over to your deputy, and then——"

" Yes ? "

" Filter through to the Antipodes—take a couple of

months. Do what our Mission did in the Western Hemisphere, or as much like it as possible."

" Oh, that sounds good."

" It *is* good. Think what it means. Our postbag shows that the A.A. spirit is spreading and spreading. We are getting inquiries from motoring organizations overseas asking this and that, and that and this—how to run a patrol force, how to prepare routes, how to get members, how to assist the growing tide of visitors to Britain, which the dear people love to call ' Home.' "

His Chief got more and more excited, and continued :

" Let your wife take all the big stuff with her. Cut your personal gear down to the lowest possible limits. You can always buy a toothbrush or an extra shirt. Then—don't you see ?—you can jump ashore at Port Said, and run along to Cairo to shoot a card, and ginger things up. We want an A.A. in Egypt one day. And do the same at Bombay, and Colombo, and Singapore. No ? Not Singapore ?—a pity, but never mind ! Australia ? Yes ? Good. We have friends in every State—tackle the lot. That's the stuff. Then New Zealand—but that's easy—you'll be at home. And when—when you're able to come back——"

" Oh ! thank you. I do hope so."

" Right—a cable will settle that—at any time. When you're able to come back, you can do so by way of South Africa, and shoot more cards, and make more friends.'

The eyes of the exile-to-be glistened.

" It's—it's fine ! Depend on me, I'll rub our beloved A.A. into the mind of everyone I meet. We'll not stop running until there's an A.A. of South Africa, and who knows ? we may live to see an A.A. in Australia, in New Zealand, in India—and—it's wonderful."

So he departed, loaded with send-off gifts, good wishes, last-minute instructions, and enthusiasm.

Every outpost of Empire was tackled according to plan. The parable of the Sower was re-enacted, with a minimum of stony ground. Sydney, Australia, proved to be the first really fruitful soil. Within seven years it boasted the largest motoring organization in Greater Britain, running towards a six-figure membership, and run on A.A. lines.

New Zealand motor organizations were linked up with Fanum, London, while the A.A. man's kith and kin were saying to each other, " How nice to be together again."

But it all had to happen according to plan. The A.A. Good Fairy saw to that.

A year later a cable to Fanum, London, from Auckland, New Zealand, asking, " Does your offer stand ; if so, quite ready to return," was answered, " Yes, but return by way of South Africa, as arranged, and clean up as you come along."

. . . . . .

The Empire Theatre of Varieties, Leicester Square, was lovingly termed the centre of the world. Fanum House, being within a stone's-throw, possibly acquired reflected glory therefrom. Anyway, it could fairly claim to be the hub of the motoring wheel—the spokes of which were thousands and thousands of miles long.

The motoring wheel never ceased turning, and the overseas membership expanded rapidly on the snow-ball system. It received impetus, for example, by a member of the Fighting Services going out to join his Unit in Iraq, or on the North-West Frontier, or China, or elsewhere. " I'm taking my little bus with me, and shan't be home for three years. It will look strange without the jolly old A.A. badge—can't I keep it ? "

" Of course you may," he was told. " We will put you on the supernumerary list, at a special subscription of half a guinea. Then, when you come home on leave, you can have the fullest possible benefits all the time for the same little half-guinea."

" Right ho ! " said the soldier, and when he got out in the Far East, or South, he would tell his brother

officers about the scheme, and chaff them for parading
with their cars " improperly dressed," until they, too,
would write home for badges to clothe them, and for
supernumerary membership.

Visitors from all parts of the Empire also gave the
snowball a hearty push. Members of the Greater
British Civil Service, and motorists from all parts of the
Empire, having enjoyed A.A. amenities at home, displayed similar reluctance to take the badge off the car.
" It has been a good friend—we'd hate to part with
it," they pleaded, and joyfully became supernumerary
members. And getting back to this or that corner of
His Majesty's Dominions, they, too, inoculated those
about to go Home with A.A. enthusiasm.

" You can't do without it, old man. You'll feel so
' off the map ' in Britain ; so do it now—it's cheaper
from this side."

．　　　．　　　．　　　．　　　．　　　．

South Africans brought matters to a head. Nice
people, travelling with nice luggage, and nice thoughts,
they flowed in and out of Fanum, London, and Fanum,
North, South, East, and West, enjoying every crowded
day, feeling less and less like a number at a big hotel,
and more and more like a brother or sister or cousin
in a great-hearted family.

Small wonder that within a few years A.A. members
were to be found, proudly flaunting their badges everywhere throughout the Union—in Natal, the Transvaal,
the Orange Free State, Queenstown, and the Cape
Province. And the leaders of motoring, most of whom
had been to Europe and to Britain, and had seen and
admired, said to each other, " Here's a Big Idea ! Why
shouldn't we federate with the Mother A.A., change the
pattern of our badge to hers—with permission, of course
—and then when we go Home we shall be under A.A.
protection from the moment we land ? "

The Big Idea did not take long to materialize.

Queenstown, in Cape Province, began it. Johannesburg chimed in. Durban carried on.

That was why and how the Union of South Africa was the first great overseas nation to federate with the A.A., and adopt the A.A. badge.

Organization didn't do it—sympathy and understanding did.

" Of course we must put things in black and white," said the ambassador from Durban, " and observe certain formalities. A gentlemen's agreement. Oh, yes ! but it's the spirit of the bond that will appeal to our people. And mind ! " he ended, " some of you fellows *must* come out to see us—and soon ! We won't let you off."

" Oh ! really now," said his hosts. " That's a charming thought, but we can't see it materializing yet. Such a long way, you know. Let's compromise by seeing you and yours off, at Southampton."

" Never mind," said " Durban." " I have second-sight, and take it from me, you'll be drinking coffee with us at the Marine Hotel one fine morning—sooner than you may think. You've simply *got* to come."

The Good Fairy of the A.A. must have been listening-in at " Durban's " elbow. There ensued a bewildering succession of coincidences.

One eventful night, in Paris, a Very Nice Girl cried herself to sleep, after reading a cable from her boy, who was keeping his end up in the Malay States. They were engaged to be married in the following Autumn. The idea had been that he should get leave to come West as far as Cairo for the wedding, in which case it would be easy. But the cable was to say that it could not be. It might spoil his prospects, and sorry—terribly sorry— but——

Girls mustn't be allowed to cry too long. So her Parent said, " For goodness' sake, darling, don't take on so. Perhaps there may be a way round. Let's try to find it. Hang it all, it's about time I took a decent holiday, after twenty-five years in the saddle. Impossible to promise, of course, but, perhaps, I might be able to take you out to him."

The tears dried up—rather sceptically—but the funny part was that it came off. An always sympathetic Committee said, " Splendid ! Off you go, and trust us and the staff not to burn Fanum down while you're away. No really efficient man is indispensable, otherwise he wouldn't be efficient.

" But," he was adjured, quite superfluously, " make it a bus-driver's holiday, and of course come back by way of South Africa. Look in at Egypt, and Bombay, and Colombo, and Penang, if only to give them the glad eye of encouragement."

And when " Durban " heard, he chuckled, and said, " What did I tell you ? "

The Good Fairy of the A.A. smiled and pretended that she had done nothing.

Ceylon was ripening to become A.A. The Vice-President and founder of the motoring body of that delightful island had been Home the year before, with his wife, to join the Fanum Brotherhood, and to return to his tea plantation full of pleasant memories and the idea of federation, saying, as " Durban " had said, " You *must* come out, you *must*," and to be laughed at for saying so. The Ceylon Secretary had followed a little later, and gone back full of the idea. Blessings on the personal touch, which costs but little and means so much.

Again, all went merrily as a marriage-bell, and this time it was a real bell.

The Very Nice Girl who, six months earlier, had cried herself to sleep in Paris, was wedded, in charming surroundings, all complete with orange-blossom, and wearing her mother's bridal veil—which the A.A. Good Fairy must have inspired to be kept—in case.

.   .   .   .   .   .

And then one wonderful morning—he who a quarter of a century earlier had stood at the Piccadilly end of

Shaftesbury Avenue, London, wondering what to do next
—said " Good-bye, children !   Good-bye, Singapore ! "
and sailed away.

Seventeen joyful, restful days across the Indian
Ocean were broken only by a quick run from Colombo
to the plantation for a night's lodging, and a talk with
the chiefs of the budding A.A. of Ceylon. And then—
Durban, and Mrs. Durban, and Miss Durban welcomed the Pilgrim, laid down the red carpet, ushered
him to the microphone, and told him, " Say what you
like. There is no censorship here—for you. We cross
our own t's and dot our own i's. Tell 'em all about the
A.A. Don't bother about sleep," said these wonderful
people, " you can make that up on the boat going
home."

Meetings, parties, dinners, visits to Natal's greatest
people—made a breathless time. The President of the
South African A.A., a Senator in the Union Parliament,
who had nobly waited hours for the ship to dock, said :
" Don't be so darned formal. We're Christian names to
each other ! "

Four more breathless days. Then in cars to 'Maritz-
burg for a meeting, luncheon, and speeches, fraternity
—A.A., sir. By sleeper to Johannesburg, nearly four
hundred miles. More wonderful people—not content
to wait at the terminus, which might be Waterloo, but
perforce must greet the Pilgrim at Germiston, which
might be Clapham Junction.

This warmth and obvious sincerity made the Pilgrim
feel a little ashamed, with memories of London and the
tyranny of the engagement diary. So often it was a
case when the Man from Beyond would drop in like the
Angel he may be—and usually is—unawares—" Oh,
bother ! Why didn't he telephone ? My day's engagement card is full, but show him up." And then, " Oh,
how do you do ? Did you have a good trip ? So glad,
and all that. I'm booked up now—someone else due,
by appointment, in five minutes—but are you free for

lunch ? Yes ? Oh, splendid ! Would you mind coming back at a quarter to one ? "

Contrast that with Dominion hospitality ! But the good fellows understood that it simply couldn't be helped, and those who were not good fellows didn't matter.

It was an agreeable part of a bus-driver's holiday to sit round Committee tables, at intervals of hundreds of miles, discussing familiar problems, and to assist at deputations to the Union Government. It was like Home to talk with sleek well-groomed officialdom about Triptyques and Carnets, and arrange for the Automobile Association of South Africa to be authorized to issue these harmless and necessary documents. "We might be back in Whitehall," said the Pilgrim, "except for that glorious blue sky."

It was good to meet big men who, three decades earlier, had been foes, but now were brother citizens and brother motorists.

"If you want wires pulled," said one of the biggest, "certainly count on me. We are the great A.A. of South Africa. We must have the fullest Government recognition. There must be no politics in motoring. Whatever the views of my papers (which are published only in Dutch), I'm all in with you good people for freedom of transit and transport."

"Well ! if you put it that way, Doctor !" said the Pretoria Divisional A.A. Chairman—himself a Government official—"our guest from Britain insists that we must be able to issue the International Driving Certificates and Passes for cars and motor cycles, like all the leading organizations in Europe are empowered to do."

"And why not ?" asked the Big Man.

"The Union Government can't authorize that procedure unless and until it subscribes to the International Convention for touring."

"This chap from London knows all about it. If he could explain it to the men who really count——"

" I see what you mean ! The Administrators of Provinces—they are the men who count and I would gladly introduce our visitor. But what a pity, my friend in Pretoria is away, and I'm off to Capetown on Monday to take my degree as Doctor of Laws ! What a pity ! "

" No, sir ! It's pure luck ! " broke in the Pilgrim. " I'm going to Capetown on Monday myself ! We might travel together."

" That's excellent ! Of course we will, and I'll take you straight to the Cape Administrator—and you can tell him all about the idea. It can't do any harm, and it may do a lot of good."

" I say ! You're a wonderful chap," said the Pilgrim.

" That's all right, my friend. I must go now. At nine-fifty then, on Monday morning, at Johannesburg," said the Big Man. " We can talk it all over in the train."

A hectic week-end of entertainment and Committee meetings, crowned by a charmingly intimate send-off dinner, served to make nine-fifty ack emma an almost painful moment. It seemed a shame to have to leave such delightful people. " Never mind ! " they said. " You're coming back. You've promised ! You must come—and bring your car."

" Yes ! and drive on South African A.A. papers— all spick and span, and printed in both languages," said the Pilgrim, trying hard to smile.

A score of affectionate friends of both sexes—chiefly Christian names—called and waved good-bye " Until our next merry meeting," and the long train pulled out for its thousand-mile run to Capetown.

The happy Warrior of Motor Legislation Committee fame had invoked the services of his South African colleague in a few pregnant words : " He's a pal of mine, so lend him a car when he wants one, and do him well."

The sportsman thus admonished did his job thoroughly and with discretion. He happened to be in Johannesburg at the very time, and to be returning to the Cape by the same train. He kept out of the way during the breathless week-end (" Didn't want to butt in, you know ! " he explained ; " there were plenty of people eager to carry you about, and they would have resented my interfering "), and duly dry-nursed the Pilgrim, his countryman, from Pretoria to the Cape.

" Don't dare to be late for breakfast," he said on retiring. " You mustn't miss the view through the Hex River Mountains, on pain of imprisonment without the option. It's unforgettable."

He knew everybody, including, of course, the big-hearted newspaper owner, and made a tactful third at all discussions. " In motoring there should be no politics ! Friends all ! Brethren of the road ! "

" Agreed ! "

" South Africa must take its rightful place in the great world of touring."

" Certainly ! "

" Now I will tell you one," said the Pilgrim. " It's a topper, and so true. Write it down, both of you, for a keepsake. It's—*Gute Seelen treffen sich zu Wasser und zu Lande.*"

.   .   .   .   .   .

Capetown was breezy, beautiful, and business-like.

" Our appointment with the Minister is fixed for to-morrow morning, at nine-thirty sharp. His A.D.C. and I will fetch you at nine o'clock," said the Big Man. " Don't dare to be late ! "

" Perhaps it would be safer not to go to bed ! " joked the Pilgrim, knowing, by this time, all about South African hospitality. " Anyway, that will leave the rest of the morning clear for a Committee Meeting."

" But we've arranged to drive you round Table Mountain," said his principal host, " and after that lunch, and after that, a rally—and tea, and after that a dinner—and then you broadcast from our Studio. And after that——"

260

" Yes ! I know—and it's perfectly splendid of you, dear people. Only one favour, though. Do let us have a meeting. If I don't attend a Committee it will spoil my record for a bus-driver's holiday."

" Oh, very well ! We'll fix one up specially for you," conceded his amiable friends.

" Thank you ! With just one tiny reservation."

" And that is ? "

" Don't have it *earlier* than nine ack emma, please ! "

. . . . . .

At a meeting in London three weeks later the proceedings were more or less informal. The chief item on the agenda being—To welcome the Pilgrim back, and wish each other a merry Christmas.

" What impressed you most about South Africa ? " he was asked.

" The sunshine ! " was the reply. " It gets you. It radiates, and permeates, and eradicates. It makes nice men nicer, and pretty women prettier. I told them so. I told them that we never have sunshine like theirs, and that our only remedy is to get synthetical. That is —when the day is cold and miserable, we make the most of a coal fire. We have to conjure up our own ultra-violet rays. They don't need any. Their place is in the sun—all the time."

" And what about the road problem ? "

" They're as keen as can be. It's already feasible to drive quite comfortably from Capetown to beyond Pretoria. Even as we are working for a Throughway —that's our own A.A. term—across Europe to Stamboul, so is South African motoring thought concentrating on a Cape-Cairo Throughway. We shall, I hope, live to see the time when people will start for the Cape, by road—not as a stunt, but for a holiday.

" I am glad to have seen them start by air, not only for the Cape, but for Australia—and, what is more, arrive. Which reminds me. How is our Aviation Department getting along ? "

" Excellently," said Aviation. " Our members have already covered over half a million miles in their aeroplanes, finding their way safely and easily by the aid of our blue and yellow Air Route Maps, the best in the world."

" Well done ! " said the Pilgrim. " And A.A. flying is yet in its childhood.

" In our eyes," he continued, " the airway is the younger sister of the road. On members' 'planes as well as cars our Badge is carried, and it has wings, even as our Good Fairy. If this is a coincidence, it is a happy one. What's our membership now ? "

" Four hundred and thirty-two thousand, five hundred and fifty-seven, at noon to-day," said the Deputy. " Not too bad, eh ? considering the awful weather."

" It's fine," agreed the Pilgrim. " It's a real welcome home. When we need ultra-violet rays let's look at our membership figures. Now, everybody ! We will just drink to the health of the world's largest motoring organization, from its respected President, Vice-Presidents, Chairman, Vice-Chairman, Treasurer, and Committee, down to the youngest messenger-boy, and then disperse for a happy Christmas. And when we've all got over the festivities, and are back at work, we will——"

" What ? "

" Go all out for the first half million." *

---

* This was reached on the 24th August, 1933.

EPILOGUE

CHRISTMAS EVE.

He was telling Her all about it.

" Singapore Cathedral made a fine setting for your big girl, and the wedding was simple and sweet. I cried— and I'm not ashamed to own it. Just fancy ! One of our children has been born, brought up, and wedded, within the lifetime of the A.A. That puts the clock on, darling, but you don't look it, and I certainly don't feel it. After all, it has meant and it does mean quite something to be . . ."

" To be what ? dear ! "

" Secretary . . . of the . . . Automobile Association."

    .   .   .   .   .   .

" Hold my hand."

CHARACTERS IN ORDER OF THEIR APPEARANCE AND PAGE NUMBER

PAGE

66	Jimmy, the Editor of Scottish paper.	James Inglis Ker.
67	R.J.	Robert John Smith.
84	First Sportsman in England.	The Earl of Lonsdale.
87	Honest John.	Rt. Hon. John Burns.
89	Editor of Britain's brightest ha'penny paper.	Tom Marlowe.
93	Arthur—regular Knight of the Round Table.	Sir Arthur du Cros.
95	Uncle George and Uncle Willie.	George du Cros and Will du Cros.
106	Jimmy.	The late Sir James Percy.
106	Arjay.	The late R. J. Mecredy.
108	" Irish born raised in New Zealand."	Arthur Dunscombe Alle (now Director of Tourin London).
126	Vice-Chairman.	The late Sir Archibald Ma donald.
127	Noble Earl.	The Earl of Lonsdale.
127	Secretary to the Road Board.	William Rees Jeffreys.
132	Chairman of the M.U.	The late Sir William Joynso Hicks (The Viscount Bren ford).
134	Chairman of the M.U. Finance Committee.	Charles McWhirter.
134	Hon. Treasurer M.U.	The late William Ball Hinde.
135	Elijah.	William Rees Jeffreys.
135	Young legal chap.	William V. Gibson (no Parliamentary Secretar London).
138	Midland Manager.	Edward Harpur Fryer (no Deputy-Secretary).
139	Junior.	Stenson Cooke, junior.
140	Kindly Scots lawyer.	The late John Kennedy.
141	Head of famous medical requisites firm.	H. S. Wellcome.
144	Assistant Road Manager.	John T. Phillips (now Roa Manager, London).

GE

8	The Reverend Member—Chaplain.	Rev. **Canon** F. W. Hassard-Short.
8	Medical Member.	Dr. J. Lewis Lock.
9	Friend on old M.U. Committee—a soldier.	The late Capt. Lucius Kingston.
1	C.T.C. colleague.	Lt.-Col. H. C. Baskerville.
2	Secretary of the Alliance.	The late G. A. Pos.
3	Bluff Midlander.	Edward M. Tailby.
5	Staff Officer.	Col. Alan Gossett, Cheshire Regt.
0	Faithful Major Domo.	Henry J. Rapson.
2	Particular Personal Secretary (Miss K.).	Mrs. M. H. Abbott (née L. S. King).
7	Head of Engineering Department.	Frank Newton.
3	Quiet watchful Motoring Industry Leader.	Selwyn Francis Edge.
2	Royalty from Southern Europe.	H.M. King Alfonso of Spain.
3	Auditor.	Frederick William Lord.
9	Young and hardly-known architect.	Andrew Mather.
1	Bright Area Secretary.	Harold G. Wigzell (now Home District Secretary, London).
2	Engineering Member.	Philip A. Sharman.
3	Chairman.	Charles McWhirter.
3	Charles, a City Magnate and World Traveller.	Charles Peto Bennett.
3	Second medical member, also a Charles.	The late Dr. Charles Buttar.
3	Yet another Charles—M.U.—one of the Vice-Chairmen. A Walter, a John or two, an Alfred, a Frederick, a Francis, a Richard and a Philip.	Charles H. Dodd, the late Lt.-Col.Sir Walter Gibbons, Dr. J. Lewis Lock, John Amery-Parkes, Alfred King-Hamilton, Rev. F. W. Hassard-Short, Selwyn Francis Edge, the late D'Arcy Richard Baker, Philip A. Sharman.
8	George.	George Monro.

267

PRINTED AT THE CHAPEL RIVER PRESS, ANDOVER, HANTS